Managing Tudor and Stuart Parliaments: Essays in Memory of Michael Graves

Michael Arthur Roy Graves 1933–2009. Photographed in London, May 2004.

Managing Tudor and Stuart Parliaments: Essays in Memory of Michael Graves

Edited by

Chris R. Kyle

WILEY Blackwell

for

The Parliamentary History Yearbook Trust

© 2015 The Parliamentary History Yearbook Trust

John Wiley & Sons

Registered Office
John Wiley & Sons Ltd, The Atrium, Southern Gate, Chichester, West Sussex, PO19 8SQ, United Kingdom

Editorial Offices
350 Main Street, Malden, MA 02148–5020, USA
9600 Garsington Road, Oxford, OX4 2DQ, UK
The Atrium, Southern Gate, Chichester, West Sussex, PO19 8SQ, UK

For details of our global editorial offices, for customer services, and for information about how to apply for permission to reuse the copyright material in this book please see our website at www.wiley.com/wiley-blackwell.

The rights of Chris R. Kyle to be identified as the editor of the editorial material in this work has been asserted in accordance with the Copyright, Designs and Patents Act 1988.

Library of Congress Cataloging-in-Publication Data
Library of Congress Cataloging-in-Publication data is available for this book.

A catalogue record for this title is available from the British Library
Set in 10/12pt Bembo
by Toppan Best-set Premedia Limited
Printed and bound in Singapore
by Markono print Media Pte Ltd

1   2015

CONTENTS

NOTES ON CONTRIBUTORS

P.R. Cavill is a lecturer in early modern British history at the University of Cambridge, and a fellow of Pembroke College, Cambridge. He has written *The English Parliaments of Henry VII, 1485–1504* (Oxford, 2009), and several articles on the political and religious history of 15th- and 16th-century England. He was joint winner of the *Parliamentary History* essay prize in 2005.

David Dean is professor of history at Carleton University where he teaches early modern British history and public history. He took degrees at the University of Auckland (where he studied with Michael Graves) and the University of Cambridge, and taught at Goldsmiths College, London, before moving to Canada. His publications include studies of law making, parliament, local politics, London companies, and the lottery in Elizabethan England, controversies in Canadian and Australian museums, and theatrical representations of the past. Forthcoming publications include: *History, Memory, Performance* (co-editor, with Yana Meerzon and Kathryn Prince, Basingstoke, 2014); *A Companion to Public History* (editor, Oxford); and *Shakespeare's England: A Cultural History, 1558–1649* (co-author, with Kathryn Prince, Oxford). Co-director of the Carleton Centre for Public History, he was company historian to Ottawa's National Art Centre's English Theatre (2008–12). He is a life member of Clare Hall, Cambridge and a fellow of the Royal Historical Society.

Lori Anne Ferrell is professor of early modern literature and history at Claremont Graduate University. She is the author of, most recently, *The Bible and the People* (New Haven, CT, 2009) as well as many articles and essays on preaching, politics, and religion in early modern England. She is currently editing volume xi of *The Oxford Sermons of John Donne* (16 vols projected, 2013–) and is at work on a monograph about the Parker Society and its editorial appropriation, in the 19th century, of the English Reformation.

Paul E.J. Hammer is professor of history at the University of Colorado at Boulder. His publications include: *The Polarisation of Elizabethan Politics: The Political Career of Robert Devereux, 2nd Earl of Essex, 1585–1597* (Cambridge, 1999); *Elizabeth's Wars: Government and Society in Tudor England, 1544–1604* (Basingstoke, 2003); *Warfare in Early Modern Europe 1450–1660* (editor, Farnham, 2007); and many articles on Elizabethan politics and political culture. He is currently completing a book on the Essex rising and the politics of treason in Renaissance England.

Paul M. Hunneyball is a senior research fellow at the History of Parliament Trust. A contributing author to the History of Parliament's volumes on the early Stuart house of commons, he now works on the house of lords during the same period. He has also published on a wide range of 17th-century topics, including electoral strategies, provincial architecture, and the cultural life of the Cromwellian court.

Norman Jones is director of general education and curricular integration as well as professor of history at Utah State University. He chaired the history department there for 18 years. He has held visiting fellowships at Harvard University, the Huntington Library (San Marino, CA), the Folger Shakespeare Library (Washington, DC), the University of Geneva, and the University of Cambridge. In 2008 he was named a visiting senior research fellow of Jesus College, Oxford. His publications include: *Faith by Statute: Parliament and the Settlement of Religion, 1559* (1982); *God and the Moneylenders: Usury and Law in Early Modern England* (Oxford, 1989); *The Parliaments of Elizabethan England* (co-editor, with David Dean, Oxford, 1990); *The Birth of the Elizabethan Age: England in the 1560s* (Oxford, 1993); *The English Reformation: Religion and Cultural Adaptation* (Oxford, 2002); *A Companion to Tudor Britain* (Oxford, 2004); *The Elizabethan World* (co-editor, with Susan Doran, 2011); *Governing by Virtue: Lord Burghley and the Management of Elizabethan England* (forthcoming, Oxford) and more than 40 articles. A native of Idaho, he attended the College of Southern Idaho before taking his BA at Idaho State University. He did his MA at the University of Colorado, Boulder, and PhD in history at the University of Cambridge.

Chris R. Kyle is associate professor of history at Syracuse University. He is the author of *Theater of State: Parliament and Political Culture in Early Stuart England* (Stanford, CA, 2011), three edited books, and over a dozen articles on 16th- and 17th-century English history. He has held fellowships from the Huntington Library (San Marino, CA), the Folger Shakespeare Library (Washington, DC) and Hughes Hall, University of Cambridge. He is currently the editor of *The Oxford Works of Francis Bacon. Volume VII: Legal and Political Writings 1613–1626* and is starting a new monograph project on Tudor and Stuart proclamations.

Glyn Parry is professor of early modern history at the University of Roehampton, London. His recent publications include *The Arch-Conjuror of England: John Dee* (New Haven, CT, 2012). He is currently working on a study of the role of magic in Elizabethan politics, and an archivally-based study of Shakespeare's Warwickshire and London context.

Jason Peacey is professor of history at University College London. His publications include: *The Regicides and the Execution of Charles I* (editor, Basingstoke, 2001); *Parliament at Work: Parliamentary Committees, Political Power and Public Access in Early Modern England* (co-editor, with Chris Kyle, Woodbridge, 2002); and *The Print Culture of Parliament, 1600–1800* (editor, *Parliamentary History*, xxvi, special issue, 2007). He is also the author of *Politicians and Pamphleteers: Propaganda during the English Civil Wars and Interregnum* (Aldershot, 2004), and most recently, of *Print and Public Politics in the English Revolution* (Cambridge, 2013).

Foreword

CHRIS R. KYLE

It was S.T. Bindoff who started Michael A.R. Graves on the path to becoming an academic historian. After completing his BA at Cambridge University in 1960, Michael worked for a private tutoring company in Holland Park, London, as he started on his PhD under Bindoff's supervision at London University. By 1962, economically stretched already with a family of four children, he asked Bindoff about the possibility of a university tutorship to which came the immortal reply: 'Graves, Graves why don't you try the colonies?' That, indeed, is what Michael did and, after obtaining a lecture-ship at the University of Otago, New Zealand, he and his family embarked on the ship *Ruahine* for the six-week voyage to New Zealand and a strange new world far away from his beloved childhood and memories of Balham High Street – always pronounced Blahm by Michael in jocular fashion.

Michael was born in Balham in 1933, but evacuated to Devon during the war. Before his education at Cambridge he completed his national service working on codes and ciphers, punching endless marks into cards for the air force. His aptitude test had singled him out for pilot training but, as quickly became apparent, Michael and technology of any kind were distant bedfellows – a situation that continued throughout his life as anyone who knew him could attest. He never learned to drive and the few half-hearted attempts he made at it invariably resulted in damage to property and psychological damage to anyone in the vicinity, although fortunately no physical harm! Until the very end of his life, computers, and even typewriters, were anathema to him, and all his books and articles were handwritten, annotated heavily in his distinctive hand, and no doubt a puzzle for even the most skilled typist or copy-editor.

Michael quickly settled into life in Dunedin and loved the quiet of the city and the beauty of the surrounding countryside, far away from what he had left behind in war-torn London. While he worked weekdays on his PhD at Otago on the house of lords in the reigns of Edward VI and Mary I, weekends were often spent on archaeo-logical digs with his great friend, the acclaimed New Zealand author, Maurice Shadbolt.

Michael had also became firm friends with the chair of the history department, a much-decorated New Zealand war hero and ex-special forces operative, Angus Ross. Daring in a department meeting to contradict Ross one day he was met with a glare and a comment: 'Graves, I've killed men for less than that.' This helps to explain the secrecy surrounding his move to Auckland University in 1966. Having given a lecture at Auckland the previous year and impressed the department, the chair at Auckland, (Sir) Keith Sinclair, travelled to Otago ostensibly to give a paper, but in reality to offer Michael a position. Fearful of Ross's anger should Keith and Michael be seen together, Keith snuck through the bushes beside the department, tapped on Michael's window through which he then emerged and a deal was struck over lunch at a local pub. A move to Auckland was offered and Keith guaranteed he could swing a promotion. Michael accepted and moved, although I never heard the story of how he broke the news to Angus Ross![1]

Apart from periods of sabbatical leave, always spent at his beloved alma mater, Cambridge University, Michael remained at Auckland University for the remainder of his career. Michael was, in fact, exceedingly happy at Auckland with the early modern resources that he could use and the material he had to hand to offer graduate students. Over the years, a number of generous research grants from the university had allowed him to order copious quantities of microfilm from what seemed like half the British Library collection through the Repertories and Remembrancia of London to the main papers of the house of lords and manuscript Commons journals. This, in combination with the willingness of the university library to purchase widely in early modern history, meant that Auckland had a collection to rival most universities in the United Kingdom.

In 1970 he entered the world of academic publishing with an article in the *Bulletin of the Institute of Historical Research* on the two Lords journals of 1542 and this was closely followed by another piece on proctorial representation in the parliaments of Edward VI.[2] The latter was a response to an article by Vernon Snow on absences and proxies in the mid-Tudor Lords. Michael's essay questioned Snow's statistical methodology, categories of absenteeism and the use of proxy votes. Snow quickly penned a rejoinder accepting some criticism but denying Graves's claim in no uncertain terms on the role of 'joint proxies'.[3] Their relationship never recovered, as is evidenced from Snow's copy of Michael's later book on the mid-Tudor house of lords which is heavily interlined and the margins covered with comments – usually along the lines of 'NO', 'check', '?', and more lengthy negative comments, most of them it must be said seem more vitriolic than substantive.[4]

Michael subtitled his book 'an institutional study', and in many ways it reflected the revisionist agenda of the 1970s – a specific desire to place the house of lords back into the parliamentary story of the Tudors and to critique the Commons-centred teleological model evinced by A.F. Pollard and J.E. Neale.[5] In this, Michael drew on the work of his great friend, Sir Geoffrey Elton, and his wife, Sheila Lambert. During his sabbatical in Cambridge in 1979–80 they plotted, planned and debated revisionist

[1] Author's personal recollection. I am grateful to Jim Frood for sending me a piece that Michael wrote about his journey to New Zealand.

[2] Michael A.R. Graves, 'The Two Lords' Journals of 1542', *Bulletin of the Institute of Historical Research*, xliii (1970), 182–9; Michael A.R. Graves, 'Proctorial Representation in the House of Lords during Edward VI's Reign: A Reassessment', *Journal of British Studies*, x (1971), 17–35.

[3] Vernon F. Snow, 'Proctorial Representation in the House of Lords during Edward VI's Reign', *Journal of British Studies*, viii (1969), 1–27; Vernon F. Snow, 'A Rejoinder to Mr Graves' Reassessment of Proctorial Representation', *Journal of British Studies*, x (1971), 36–46.

[4] Michael A.R. Graves, *The House of Lords in the Parliaments of Edward VI and Mary I: An Institutional Study* (Cambridge, 1981). Snow's copy of the book is now in my possession.

[5] A.F. Pollard, *The Evolution of Parliaments* (2nd edn, 1926); J.E. Neale, *Elizabeth I and her Parliaments, 1559–81* (1953); J.E. Neale, *Elizabeth I and her Parliaments, 1584–1601* (1957); see also Wallace Notestein, 'The Winning of the Initiative by the House of Commons', *Proceedings of the British Academy*, xi (1924–5), 125–75.

parliamentary politics with a fervour only matched by a legendary consumption of tobacco, whisky and wine. Although Michael specifically noted that he was not writing a 'political study', he was not blind to the importance of the political process and potential for conflict and mismanagement. Indeed, Michael concluded that the infighting of the nobility during Mary's reign adversely impacted upon the prestige and power of the Lords and this led to a decrease in procedural importance and efficiency.[6] In combination with Elizabeth Read Foster's *The House of Lords, 1603–1649* (Chapel Hill, NC, 1983), Michael's work put the upper House firmly back into its rightful place in the parliamentary trinity.

Rehabilitating the Lords as an important part of parliament was a natural step in demolishing Neale but it still left in place the central tenet of a rising powerful house of commons, dominated by an Elizabethan puritan faction, winning the initiative and forming a hard-core opposition to crown policies that inevitably ended in the civil wars of the 1640s and parliamentary executive power. One of the key points of Neale's argument was the emergence of a 'puritan choir' in the Commons led by the 'radical' puritan, Thomas Norton. Much of the foundation of Neale's argument was based on a manuscript in Cambridge University Library entitled 'the lewde pasquyle', a document which Neale associated with an organised puritan opposition that planned radical religious legislative reform before each of the 1560s' parliaments.[7] As Michael argued in an article published in *Parliamentary History* in 1983:

[The manuscript] lists 43 members, each one with accompanying descriptive tags. Some describe parliamentary episodes, but nowhere is there a hint that these men were members of a Puritan party engaged in organized and rebellious courses against the Queen. The list excludes zealous Protestants and Marian exiles such as Nicholas and Clement Throckmorton, Anthony Cooke and James Morice; yet it includes moderate loyalists such as William Fleetwood, inveterate conservatives like Francis Alford, and such courtier-politicians as Robert Newdigate and Henry Goodere. Moreover, amongst the most prominent of this motley 'choir' were several lawyers and a City merchant who will shortly appear in a very different guise: Robert Bell, William Fleetwood, John Marshe, Thomas Norton and Christopher Yelverton.

At the very end of the pasquil the anonymous author provides a vital clue as to its meaning:

> As for the reste
> theye be at Devotion
> and when theye be prest
> theye crye a good motion

He derides the majority, mindlessly following the bold and articulate who are described variously as 'orator, jangler, wrangler, glorious [i.e., boastful], merry, weary, pacifier, crier, earnest, hottest' and even 'drudger' – one remembers a bore as much as an orator. The pasquil is neither a party list nor a serious commentary

---

[6] Graves, *House of Lords*, 202.
[7] Cambridge University Library, MS Ff, V, 14.

on the politics and religion of those named, but a frivolous lampoon. 'Choir' does not mean collaboration, marching in unison to a Puritan battle hymn, but the fact that these men were vocal, not silent. The pasquil should be assigned to the world of political graffiti, not to that of organized parliamentary parties.[8]

This work led to what, perhaps, defines Michael's legacy as an early modern historian – the concept of 'men-of-business' in the mid-Elizabethan parliaments – an idea which has stood the test of time and is widely acknowledged today. Far from forming an opposition party, men such as Norton, William Fleetwood, Robert Beale and others named above were, he concluded, acting on behalf of the privy council and led by William Cecil, Lord Burghley. The government, anxious to distance itself from the wrath of Elizabeth I in matters of marriage, succession and religion, 'employed' these 'men-of-business' to act in accordance with the wishes of Burghley *et al.* Although the relationship could be said to be that of 'patron and client', as Graves pointed out, this did not mean that these men always followed the wishes of the council, or that they did not occasionally overstep the line. Michael developed this analysis over a number of articles starting with 'Thomas Norton: The Parliament Man' in 1980 through a debate with Patrick Collinson over the effectiveness of their role in parliament, in 'Elizabethan Men of Business Reconsidered' (1996).[9] To quote Michael again: 'the outlines are clear: that the Privy Council had to secure its objectives in the teeth of too much business, too little time, an inefficient House of Commons and an obstinate Queen; . . . men-of-business were crucial to its success'.[10]

Work on men-of-business also led to another monograph, this time a biography of Thomas Norton, which looked well beyond his parliamentary career to his service for the privy council, as well as to his role as co-author of the first blank verse drama in English, *Gorboduc*, numerous pamphlets that he authored against catholicism, and his use by the government as an 'examiner' of jesuit priests and those who surreptitiously printed catholic works in England.[11] This led to the epithet applied to him by Robert Parsons of 'Rackemaister'.[12] The Norton of Graves' biography was, in many ways, a typical Elizabethan official in service of his country and his beloved City of London but, as the biography reveals in detail, what set him apart were 'his professionalism, his

[8] Michael A.R. Graves, 'The Management of the Elizabethan House of Commons: The Council's Men-of-Business', *Parliamentary History*, ii (1983), 12.

[9] Michael A.R. Graves, 'Thomas Norton the Parliament Man: An Elizabethan M.P., 1559–1581', *Historical Journal*, xxiii (1980), 17–35; Graves, 'The Management of the Elizabethan House of Commons'; Michael A.R. Graves, 'Patrons and Clients: Their Role in Sixteenth Century Parliamentary Politicking and Legislation', *Turnbull Library Record*, xviii (1985), 69–85; Michael A.R. Graves, 'The Common Lawyers and the Privy Council's Parliamentary Men-of-Business, 1584–1601', *Parliamentary History*, viii (1989), 189–215; Michael A.R. Graves, 'Managing Elizabethan Parliaments', in *The Parliaments of Elizabethan England*, ed. David M. Dean and Norman L. Jones (Oxford, 1990), 37–63; Michael A.R. Graves, 'Elizabethan Men of Business Reconsidered', *Parergon*, xiv (1996), 111–27. For Collinson's article, see Patrick Collinson, 'Puritans, Men of Business and Elizabethan Parliaments', *Parliamentary History*, vii (1988), 187–211.

[10] Graves, 'The Management of the Elizabethan House of Commons', 32.

[11] Michael A.R. Graves, *Thomas Norton: The Parliament Man* (Oxford, 1994).

[12] Graves, *Thomas Norton*, 272.

prodigious energy and output even in the most discouraging circumstances, his seem-ingly inexhaustible capacity to come up with ideas, schemes and solutions, and an ability to order his advices and proposals with clarity and cogency, both in speech and with pen'.[13] Much of the book was written on sabbatical at Cambridge between a flat that overlooked the Cam and the Fort St George pub on the edge of Midsummer Common, his daily, and favourite, haunt. As lunchtime approached so, too, did Michael, and the staff soon came to reserve a table for him overlooking the river and the resident population of swans. A pichet of dry white wine arrived and Michael would settle down to write amid wine refills and the ubiquitous ploughman's lunch.

One of Michael's greatest passions was teaching, and amidst his academic writing he co-authored an advanced school/undergraduate textbook with a schoolteacher in New Zealand, Robin Silcock. *Revolution, Reaction and the Triumph of Conservatism: English History 1558–1700*, appeared in 1984 as a general narrative of Tudor and Stuart history. It was designed to fit in with the New Zealand school syllabus for students in their final year of secondary education and was rapidly adopted by students throughout the country. In latter years, in co-operation with his great friend, Jim Frood, a King's College (Auckland) schoolteacher, Michael produced a series of pamphlets and studies on specific Tudor and Stuart subjects within the curriculum which offered students and educators alike the chance to examine case studies in some depth. He combined this with innumerable visits to schools to talk to pupils, meetings with groups of teachers, and consultation with the department of education to set, and mark, national history exams. It was a remarkable record of service to New Zealand secondary education.

Michael also put his facility in writing to use at the university level. He wrote two books for the Longman 'Seminar Studies in History' series. *Elizabethan Parliaments, 1559–1601* appeared in 1987 and a companion volume, *Early Tudor Parliaments, 1485–1558*, came out three years later.[14] Both these combined short analytical sections covering various aspects of the parliaments from management to procedure and legis-lation followed by a series of primary source documents illustrative of the parliaments. But perhaps his greatest contribution in this form of pedagogical writing was *The Tudor Parliaments: Crown, Lords and Commons, 1485–1603* (1985). The book is very indicative of Michael's parliamentary interests, opening with a review of the historiography of Tudor parliaments in which Neale's view of a rising house of commons was severely critiqued again. Sections followed on procedures, privileges and the records of parlia-ment before an analytical narrative of the institution throughout the century that places due emphasis on the role of the house of lords.

Michael's long association with Longmans (now Pearson) continued throughout the 1990s and beyond. A study of William Cecil, Lord Burghley, appeared in 1998 in the 'Profiles in Power' series and, as Michael himself noted: 'it was not a biography but a study of [Burghley's] role as Elizabeth's long-serving chief adviser, meticulous administrator and lord treasurer – for forty years he was the heart of her government'.[15] Then in 2003, a

[13] Graves, *Thomas Norton*, 409.
[14] A second edition of *Elizabethan Parliaments* appeared in 1996.
[15] Private communication.

similar study of Henry VIII, who had long been one of Michael's favourite historical characters, emphasized Henry's kingship and personal interventions in Church and state affairs.

Shortly before *Henry VIII*, Michael ventured into much wider territory. For many years he had taught an undergraduate class on early modern European parliaments which, perhaps surprisingly, was a perennial favourite at Auckland drawing large numbers. Far from just being interested in England, he had always loved comparative studies of representative institutions from the Polish *Sejm* to the Sicilian *Parlamento*. The *Parliaments of Early Modern Europe* (2001) was a much-needed update to the previous classic, A.R. Myers's *Parliaments and Estates in Europe to 1789* (1975). It would have been an easy path to concentrate on the major assemblies of England, France, the Netherlands, Sweden and Spain, but the book ranged widely through the northern Italian assemblies in Montferrat, Piedmont and Friuli to the *Rigsdag* of Denmark, the Hungarian Diet and the *Bundestag* of the Swiss Confederation.

In the midst of all this writing, Michael's sense of mischievous humour was never far from the surface. Whether it be dressing as a window cleaner to wash the windows while one of his colleagues lectured in the room, to a bet with Jason Peacey that he would work Stamford Bridge into a paper at the Cambridge early modern history seminar if Jason would wear a Chelsea shirt to the talk – both were achieved and certainly left a few puzzled faces around the room, both at Jason's dress and what Chelsea's football ground had to do with Tudor parliaments. Michael and Jason shared a lifelong passion for Chelsea and they returned to Stamford Bridge later that year to watch the team. In fact, Michael had not been back since the war ended and as a small boy was one of the over-100,000 people who packed the Bridge for the famous game between Chelsea and Dynamo Kiev. Irreverent to the last, he never really lost his sense of the Balham working-class boy. No doubt the fellows of Trinity College, Cambridge, were a little bemused as to why their high table guest wore Reebok trainers and, if I hadn't been nervous enough on the day of my PhD viva, ominously held in the Spain and Portugal room of the Institute of Historical Research, then the sight of Michael in a suit and tie certainly emphasized the seriousness of the occasion.

Although Michael in far-flung New Zealand had few opportunities to supervise graduate students at PhD level, he guided with an expert hand, numerous MA theses and independent studies at advanced undergraduate level. Two of the most notable students were David Dean and Paul Hammer (both contributors to this volume) and both of whom went on to do PhDs at Cambridge with Geoffrey Elton, and subsequently into highly-successful careers in academia.

Michael retired as an associate professor. Although friends and colleagues had long tried to persuade him to go up for full professor (and certainly his publication level warranted it) promotion at Auckland to 'full' would have brought with it significant administrative responsibilities – unlike Norton, Michael was not a committee man – and he always felt his talents were best put to teaching and writing. After retirement, he purchased a small flat in the fashionable area of Mount Eden Village, where he could walk to restaurants, coffee shops and boutique food stores. A lifelong gourmet cook, there were few things he liked better than a day in the kitchen in meticulous preparation followed by a multiple-course spectacular dinner for his guests with conversation and wine flowing long into the evening. Sadly, after a few years, he suffered from a stroke, made dramatically worse in that he lay stricken for several days before being found. This eventually necessitated assisted care and the use of a walker to get around. However, Michael remained, by and large, in good spirits and was soon organising wine tastings for the inhabitants of the assisted living care facility (especially the ladies) and developing his skills with a computer – although it must be said these remained limited and in frequent need of outside intervention!

Michael Arthur Roy Graves passed away on 27 October 2009 – a great friend and mentor.

Introduction

CHRIS R. KYLE

In the wave of late 1970s and 1980s revisionism, the management of parliament took centre stage. As Geoffrey Elton systematically cut down J.E. Neale's notions of an Elizabethan house of commons increasingly in confrontation with a beleaguered crown and government, so, too, Michael Graves replaced Neale's 'puritan choir' with his model of 'men-of-business', acting at the behest of, and in collusion with, William Cecil, Lord Burghley and other members of the privy council.[1] Graves, too, wrote a highly influential essay, 'Managing Elizabethan Parliaments' which extended the concept that parliaments required managing not just by the government, but also by all sectional interests from individual boroughs to the City of London. As Graves noted, success in parliament required 'practicing the mixed managerial arts of surveillance, canvassing, persuasion, propaganda and opposition'.[2] For Graves, though, success was about the pursuit of a legislative agenda and management of the key strategy to this end. Legislation and management was also represented in the work of other notable parliamentary scholars, including several represented in this volume, namely David Dean's study of the later Elizabethan parliaments, *Law-Making and Society* (Cambridge, 1996) and Norman Jones's revision of the religious settlement of 1559, *Faith by Statute* (1982).

Across the 1603 dividing line, those in early Stuart studies using similar tools, pressured and then broke the whig orthodoxy most clearly articulated in Wallace Notestein's *The Winning of the Initiative by the House of Commons* (1924). In particular, Conrad Russell's *Parliaments and English Politics, 1621–1629* (Oxford, 1979) mixed the high politics of whigs with parliamentary management, an emphasis on legislation and the wider political world in which parliaments assembled at Westminster. Although the success of legislation as managed by the privy council, local and sectional interest was a key component of revisionism, it was not the only rewriting of management that took place. Patronage and elections came under intense scrutiny, most especially in Mark Kishlansky's radical departure from a focus on contested elections to the idea that contests were rare and most MPs were 'elected' by selection.[3] Further work, most

---

[1] G.R. Elton, *The Parliament of England, 1559–1581* (Cambridge, 1986); G.R. Elton, 'Parliament in the Sixteenth Century: Functions and Fortunes', *Historical Journal*, xxii (1979), 255–78; G.R. Elton, 'Parliament', in *The Reign of Elizabeth I*, ed. Christopher Haigh (1984); Michael A.R. Graves, 'Elizabethan Men of Business Reconsidered', *Parergon*, xiv (1996), 111–27; Michael A.R. Graves, 'Managing Elizabethan Parliaments', in *The Parliaments of Elizabethan England*, ed. David M. Dean and Norman L. Jones (Oxford, 1990), 37–63; Michael A.R. Graves, 'The Common Lawyers and the Privy Council's Parliamentary Men-of-Business, 1584–1601', *Parliamentary History*, viii (1989), 189–215; Michael A.R. Graves, 'The Management of the Elizabethan House of Commons: The Council's Men-of-Business', *Parliamentary History*, ii (1983), 11–38.

[2] Graves, 'Managing Elizabethan Parliaments', 38.

[3] Mark Kishlansky, *Parliamentary Selection: Social and Political Choice in Early Modern England* (Cambridge, 1986).

notably by Sheila Lambert, challenged the prevailing view that procedural changes in the early Stuart house of commons were deliberately instituted to wrestle parliamentary control from an increasingly despotic crown.[4] Other scholars emphasized the importance of patron–client relationships, the neglect of the house of lords,[5] the role of faction in parliamentary politics,[6] and the importance of lobbying.[7]

The turn of post-revisionism placed a different emphasis on management as high politics and foreign policy were written back into parliamentary history, with the concomitant result that parliament became an increasingly important site of discourse and a reaffirmation that successful parliamentary management could be the key to either stifling royal policy or bending it in another direction. Thomas Cogswell, in particular, did much to highlight this view with the identification of the 'patriot coalition' in the 1620s.[8] The more recent emphasis on the post-Reformation public sphere, the impact of propaganda, and the importance of image and ceremonial, has added another layer to how we must account for the myriad devices available for exploitation of parliamentary management. One of the most important early essays in this context was David Dean's 'Image and Ritual in Tudor Parliaments' which emphasized how the crown projected images of majesty, power, splendour and control through the elaborate and crowd-pleasing rituals of the opening and closing of parliament. It illustrated that management could take many forms, especially those more subtle than packing the house of commons with crown nominees.

What all this has denoted is a shift from a largely chamber-centric perspective of management to one focused on preparations for a session, the public perception of what was taking place during the parliament and how various bodies, from the crown and government to interest groups and individuals, reacted to ever-changing events. The articles in this volume reflect both the need for a fresh examination of more traditional modes of management, such as elections, procedure, and conciliar management of the 'men-of-business', but also how state openings of parliament, sermons, and proclamations could form part of a managerial strategy.

[4] Sheila Lambert, 'Committees, Religion, and Parliamentary Encroachment on Royal Authority in Early Stuart England', *English Historical Review*, cv (1990), 60–95; Sheila Lambert, 'Procedure in the House of Commons in the Early Stuart Period', *English Historical Review*, xcv (1980), 753–81.

[5] See, in particular, Elizabeth Read Foster, *The House of Lords 1603–1649: Structure, Procedure, and the Nature of its Business* (Chapel Hill, NC, 1983); Michael A.R. Graves, *The House of Lords in the Parliaments of Edward VI and Mary I: An Institutional Study* (Cambridge, 1981); James S. Hart, *Justice upon Petition: The House of Lords and the Reformation of Justice 1621–1675* (1991).

[6] See, in particular, the essays in *Factions and Parliament*, ed. Kevin Sharpe (Oxford, 1978).

[7] David M. Dean, 'Parliament, Privy Council, and Local Politics in Elizabethan England: The Yarmouth-Lowestoft Fishing Dispute', *Albion*, xxii (1990), 39–64; David M. Dean, 'London Lobbies and Parliament: The Case of the Brewers and Coopers in the Parliament of 1593', *Parliamentary History*, viii (1989), 341–65; David M. Dean, 'Public or Private? London, Leather and Legislation in Elizabethan England', *Historical Journal*, xxxi (1988), 525–48; David M. Dean, 'Pressure Groups and Lobbies in the Elizabethan and Early Jacobean Parliaments', *Parliaments, Estates and Representation*, xi (1991), 139–52; Ian Archer, 'The London Lobbies in the Sixteenth Century', *Historical Journal*, xxxi (1988), 17–44; Edwin Green, 'The Vintners' Lobby, 1552–1568', *Guildhall Studies in London History*, i, 2 (1974), 47–58; Chris R. Kyle, 'Parliament and the Politics of Carting in Early Stuart London', *London Journal*, xxvii (2002), 1–11.

[8] Thomas Cogswell, *The Blessed Revolution: English Politics and the Coming of War, 1621–1624* (Cambridge, 1989).

Paul Cavill's opening article examines the anticlericalism debate in the early 16th century, specifically in relation to parliament. Taking as a starting point Christopher Haigh's hugely influential article, 'Anticlericalism and the English Reformation', Cavill traces lay attitudes towards the Church in parliaments from 1485 to 1529. In particular, given the scarcity of sources, Cavill critiques Haigh's argument 'from silence', noting that, because neither the Lords journals or original acts survive from the 1523 parliament, it is too easy to make the assumption that anticlericalism did not rear its head in this parliament. In fact, Cavill demonstrates that parliament was the natural venue of the lay push for clerical reform and that it served both as a sounding board for criticism of the Church and did advance legislative solutions towards those aims. Using the scant sources available, Cavill provides a masterful reconstruction of how anticlericalism played out at Westminster and, in doing so, emphasizes the important corrective to Haigh – that parliamentarians held the 'conviction that the reform of the Church was too important a matter to be left to the clergy'.

David Dean takes us away from more conventional early modern history to examine the portrayal of the Elizabethan religious settlement in parliament as captured in Shekhar Kapur's 1998 film *Elizabeth*. Dean's analysis revolves around the extended scenes in which Elizabeth (not quite single-handedly but almost) quells parliamentary opposition to the reintroduction of protestantism to England, faces down the hostile house of lords led by the bishops and the duke of Norfolk and earl of Sussex, and wins the vote to ensure the passage of the Acts of Uniformity and Supremacy. While Dean is quick to acknowledge the historical anachronisms and outright errors introduced by Kapur, he argues that the film-maker caught the right tone and the key point that the settlement would not have been enacted without good parliamentary management. This comes both from the increasingly powerful and confident presence of the queen, but also the machinations undertaken by Walsingham [*sic*.] to keep vital opposition away including Gardiner [*sic*.] and under lock and key – a tried and trusty, if somewhat controversial, style of management. Furthermore, Kapur's staging represents the historical reality that a young and untested queen faced considerable opposition from an entrenched catholic nobility and clergy determined to stop her through their actions in parliament. Playing with the themes of light and dark – surely a familiar early modern trope – Kapur and Dean walk us through the centrality of parliament to the film and the catholic *versus* protestant hostility that forms the central dramatic tenet. In doing so, while Kapur is providing entertainment and commercial interest, Dean is ensuring that we take seriously historical films as a mode of historical analysis.

Norman Jones's article takes a broad view of the concept of 'managing England' through multiple perspectives of contemporary treatise writers, networks of kinship, social status and William Cecil, Lord Burghley's translation of his understanding of the governing system of Elizabethan England into 'managing parliament'. Crucial to this enterprise was the idea of individual morality and trust between the different parts of the state. Jones's analysis of Burghley reveals the consummate manager, a 'governor' continually reinforcing the remnants of medieval codes of honour, fidelity and chivalry to hold together a state on the verge of Baconian individualism. Burghley then conceived 'governance in terms of those who have the right to govern . . . [which] meant that the state could not be separated from the people born to run it'. Thus it was the network of connections that Burghley understood that held England together and one of the reasons he so avidly tracked genealogy and cultivated contacts, epitomised in the men-of-business working to enact the government's agenda in parliament and in the country at large. Managing England was obviously a more daunting task than the contained chambers of parliament, but both required the same techniques of watchfulness and reliance on contacts, kin and the emphasis of a devotion to duty.

Glyn Parry turns to the 1576 session of parliament to stress how the divide in English foreign policy was manifested in the attempts by the privy council and the queen to control the debate. Parry argues that the parliament became a 'great council of the realm', advising both the government and crown on England's strategic interest. Should England follow the path of a protestant *res publica* and, hence, Elizabeth accept the offer of sovereignty over the Netherlands at the very definite risk of war with Spain, or pursue a more cautious path of covert support for the Dutch? This ideological divide strained the now well-established conciliar management techniques of men-of-business acting (by and large) in cohorts with the council and, indeed, revealed the split within the council itself. Parry's close analysis of these debates and their domestic and international context, reveals the council's inability to manage the debates of 1576 as a unified body or to control a somewhat fractious House. Despite this, the 1576 foreign policy debates that occurred despite the fervent opposition of the queen, were not an attempt to 'seize the initiative' but, rather, manifestations of this ideological tension between a broader protestant allegiance and those, such as Burghley, who wished to see the queen focused on the British Isles.

Paul Hammer turns his attention to revisiting the parliamentary patronage of Robert Devereux, 2nd earl of Essex. Hammer challenges the still dominant (or at least unchallenged) view of J.E. Neale that Essex was a parliamentary patron driven by 'megalomania'. Hammer also issues a timely reminder that patron-client relationships were not a one-way street; in particular, that while it is certainly possible to identify many Essex clients and supporters in the parliaments of the 1590s, many of these expressed their own desire to be returned as MPs and used Essex's influence to improve their electoral chances. In other words, we need to be cautious that connections between an aristocrat and those in the Commons were not solely initiated and manipulated by the patron. In the final section of the article, Hammer looks at the earl's preparations for a parliament in 1601 – a parliament, of course, that finally assembled after his execution. But it is clear that Essex was in the process of extensive preparations for the session and hoped to use the parliament as a means to dispose of his enemies at court once and for all. In this, Hammer sees the Essex circle in a last gasp measure of desperation, willing to use the justification in 'The State of Christendom' for the nobility and parliament to override the authority of the monarch – a position that John Adamson has argued was also held by the 12 peers against Charles I in August 1640. Although this conclusion must remain speculative, it does point to the importance Essex attached to managing a parliament and advancing his position and policies.

Paul Hunneyball revisits the importance of procedure to the management of parliament. Procedural developments have often been utilised as a tool of 'winning the initiative' and as a deliberate policy, especially in the house of commons, to illustrate how the lower House gained the upperhand in disputes with the crown and the house of lords. Hunneyball's detailed examination of the early Stuart period illustrates how parliamentary privilege was viewed differently in the Lords and Commons. In particular, the article highlights the Lords, the oft-neglected part of the bicamerality of parliament, and shows how the Lords' use of privilege mimicked its elevated status in society and made it 'the one body the Crown could not afford to alienate'.

In 1621, the management of parliament took on an extra dimension. After the abortive last session of the 1604–10 parliament and the failure of its successor in 1614, both James and his newly-appointed lord chancellor, Sir Francis Bacon, Viscount St Alban, were desperate for a peaceable and tractable parliament. Chris Kyle's article examines the steps taken by Bacon and James to ensure success. In particular, it discusses the relatively rare technique of using proclamations to manage the elections and to ensure that controversial Jacobean foreign policies did not became the 'talk of the town' or, indeed, the 'common people'. It was a process that led to clashes between James and Bacon and one that, Kyle argues, may have contributed to Bacon's subsequent downfall. Bacon, as one of the foremost advocates of parliamentary governance, recommended that James publish in print his policy on the Palatinate and enlist the aid of the governing class in deliberating and enacting that policy. This, however, was not how the king thought a monarch should act and Bacon's election proclamation was torn apart by James. In a moment of astonishing authorial control, James wrote the proclamation in his own hand, injecting himself directly into the process of management. Kyle argues that, far from standing aloof from the day-to-day machinations of parliamentary management and debate, James's overt intervention was an act of 'unkingly' folly in which he ignored the experience and advice of his senior government advisor.

Lori Anne Ferrell also looks at parliamentary preparation and the opening days, but through the lens of the newly-emerging market in parliamentary sermons. As Ferrell notes, some 240 sermons preached to the Long Parliament went into print but this religious propaganda war actually started under government auspices in the early Caroline period. From 1625, the opening sermon to the parliament was published and these served as an '*agent provocateur* to England's fractured politics in the opening years of Charles I's reign'. Notably, not only did the crown express its viewpoint in print, but the choice of William Laud as the preacher in every parliament can be read as provocative in, and of, itself. Nor, as Ferrell illustrates, were these sermons uncontroversial or general in tone. In fact, they were highly inflammatory and specifically targeted warnings. Laud's opening sermon played upon the theme of dissolution and, in 1625 and subsequent parliaments, Laud's key point was that parliament was called to express the will of the king. Although slow to respond, by 1628 the Commons had become wise to this overt government propaganda and began responding in kind through fast sermons, which were equally provocative in declaring the dire state of England and the need for a general fast. They, too, went into print and, like their crown/court counterparts, found a ready market.

In the final article in this volume, 'The Street Theatre of State', Jason Peacey examines the state opening of parliament between 1603 and 1660. Peacey looks not only at how the ceremony was stage-managed by the government to project a stately and powerful image of Charles I (and later Oliver Cromwell) but, crucially, the audience reaction to the procession. The state opening was one of the most anticipated and watched public appearances of the monarch and closely read by the audience for omens and signs of how the parliament would go. Important foreign dignitaries and the English public jostled for the best view along a route lined with railings designed to keep the crowd back. Indeed, one of the problems of the opening ceremony was that it could be marred by crowd disorder and missteps by the monarch, from James's unfortunate cry of 'a pox take ye' in 1621 to those wearing clothes of which he disapproved and Charles's last-minute decision to proceed to the opening of the Long Parliament, not in the traditional way via the streets but by barge from Whitehall to Westminster. Occasioned both by Charles's distaste for crowds and fears for his safety at such a turbulent time in London, it, nevertheless, sent out a political message that all was not well in the realm. Cromwell in the 1650s was accused of adopting a 'quasi-monarchial' attitude to ceremony but, as Peacey illustrates, Cromwell's parliamentary processions, although following many of the trappings of his crowned predecessors, differed in important ways. The presence of MPs in the procession, an overt military presence, and the inclusion of commoners in the ritual, sent out a very different message. But whether the opening of parliament was in the full grandeur of the old medieval tradition or the borrowed and altered nature of Cromwellian England, it required considerable attention to detail, management and was subject to intense public scrutiny.

Anticlericalism and the Early Tudor Parliament*

P . R . C A V I L L

This article reconsiders one aspect of Christopher Haigh's influential article 'Anticlericalism and the English Reformation'. His article argued that anticlericalism in early 16th-century England had been exaggerated, mislabelled and (in effect) invented as a scholarly construct. Dr Haigh proceeded to dismantle the foundations of anticlericalism in literature, in litigation, and in legislation. Evidence of anticlericalism in parliament, he maintained, was discontinuous, opportunistic and unrepresentative. This article suggests, however, that Haigh's claim makes insufficient allowance for the scarcity of the sources, underestimates the degree of continuity before and after 1529, and fails to take into account the inherently public character of parliamentary petitioning. It proposes, instead, that the challenging of the Church's wealth, the criticizing of clerical abuses, and the questioning of ecclesiastical jurisdiction recurred in early Tudor parliaments, and that the significance of such thwarted attempts at legislative reform crossed sessions and became cumulative.

Keywords: anticlericalism; the Reformation parliament; probate; mortuary payments; pluralism; disendowment; Lollardy; hospitals; almshouses; convocation

In 1983, Christopher Haigh presented a compelling assault on the established narrative of the Reformation.[1] A revisionist *tour de force*, 'Anticlericalism and the English Reformation' denied that widespread resentment of the Church and the clergy in the early 16th century played any part in this religious revolution. Existing accounts, Dr Haigh argued, had lumped together indiscriminately a mass of different sources: denunciations of clerical excess in literature, criticisms of the Church courts, and legislation by the Reformation parliament. By disaggregating and depreciating this material, Haigh sought to abolish the concept of anticlericalism – at least before the break with Rome, for, in a startling inversion, he concluded that anticlericalism, rather than being a cause of the Reformation, was a consequence. His argument, however, was based on a questionable assumption: that if anticlericalism did not cause the Reformation, then the concept played no part in explaining the process of religious change. While accepting Haigh's first contention, subsequent contributors have rehabilitated anticlericalism as a catch-all label for a set of attitudes, behaviours, and discourses.[2] Peter Marshall has explained anticlericalism as the reaction to the unstable clerical compound of exalted station and

---

* I am very grateful to Carole Rawcliffe and John Watts for their advice. I also thank Michael Everett, Tracey Sowerby and a seminar audience at the Institute of Historical Research for their comments.

[1] Christopher Haigh, 'Anticlericalism and the English Reformation', in *The English Reformation Revised*, ed. Christopher Haigh (Cambridge, 1987), 56–74. The article first appeared in Christopher Haigh, 'Anticlericalism and the English Reformation', *History*, lxviii (1983), 391–407.

[2] Peter Marshall, 'Anticlericalism Revested? Expressions of Discontent in Early Tudor England', in *The Parish in Late Medieval England*, ed. Clive Burgess and Eamon Duffy (Donington, 2006), 365–80.

mundane fallibility.[3] Ethan Shagan has suggested how, from the 1530s, government policy and the evangelical message energised this latent and reactive, broad if not deeply-held, sensibility. The case for post-Reformation anticlericalism, Professor Shagan added, is open to the same evidential objection that Haigh had brought for the earlier period.[4] George Bernard, while accepting that anticlericalism 'in no way made the reformation inevitable', has insisted that 'nonetheless it was important'.[5]

This article, therefore, starts from the premise that anticlericalism was neither a cause nor a consequence of the Reformation, but a catalyst. While other analyses have ranged broadly over the subject, drawing on a range of sources, this article is concerned only with one, hitherto neglected, dimension of Haigh's case: the role of parliament. Haigh made two criticisms of the legislative evidence for anticlericalism. First, he advanced a 'political' account of the Reformation parliament.[6] The laws of 1529 concerning mortuaries, pluralism and probate and the manœuvrings of 1532 around the 'Supplication against the Ordinaries' did not voice widely-felt grievances. Rather, he maintained, these complaints originated with the crown's attempts to pressurise the Church into granting the king's divorce, and they drew support from a narrow range of special interests – especially common lawyers and Londoners – that were, however, over-represented in the Commons.[7] Haigh's second point followed naturally from his belief that the anticlericalism of the Reformation parliament was contingent, opportunistic and unrepresentative. In the absence of royal sponsorship, criticism of the Church in earlier parliaments was, he claimed, rare, transient and hardly deserving of the importance it had been accorded. A fuss had been made in the contentious parliament of 1515 over the statutory restriction of benefit of clergy and over the death (in the Church's custody) of the London citizen, Richard Hunne, but both issues soon petered out.[8] Because 'agitation about spiritual jurisdiction died down after 1515', the Reformation parliament was thus not the crescendo of a growing chorus of lay criticism. Discontinuity marked the parliament of 1523, which, 'despite its struggle with Wolsey over taxation, had nothing to say about the Church'.[9]

The simple fact that only one parliament met between 1515 and 1529 helps to make the case against 'a rising tide of lay discontent', but it also suggests considering alternative means by which such sentiment could be expressed (as Haigh and others have) and studying parliament over a longer timescale (as is attempted here).[10] Because they lacked the royal impetus behind the 1529 session, previous parliaments may better typify lay

---

[3] Peter Marshall, *The Catholic Priesthood and the English Reformation* (Oxford, 1994), esp. ch. 8.

[4] E.H. Shagan, *Popular Politics and the English Reformation* (Cambridge, 2003), ch. 4.

[5] G.W. Bernard, *The Late Medieval English Church: Vitality and Vulnerability before the Break with Rome* (New Haven, CT, 2012), 152.

[6] Haigh, 'Anticlericalism', 60–6.

[7] Broadly supportive of this interpretation is Richard Rex, 'Jasper Fyloll and the Enormities of the Clergy: Two Tracts Written during the Reformation Parliament', *Sixteenth Century Journal*, xxxi (2000), 1043–62. Dr Rex places these tracts in their 'immediate political context' as attempts by the crown to 'manipulate' public opinion (1046).

[8] This episode is recounted in Christopher Haigh, *English Reformations: Religion, Politics, and Society under the Tudors* (Oxford, 1993), ch. 4.

[9] Haigh, 'Anticlericalism', 56–7.

[10] Haigh, 'Anticlericalism', 56.

attitudes to the Church. Although it will draw attention to some little-remarked pieces of evidence, this article cannot marshal significant archival discoveries about the early Tudor parliament. Instead, it will propose a maximalist, rather than Haigh's minimalist, reading of existing sources, and it will challenge arguments from silence about the spasmodic nature of parliamentary activity. Thus the interpretation rests on looking more searchingly at the evidence and on extending the period under examination.

This reasoning depends on recognizing how little is known about the early Tudor parliament. The parliament rolls recorded the texts of acts but not much else.[11] The single extant volume of the Lords journals covers only four of the 20 sessions from 1485 to 1523.[12] Only a few draft bills have survived among the governmental archives, and there is rarely proof that they were presented to a parliament.[13] What have not survived are documents comparable to the sequences of drafts, the successive revisions, the legislative memoranda and the unsolicited commonwealth initiatives that passed through Thomas Cromwell's hands in the 1530s.[14] When the limits of the evidence are properly acknowledged, arguments from silence must, therefore, be qualified.

In particular, Haigh's stark contrast between the parliaments of 1515 and 1523 – the former deeply concerned with Church-state relations, the latter not at all – may be questioned. Admittedly, the earlier parliament was dominated by ecclesiastical controversies, the later by Wolsey's huge tax demand. But warfare against Scotland was seriously considered, if not ultimately pursued, in 1515; two taxes were granted, albeit to make up an earlier shortfall.[15] In 1523, taxation did remain uppermost in people's minds across the 17 weeks; as the Commons proved intractable and the cardinal stubborn, the parliament overran through the summer into August. The controversy crowded out other business: even in July no opportunity to pursue private legislation had yet arisen.[16] The chronicler, Edward Hall (probably a member of the Commons), sourly contrasted Bishop Tunstall's promise in his opening sermon of reforming laws with the sessions' actual achievements: 'This was the cause of the Parlyament he sayd, but surely of these thinges no worde was spoken in the whole Parlyament, and in effect no good act made except the graunt of a great subsidie were one.'[17] Yet in its immediate aftermath, Thomas Cromwell (also an MP) complained wearily that the 1523 parliament had touched on an almost inexhaustible range of possible reforms, however inconclusively.[18]

In contrasting the two parliaments, Haigh therefore made insufficient allowance for the vagaries of the sources. Neither the Lords journals nor the 'original acts' have

[11] G.R. Elton, 'The Rolls of Parliament, 1449–1547', in G.R. Elton, *Studies in Tudor and Stuart Politics and Government* (4 vols, Cambridge, 1974–92), iii, 110–42.

[12] M.F. Bond, *Guide to the Records of Parliament* (1971), 30–1.

[13] E.g., *Letters and Papers, Foreign and Domestic, of the Reign of Henry VIII*, ed. J.S. Brewer, James Gairdner and R.H. Brodie (21 vols in 36 pts with addenda, 1862–1932) [hereafter cited as *LP*], i, pt 2, nos 3599–600; John Guy, 'Wolsey and the Parliament of 1523', in *Law and Government under the Tudors*, ed. Claire Cross, David Loades and J.J. Scarisbrick (Cambridge, 1988), 10–12.

[14] These sources underpinned much of Sir Geoffrey Elton's work: e.g., *Studies in Tudor and Stuart Politics*, ii, chs 23–6; *Reform and Renewal: Thomas Cromwell and the Common Weal* (Cambridge, 1973).

[15] *LJ*, i, 21b; *CSP Ven., 1509–19*, pp. 241, 270; Sebastian Giustinian, *Four Years at the Court of Henry VIII*, ed. Rawdon Brown (2 vols, 1854), i, 142; 6 Hen. VIII, c. 26; 7 Hen. VIII, c. 9.

[16] TNA, SP1/28, f. 105 (*LP*, iii, pt 2, no. 3164).

[17] Edward Hall, *Chronicle*, ed. Henry Ellis (1809), 652.

[18] *Life and Letters of Thomas Cromwell*, ed. R.B. Merriman (2 vols, Oxford, 1902), i, 313–14.

survived for the parliament of 1523 as they have for the earlier parliament. Whether the issues that had provoked controversy in 1515 resurfaced eight years later is thus a matter for conjecture. Might the Hunne case have been raised once more? In 1515, the Commons had attempted to protect Hunne's children from the material loss consequent upon his posthumous conviction for heresy. The Commons may have renewed its petitioning in 1523, for during the fourth week of the parliament the king re-granted Hunne's forfeiture to his surviving daughter and her husband.[19] Haigh's stark contrast between the two parliaments was, therefore, too sharply drawn.

A similar point could be made when comparing the first session of the Reformation parliament with previous parliaments. According to Hall, in November 1529 the Commons identified six principal grievances against the Church, which a committee then condensed into three bills: on probate, on mortuaries, and on secular employment, pluralism and absenteeism. Approved by the Commons, these bills were opposed by the lords spiritual but backed by the king; following conferences between representatives of the two Houses, the bills were either redrafted or amended; only when the lords temporal had sided with the lower House were the measures passed.[20] In Hall's version, these three acts remedied the Commons' six articles. Our knowledge of legislative proceedings in the Reformation parliament, however, is incomplete, especially as the Lords journals have survived for only the sixth session (in spring 1534). Through an analysis of draft bills, modern scholarship has revealed that criticisms of convocation's legislative power, of the ecclesiastical courts, and of the Church's wealth, were probably also raised in 1529.[21] Evidently, the full range of anticlerical grievances aired in this first session is unknowable. Haigh's supposed discontinuity – issues that had mattered in earlier parliaments were not raised in 1529 – is unproven.

Reflecting on this first session of 1529, Edward Hall emphasized its unprecedented character: no one had hitherto dared to criticize clerical abuses. 'These thinges', he wrote, 'before this time might in nowise be towched nor yet talked of by no man except he would be made an heritike, or lese al that he had.'[22] Had he been present in 1515, Hall could hardly have asserted that; but the parliament of 1523 was the first assembly in which Hall, who was born in 1496 or 1497, could have sat.[23] Of course, his comment was polemical in purpose and informed by hindsight: for Hall, the clergy's repressive reaction to legitimate complaint, especially under Wolsey's iniquitous regime, ended abruptly and conclusively in November 1529 when God opened the king's eyes, whereupon the Commons at long last could discuss the 'grefes wherwith the spiritualtie had before tyme greuously oppressed them'.[24] Foremost among these grievances were the issues of probate, mortuary payments, and pluralism that became the subject of new legislation. Haigh also implied that these three issues were first aired in 1529 – not

[19] P.R. Cavill, 'Heresy, Law and the State: Forfeiture in Late Medieval and Early Modern England', *English Historical Review*, cxxix (2014), 284–8.

[20] Hall, *Chronicle*, 765–7.

[21] S.E. Lehmberg, *The Reformation Parliament, 1529–1536* (Cambridge, 1970), 83–6. For the third aspect, see the discussion of disendowment below.

[22] Hall, *Chronicle*, 765.

[23] *The History of Parliament: The House of Commons, 1509–1558*, ed. S.T. Bindoff (3 vols, 1982) [hereafter cited as *HPC, 1509–58*], ii, 279–82.

[24] Hall, *Chronicle*, 765.

because they reflected long-suppressed grievances, but rather because they 'arose from Wolsey's own career and may have been part of a campaign to secure his permanent exclusion from power'.[25] Each issue probably had, however, been debated in an earlier parliament.

In 1529, the Commons' principal complaint concerning probate was the excessive charges that bishops and their officers demanded, to which the legislative remedy would be the fixing of fees based on the value of testators' estates.[26] Twenty-five years earlier, on 17 February 1504, London's court of aldermen decided to draw up a bill 'for the probate of testamentes'.[27] Parliament was in its fourth week when this decision was taken; when the bill was presented and how it fared over the session's remaining seven weeks are not known. The likelihood is that the city's efforts were concentrated, unsuccessfully, on opposing two bills judged highly detrimental to the capital's interests rather more than on promoting this proposal.[28] The entry in the repertory book for 1504 did not state the city's particular concern; that this related to fees seems plausible, for in 1529 the Mercers' Company would describe Londoners as 'polled and robbed without reason or conscience by th'ordenarys in probatyng of testamentes'.[29]

The bill of 1504 also addressed the administration of the estates of those who had died intestate and of those whose executors had refused the role. It proposed some regulation of the letters *ad colligendum* that ordinaries issued for the collection of the goods of the deceased; possibly the fees demanded had given rise to complaint, as they would also be restricted by the statute.[30] Letters of administration would feature, too, on the list that Thomas, Lord Darcy prepared of Wolsey's abuses in his memorandum of July 1529.[31] London's bill also sought to overturn the court's practice of naming a date upon which creditors should stake their claims, whereby those who failed to appear on that day forfeited their rights; as a result, the aldermen complained, the ordinaries 'kepe all the goodes'. This issue did not appear in the act of 1529, so a direct connection between the two bills seems unlikely; but the abuse of probate, therefore, had been aired in at least one previous session.

Also raised in early Tudor parliaments before being the subject of legislation in 1529 was probably the issue of mortuary payments.[32] The repercussions of the Hunne case provided a plausible – but not the only conceivable – context. Richard Hunne's refusal in March 1511 to give the rector of St Mary Matfelon (Whitechapel) his infant son Stephen's winding sheet began the chain of events that culminated in his suspicious death and posthumous condemnation for heresy in December 1514.[33] There has survived among the governmental archives a corrected draft petition to the Commons that

[25] Haigh, 'Anticlericalism', 60.

[26] 21 Hen. VIII, c. 5.

[27] Helen Miller, 'London and Parliament in the Reign of Henry VIII', *Bulletin of the Institute of Historical Research*, xxxv (1962), 134.

[28] Miller, 'London', 132–4.

[29] Miller, 'London', 144.

[30] 21 Hen. VIII, c. 5, s. 2.

[31] *LP*, iv, pt 3, no. 5749.

[32] 21 Hen. VIII, c. 6.

[33] Susan Brigden, *London and the Reformation* (Oxford, 1989), 98–103.

reflected Hunne's grievance, but made no reference to his case or to any other.[34] This petition's preamble complained how parish priests and farmers (i.e., lessees of parochial lands) were suing for mortuary dues. It censured the cruelty, pitilessness and lack of charity of parish priests and their curates in making burial conditional on receiving their dues. The bill, therefore, proposed to exempt from mortuary and other death duties, children under the age of 14 years (such as Stephen Hunne) and also married women, those in religious orders, and anyone having no goods within the parish. Anticipating the possibility that these groups might henceforth be denied burial, the bill obliged priests to receive the bodies of anyone who died in their parish. It also required clergymen to administer the sacraments to the parish's sick, by implication in their own homes. Churchwardens were empowered to enforce these regulations by bringing actions in any royal court of record; breaches were to be punished by a £40 fine, to be divided between the parish church and the crown.

The date and provenance of this bill are both uncertain. No reference to such a measure is found in the extant Lords journals (for 1510, spring 1512, and 1515). The dates proposed in *Letters and Papers* – 1514 or December 1515 – seem to be based on the Hunne case.[35] As the document is damaged, the opening clauses that might have disclosed the petitioners' identity have been lost. That such a bill is now found in the governmental archive need not imply royal initiative: a petition about tithes in Romney Marsh, for instance, originated locally.[36] Although the editors of *Letters and Papers* linked the bill to a complaint from Londoners against other oblations demanded by the city's clerics, this complaint may rather date to the controversy over tithes in the 1530s.[37] The bill is unlikely to have been a preliminary draft of the Mortuary Act of 1529, for the two texts differed markedly. The act fixed mortuary dues for everyone, whereas the bill was concerned only with those who should pay nothing. The identities of those exempted also differed; here the bill was the better drafted, as it defined childhood by age. Moreover, the act's preamble expressed no concern over unburied bodies, while the requirement that priests minister sacraments to the sick did not appear. Additionally, the act vested the right to sue in the aggrieved party rather than in the churchwardens of the affected parish. Therefore, this bill was most likely prepared for an earlier parliament.

The third statute passed in 1529 encompassed four of the six articles formulated in the Commons' committee in three parts: clergymen's worldliness, pluralism and non-residence.[38] While the earlier probate and mortuaries bills had been rewritten during their progress through the two Houses, this later measure – according to Hall – underwent only 'a litle qualifiyng'.[39] Its disjointed sequence of clauses, nevertheless,

[34] TNA, SP1/12, f. 20.

[35] *LP*, i, pt 2, no. 3602; ii, pt 1, no. 1315.

[36] TNA, E175/6/21; Lehmberg, *Reformation Parliament*, 189 n. 5; *HPC, 1509–58*, i, 258–9.

[37] *LP*, i, pt 2, no. 3602. The complaint had been included in the first edition (1862), but could no longer be found in the Public Record Office when the second edition (1920) was compiled. A copy has been credibly identified: Brigden, *London*, 50–1, citing Lambeth Palace Library, CM viii/2d (which is bound as CM viii/1–3, ff. 64–72). This is a 17th-century transcript of a schedule annexed to a replication in a chancery case between three London parishes and their parsons in 1533. The schedule and accompanying documents do not suggest that the complaint was other than contemporaneous with the chancery proceedings. The original bill, without the schedule and other documents, is TNA, C1/754/8.

[38] 21 Hen. VIII, c. 13.

[39] Hall, *Chronicle*, 767.

implies a complex passage.[40] Scholarly attention has focused on two of the act's three parts: the setting of limits to the number of benefices churchmen could hold and the requirement that they be resident in one of those benefices. Although multiple exemptions were thought to have rendered these provisions ineffectual, recently Robert Palmer has shown how, in the years after enactment, many actions were brought in the royal courts.[41] Professor Palmer has also drawn attention to the act's third and complementary element: restrictions on commercial activity. Taken together, these measures represented, he proposed, a reorientation of 'the English parish from a commercial enterprise into a pastoral institution'.[42]

The principal problem requiring reform, according to Palmer, was the practice by rectors and perpetual vicars of leasing out parishes' glebe lands, other property rights and spiritual dues (including mortuaries) to laymen or other churchmen.[43] At the time, however, as pressing a grievance may have been clergymen farming land themselves, for this practice appeared as the Commons' third article, and its prohibition was given pride of place in the act. Under this statute, clergymen were required to divest themselves of such leases by September 1530, but continued to be able to lease out lands to laymen. Thus it was not so much that the parish lost its commercial dimension, as that the clergy were largely excluded from that aspect of its life. Seventeen years earlier, this same restriction had been proposed in parliament. In March 1512, the Commons had approved a bill stating that 'spiritual persons should not occupy farms of lands and tenements'. Sent to the upper House, the bill was read once by peers and rejected straight away.[44] Nothing is known of either the measure's origins or its contents. Conceivably, this bill might even have formed the basis for the discrete measure in the statute of 1529, for that was the only part to contain all elements necessary in an act.[45]

Therefore, some aspect of each of the three laws of 1529 had been aired already. When viewed in isolation, this evidence might be dismissed as fragmentary; but because only a fraction of parliamentary business has been preserved, these instances ought to be scaled up. Bills presented in one parliament were sought in the next: for example, decades of lobbying preceded the passing of the first Enclosures Act in 1490.[46] Corporations demonstrably pursued objectives decade after decade.[47] Where records are not extant, such persistence can only be surmised. A list of bills in 1495 reveals that Newcastle came close to securing an act concerning the River Tyne; how many further attempts were made before the borough secured legislative relief in 1529 are not

---

[40] A subsidiary complaint in the third of the Commons' articles – priests serving as stewards, surveyors, and other secular officers – did not feature in the act. The fourth article – spiritual men running tanning houses and selling merchandise – was separated in the act (sections 5, 21). The number of chaplains allowed to archbishops and bishops was evidently revised (sections 11, 13). The act's final proviso carried its own internal saving clause (section 24).

[41] R.C. Palmer, *Selling the Church: The English Parish in Law, Commerce, and Religion, 1350–1550* (Chapel Hill, NC, 2002), 144–8, 173–208.

[42] Palmer, *Selling the Church*, 1.

[43] Palmer, *Selling the Church*, chs 2, 4.

[44] *LJ*, i, 14b–15a.

[45] 21 Hen. VIII, c. 13, s. 1.

[46] John Rous, *Historia Regum Angliae*, ed. Thomas Hearne (2nd edn, Oxford, 1745), 120–1; 4 Hen. VII, c. 19.

[47] P.R. Cavill, *The English Parliaments of Henry VII, 1485–1504* (Oxford, 2009), 157.

known.[48] Rejection, therefore, need not have put an end to such efforts. In his last parliament, Henry VII vetoed a customs bill; undeterred, the bill's proponents tried again in Henry VIII's first parliament.[49] If issues were felt to be important enough to pursue once, then they were likely to reappear in other parliaments. And if, competition for legislative time notwithstanding, some bills were sufficiently appealing to be passed by one House (if not the other), then the likelihood that they would be pursued in subsequent sessions possibly increased.

However often such issues recurred, the grievances raised have been thought unrepresentative. One, or possibly two, of the three bills that anticipated the statutes of 1529 had originated with the city of London. Thus Haigh treated this legislation as the work of particular interest-groups rather than as the reflection of wider concerns. The distinction between a (common) public interest and a (singular) private interest was a staple of petitionary rhetoric.[50] Yet as a means of analysing law-making, this division misleads because statutes usually reflected the current concerns of specific groups. For instance, in 1467 pyxes had been stolen from many of London's churches; assumed to be heretics, the culprits turned out only to be common criminals.[51] The following year, the Commons complained of a spate of thefts of pyxes and other holy vessels from churches.[52] While this episode could be further evidence of the city's disproportionate influence on law-making, it also illustrates how the public forum transformed the particular into the universal: however local or vested their motivation, proponents of legislation assumed a communal petitionary identity. Peculiar grievances were reformulated as all-embracing reforms: the 1468 bill referred to a nationwide problem rather than the capital's crime wave, for which it proposed a standard punishment. This universalising impulse helped to secure priority in the legislative schedule and also to garner support. As they passed through parliament, bills could thus become genuinely (and not just rhetorically) public and collective.[53]

One issue that apparently did not feature in the early Tudor parliaments but loomed large from 1529 was the confiscation and reallocation of the Church's material wealth. In 1533, Sir Thomas More emphasized this discontinuity. He could think of no precedent for the present murmur around disendowment, except 'onys in the tyme of the famouse prynce kyng Henry ye fourth, aboute the tyme of a greate rumble that the heretykes made [Oldcastle's rebellion] . . . there was a folysshe byll & a false put into a parleament or twayn'.[54] More's purpose was to discredit such talk by association with outright heresy and open rebellion. In similar terms, Haigh stressed the gulf between the Lollard petition of (probably) 1410 and the opening of the Reformation parliament: 'Disendowment had not been a popular slogan in the meantime, which should remind

[48] *The Parliament Rolls of Medieval England, 1275–1504*, ed. Chris Given-Wilson *et al.* (16 vols, Woodbridge, 2005) [hereafter cited as *PROME*], xvi, 279; 21 Hen. VIII, c. 18.

[49] Cavill, *English Parliaments*, 58.

[50] *PROME*, xvi, 91, 96–7, 132–3.

[51] *The Historical Collections of a Citizen of London in the Fifteenth Century*, ed. James Gairdner (Camden Society, new ser., xvii, 1876), 234–5.

[52] TNA, C49/36/4; *PROME*, xiii, 383–4.

[53] Cavill, *English Parliaments*, 156, 161–72.

[54] Thomas More, *The Apology*, ed. J.B. Trapp, in *The Complete Works of St. Thomas More* (15 vols, New Haven, CT, 1963–97), ix, 84.

us that there was no crescendo of heresy and protest from the time of Wycliffe to that of Wolsey.'[55] Margaret Aston, by contrast, saw disendowment as a potent idea for the century between the 1350s and the 1450s.[56] The concept could be traced from the controversy between Archbishop Fitzralph and the friars through the war parliaments of the 1370s via the 'Twelve Conclusions' of 1395 to the petition of 1410. It remained topical in Henry VI's reign, for Bishop Pecock treated the matter at length, while Kentish protestors in 1452 demanded that priests should own nothing 'save a chair and candlestick to look upon their books'.[57] But interest thereafter, by implication, waned.

This story resumes in the Reformation parliament, where assaults on clerical wealth culminated in the dissolution of the lesser monasteries in the eighth and final session of 1536.[58] Through an important archival discovery, Richard Hoyle has traced this issue back to the very first session of this parliament.[59] In 1529 a new petition, prefaced by a copy of the Lollard petition of 1410, invited the king through parliament to resume some of the Church's temporalities and also to assume (on a trial basis) responsibility for clerical discipline.[60] Professor Hoyle suggests that this petition may have originated within the coalition of nobles that had emerged in opposition to Cardinal Wolsey that summer.[61] He interprets dissolution as a policy pursued 'from above' for the crown's financial gain rather than demanded 'from below' on reformist grounds.[62] The criticism of Wolsey's own monastic dissolutions in parliament and elsewhere substantiates this idea.[63] In the face of such reluctance, the crown – having perhaps floated dissolution in 1529 and in 1534 – then dressed its policy up as a remedy for the supposedly irredeemable failings of the lesser monasteries.[64]

It would be possible, however, to put a different slant on the evidence that Hoyle has assembled. His argument implies that, while dissolving monasteries did not command great support, the principle of redistributing clerical wealth proved more palatable. After all, the Church's possessions were widely interpreted as a conditional lay endowment, which might be resumed if misused.[65] Thus the 1410 text continued to circulate: it was

---

[55] Christopher Haigh, 'The English Reformation: A Premature Birth, A Difficult Labour and a Sickly Child', *Historical Journal*, xxxiii (1990), 452.

[56] Margaret Aston, ' "Caim's Castles": Poverty, Politics, and Disendowment', in *The Church, Politics and Patronage in the Fifteenth Century*, ed. Barrie Dobson (Gloucester, 1984), 45–81.

[57] Roger Virgoe, 'Some Ancient Indictments in the King's Bench referring to Kent, 1450–1452', in *Documents Illustrative of Medieval Kentish Society*, ed. F.R.H. Du Boulay (Kent Records, xviii, 1964), 258. The protestors alluded to 2 Kings 4.10.

[58] 27 Hen. VIII, c. 28.

[59] R.W. Hoyle, 'The Origins of the Dissolution of the Monasteries', *Historical Journal*, xxxviii (1995), 275–305.

[60] Hoyle, 'Origins', 301–5.

[61] Hoyle, 'Origins', 287–9.

[62] Cf. Rex, 'Jasper Fyloll', 1058–9.

[63] *LP*, iv, pt 3, nos 5749, 6075; Greg Walker, 'Cardinal Wolsey and the Satirists: The Case of *Godly Queen Hester* Re-opened', in *Cardinal Wolsey: Church, State and Art*, ed. S.J. Gunn and P.G. Lindley (Cambridge, 1991), 239–60.

[64] Hoyle, 'Origins', 289, 293–4, 297.

[65] Benjamin Thompson, '*Habendum et Tenendum*: Lay and Ecclesiastical Attitudes to the Property of the Church', in *Religious Belief and Ecclesiastical Careers in Late Medieval England*, ed. Christopher Harper-Bill (Woodbridge, 1991), 197–238.

re-presented four years later, distributed during the risings of 1431, disseminated in London in the 1470s, and preserved by the city's chroniclers.[66] In 1516, a detailed summary appeared in print in Fabyan's chronicle, which might explain why Wolsey purportedly had this book burnt for exposing the clergy's excessive wealth.[67] Perhaps the Lollard petition's wider appeal lay in its proposals for the redistribution of clerical resources towards more deserving causes, such as the defence of the realm, the recruitment of new blood to the nobility and gentry, and the erection of more universities.[68] Advocates of disendowment continued to suggest ways in which the crown should deploy this windfall – on a crusade against 'the greate Turk', the petition of 1529 thought.[69] The thwarting of such long-cherished aspirations may account for evangelical disenchantment with the dissolutions of 1536 onwards.[70]

Defending his policy that year, Henry VIII appealed not only to present exigency but also to precedent.[71] Had not Edward III dissolved a whole order; had not Henry V confiscated the alien priories; had not the saintly Henry VI, the king's own grandmother and his leading prelates suppressed houses in order to erect new colleges within the universities?[72] However disingenuous the king's reasoning appears in the light of the subsequent total dissolution of the monasteries, in its immediate context his case for continuity was not implausible.[73] The earlier royal appropriations and the recycling of ecclesiastical wealth may have helped to maintain the currency of resumption. In endowing his Oxford college, Wolsey told the king in 1525, he had dissolved only 'certain exile and small monasteries, wherein neither God is served, ne religion kept'.[74] Elements of Wolsey's more extensive dissolution scheme of 1528–9, such as the erection of new bishoprics, were implemented after the break with Rome, with the avowed intention of improving educational provision and poor relief.[75] The redistribution of clerical wealth was not tainted by association with Lollardy in the way that biblical translation had become in the 15th century. Thus 1529 did not simply take up where 1410 had left off: if not a movement, disendowment was more than a moment.[76]

In the case of hospitals and almshouses, it is possible to move beyond the conjectural. Over the 14th and 15th centuries, the balance of resources within these institutions had shifted from provision for the poor and sick towards the payment of clerical stipends

---

[66] Thomas More, *Letter to Bugenhagen, Supplication of Souls, Letter against Frith*, ed. Frank Manley *et al.*, in *Complete Works*, vii, 143–4, 346–8; Wendy Scase, *Literature and Complaint in England, 1272–1553* (Oxford, 2007), 148.

[67] Robert Fabyan, *The New Chronicles of England and France*, ed. Henry Ellis (1811), pp. xviii, 575–6; John Bale, *Index Britanniae Scriptorum*, ed. R.L. Poole and Mary Bateson (Oxford, 1902), 370–1.

[68] *Selections from English Wycliffite Writings*, ed. Anne Hudson (Cambridge, 1978), 135–7.

[69] Hoyle, 'Origins', 303.

[70] Alec Ryrie, *The Gospel and Henry VIII: Evangelicals in the Early English Reformation* (Cambridge, 2003), 155, 161–5, 216.

[71] *Answere made by the Kynges Hyghnes to the Petitions of the Rebelles in Yorkeshire* (1536), sigs A2v–A3.

[72] The reference to Edward III may be an approximate allusion to the Templars (a suggestion I owe to Martin Heale): cf. John Wyclif, *Tractatus de Ecclesia*, ed. Johann Loserth (1886), 331–2.

[73] G.W. Bernard, 'The Dissolution of the Monasteries', *History*, xcvi (2011), 390–409.

[74] *State Papers: King Henry VIII* (11 vols, 1830–52), i, 154.

[75] 31 Hen. VIII, c. 9; Hoyle, 'Origins', 282–3.

[76] Cf. Hoyle, 'Origins', 289; Marshall, 'Anticlericalism Revested', 379.

supporting the round of spiritual services.[77] Foremost among the critics of this development were the Lollards, who twice petitioned parliament on this subject. The 'Twelve Conclusions' of 1395 denounced existing almshouses as the product of the almost-simoniacal practice of selling prayers for individuals, adding that 100 such establishments would have sufficed for the whole realm. By contrast, in 1410 the second petition proposed using the proceeds of disendowment to found 100 new almshouses exclusively in order to support 'alle the nedefull pore men'.[78] Their origins notwithstanding, these criticisms evidently resonated: in 1414 a petition of the Commons was enacted – remarkably, by the parliament meeting shortly after Oldcastle's rebellion.[79] This petition explained how the misapplication of hospitals' goods and profits had undermined the founders' charitable intentions. The resulting statute, therefore, commissioned the ordinaries to inquire into the state of royal hospitals and to reform other institutions.[80]

One hundred years later, another petition to parliament raised this same issue.[81] This petition can be securely dated to the two sessions of 1512. According to a contemporary endorsement, the document was presented in the king's fourth regnal year and hence in the November and December session.[82] The petition, however, is probably also the bill 'concerning masters and keepers of hospitals and other almshouses' that had reached the Lords in March 1512 in the king's third regnal year.[83] The petitioners – '[the poor] blynd lame sore miserable and impotent people of this [land that may nott labour]' – complained how daily they were dying in the streets because hospitals and almshouses had been diverted from their true calling. Not only had self-interested masters and wardens failed to maintain their institutions: they had also converted many into free chapels supporting confraternities, from which the truly deserving were excluded. Some institutions took money for men's admissions; others recruited men to join these fraternities by promising masses and orisons that, scandalously, were then not said. Therefore, every governor should make certification in chancery of his institution's statutes, income and inhabitants, and then should reform the institution in accordance with its foundation ordinances. Should no certificate be returned or no reform ensue, then the founders or their heirs were entitled to re-enter the institutions in order to reform them; should the founders or their heirs fail so to do, then the crown would re-enter in their stead.

This proposal, Carole Rawcliffe suggests, may have originated in the civic, courtly and humanist milieux of men such as the royal physician, Thomas Linacre.[84] It reflected the way in which religious institutions – competing to provide spiritual services and

---

[77] Nicholas Orme and Margaret Webster, *The English Hospital, 1070–1570* (New Haven, CT, 1995), ch. 7; Carole Rawcliffe, *Urban Bodies: Communal Health in Late Medieval English Towns and Cities* (Woodbridge, 2013), 316–49. I am grateful to Professor Rawcliffe for sight of her work ahead of publication.

[78] *English Wycliffite Writings*, ed. Hudson, 26, 136–7.

[79] *PROME*, ix, 45–6.

[80] 2 Hen. V, st. 1, c. 1.

[81] TNA, E175/11/65. The opening lines are lost; missing text is supplied from the transcript in BL, Add. MS 24459, pp. 157–60.

[82] The journal for this session has not survived: *LJ*, i, 17b.

[83] *LJ*, i, 14b. This bill arrived on the same day as that to prohibit clerical lessees.

[84] Rawcliffe, *Urban Bodies*, 296–9, 349–52; Paul Slack, *From Reformation to Improvement: Public Welfare in Early Modern England* (Oxford, 1999), ch. 1, esp. 14–23.

thereby to secure lay support – were torn between their original purpose at foundation and the pressure of current lay demands, of which the most significant was the provision of masses for the souls of the present generation.[85] Its criticism of the diversion of charitable provision from poor relief towards prayer echoed Lollard complaint and anticipated the 'commonweal' case of men such as Thomas Starkey for the Henrician dissolution.[86] Although it proposed to employ the patronal relationship in order to enforce institutional reform, the petition (unlike the statute of 1414) vested in the crown the power to intervene, which power would be assumed in the Chantries Act of 1545.[87] Absent from the proposal, however, was any role for the Church. In 1416 the Commons, complaining that the two-year-old statute had not been implemented, had proposed fining ordinaries who failed in their responsibilities; a century later, the ordinaries were bypassed entirely.[88] The 1512 petition therefore suggests a gradual erosion of confidence in the Church's administrative capacities and reflects the consequent trend towards greater lay control of new religious foundations.[89]

This petition, however, ran up against the legislative independence of the Church. The defects described, the lords spiritual declared, 'ought to be reformed in convocation'.[90] There is no evidence that any action was taken by convocation; masters of those hospitals represented in its lower House presumably would, if present, have opposed such a measure.[91] This rebuff raises the constitutional issue that became prominent in the 'Supplication against the Ordinaries' in 1532: the relationship between two assemblies that both sought through legislation to reform the ecclesiastical estate. Defending themselves against the charge of meddling with secular matters, the bishops reasoned, in December 1515, that it was 'as lauful to them in the Conuocation howse to common and treate of thinges concernyng bothe laye men and also the lawes of the land . . . as it is for them of the parliament to common or treate of any causys sownyng ayenst the clergy and the lawes of the churche'.[92] Therefore, assessments of anticlericalism in the early Tudor parliament should consider relations with convocation.

In institutional, as well as in jurisdictional, terms, convocation and parliament were entwined. Their many structural resemblances – joint summonses, bicameral nature, the speakership and members' privileges – served as a reminder that, in the early 14th century, the two assemblies had met as one body.[93] Parliament and the convocation of Canterbury often convened at the same time at other ends of the same city (at Westminster and St Paul's Cathedral).[94] While John Taylor's dual role in 1515 as clerk

---

[85] This tension is the central theme of Benjamin Thompson's work on monasteries: e.g., 'Monasteries, Society and Reform in Late Medieval England', in *The Religious Orders in Pre-Reformation England*, ed. J.G. Clark (Woodbridge, 2002), 165–95.

[86] Joyce Youings, *The Dissolution of the Monasteries* (1971), 168–9.

[87] 37 Hen. VIII, c. 4, s. 6.

[88] *PROME*, ix, 157–9.

[89] R.N. Swanson, *Church and Society in Late Medieval England* (rev. edn, Oxford, 1993), 255–60; M.K. McIntosh, *Poor Relief in England, 1350–1600* (Cambridge, 2012), 89–94.

[90] *LJ*, i, 15a.

[91] *Records of Convocation*, ed. Gerald Bray (20 vols, Woodbridge, 2005–6), xix, 251.

[92] TNA, SP1/12, f. 17v (*LP*, ii, pt 1, no. 1314), printed in *Records of Convocation*, ed. Bray, xix, 136–7.

[93] *Records of Convocation*, ed. Bray, xix, 7–10, 245–80; 8 Hen. VI, c. 1.

[94] *Handbook of British Chronology*, ed. E.B. Fryde *et al.* (3rd edn, 1986), 572–3, 603–4.

of parliaments and Speaker of the lower house of convocation was remarkable, others served in both assemblies as a matter of course.[95] The Lords adjourned 20 times in 1510, spring 1512, and 1515, because spiritual members were attending convocation.[96] Given this overlap in personnel, the timing of sessions, and the proximity of meetings, the transactions of one assembly were likely to influence the other. Indeed, Polydore Vergil drew attention to the co-ordination of the parliament of 1523 with the concurrent legatine synod and southern convocation (of which he was a member).[97]

As Vergil's account reveals, grants of clerical and lay taxation were interdependent.[98] While the two convocations offered supply independently, royal officers presented the crown's demands to parliament and to the southern convocation simultaneously, and the resultant grants took similar forms.[99] In 1523, the crown, through parliament, dictated the terms of the Church's grants. In an ostensible concession, the parliamentary subsidy authorised the two convocations to assess clerical wealth (essentially temporalities acquired after 1291) on which lay taxes were normally paid.[100] This delegation was made conditional, however, on the clergy's grant exceeding the value of the lay assessment.[101] As a result, the exemptions allowed by parliament were also to apply to any grants made by the convocations.[102] Moreover, as the crown presented its requirement as a global sum, the proportion to be borne by the clergy could become a subject of dispute. Parliaments limited the exemption of religious communities in order not to overburden 'the pore Comen people of this Realme'.[103] In 1489, MPs had proposed that the Church should pay two-thirds of the total figure requested; in the end, however, it contributed only a quarter.[104] Apportioning the tax burden may thus have kept alive the issue of the Church's wealth. The imposition in 1534 of regular and permanent royal taxation of benefices (first fruits and tenths) may have made laymen more sympathetic towards clerical complaints about excessive taxation than they had previously been.[105]

In other controversial areas, the two assemblies interacted. In November 1509 – a fortnight after the parliamentary writs had gone out – Archbishop Warham took the unusual step of summoning the southern province on his own authority without the usual royal mandate.[106] The reason given was the defence of the liberties of the Church.

---

[95] BL, Cotton MS, Vitellius B II, f. 88 (*LP*, ii, pt 1, no. 1312/6); *LJ*, i, 57b.

[96] *LJ*, i, 3–57 *passim*.

[97] *The Anglica Historia of Polydore Vergil, A.D. 1485–1537*, ed. Denys Hays (Camden Society, 3rd ser., lxxiv, 1950), 304–9.

[98] For the period after the break with Rome, when the Church's grants received parliamentary ratification, see Patrick Carter, 'Parliament, Convocation and the Granting of Clerical Supply in Early Modern England', *Parliamentary History*, xix (2000), 14–26.

[99] Cavill, *English Parliaments*, 62–4.

[100] Roger Schofield, *Taxation under the Early Tudors, 1485–1547* (Oxford, 2004), 60–1, 109–10.

[101] 14 & 15 Hen. VIII, c. 16, s. 20.

[102] 14 & 15 Hen. VIII, c. 16, ss. 21, 24.

[103] 4 Hen. VII, c. 5; 7 Hen. VII, c. 5; Schofield, *Taxation*, 65–9.

[104] Cavill, *English Parliaments*, 62–3.

[105] P.R.N. Carter, 'The Fiscal Reformation: Clerical Taxation and Opposition in Henrician England', in *Reformations Old and New: Essays on the Socio-Economic Impact of Religious Change, c.1470–1630*, ed. B.A. Kümin (Aldershot, 1996), 92–105.

[106] *Records of Convocation*, ed. Bray, vii, 1–4. This assembly was therefore a provincial council, rather than a convocation.

Prelates may have hoped to include the reassertion of ecclesiastical rights in the parliamentary reaction against Henry VII's 'unconstitutional' rule.[107] Thus, when parliament assembled in January 1510, the first bill read in the Lords concerned these liberties.[108] The upper House unanimously approved this measure and sent it to the Commons; the revised bill that the lower House returned appears to have been so unacceptable to the Lords that it was set aside.[109] Would-be legislators needed to frame bills that respected ecclesiastical and secular liberties in areas (such as usury) where jurisdictions overlapped.[110] For example, the bill of 1468 against thefts from churches had proposed an especially ingenious solution: such robbers would be burnt, not as heretics, but as traitors, which was apparently acceptable to spiritual lords (perhaps because the canon law of heresy was untouched), but not to the king, who vetoed the measure.[111]

Even where a final bill was couched in terms suitably respectful of ecclesiastical independence, such self-restraint need not have applied to the preceding debate. What might, for instance, have been said in the first Tudor parliament during the reading of a bill for the 'reformacion of Preestis Clerkys and religious men culpable or by their demerites openly noised of incontinent lyvyng'?[112] As the bishops protested in 1515, 'at sundry tymes diuers of the parliament speketh diuers and many thinges not only ayenst men of the churche and ayenst the lawes of the churche but also somtyme ayenst the kinges lawes'.[113] Disclaiming any desire to punish any parliamentarian so offending, the bishops argued that words spoken in convocation ought likewise to be privileged: thus they were not guilty of *praemunire*.[114] This protestation related to the controversy over benefit of clergy, from which the bishops (temporarily, as it turned out) emerged victorious in this parliament.[115] When the jurisdictional overlap between convocation and parliament is acknowledged, however, the statement may apply to the early Tudor assemblies in general.

The rejection of reform on the grounds that it lay outside parliament's competence provided one proof for Simon Fish of the Church's overweening influence. His *Supplication of Beggars* drew on the same convention of complaint literature as had the hospitals bill of 1512 and the Lollard petition of 1410, one in which the excessive poverty of the speakers amplified the greed of their (often clerical) oppressors.[116] This evangelical polemic of late 1528 or early 1529 presented ecclesiastical power and wealth as a threat to royal authority: the Church became a corporate 'overmighty subject'. Fish showed the king to be powerless to legislate against the litany of clerical abuses, for

---

[107] P.R. Cavill, 'Debate and Dissent in Henry VII's Parliaments', *Parliamentary History*, xxv (2006), 173–5.

[108] *LJ*, i, 4b.

[109] *LJ*, i, 5a, 6b. The rejected bill was handed to the usher of the parliament chamber. Had the Lords expected to proceed, the text would possibly have been handed, instead, to a common lawyer for revision.

[110] 3 Hen. VII, c. 7; 11 Hen. VII, c. 8.

[111] Cf. *Chronicles of London*, ed. C.L. Kingsford (Oxford, 1905), 188.

[112] 1 Hen. VII, c. 2. This statute was invoked in the 1529 disendowment petition: Hoyle, 'Origins', 302.

[113] TNA, SP1/12, f. 17v (*Records of Convocation*, ed. Bray, xix, 136).

[114] *Reports of Cases by John Caryll*, ed. J.H. Baker (2 vols, Selden Society, cxv–cxvi, 1999–2000), ii, 690.

[115] P.R. Cavill, 'A Perspective on the Church–State Confrontation of 1515: The Passage of 4 Henry VIII, c. 2', *Journal of Ecclesiastical History*, lxiii (2012), 655–70.

[116] Scase, *Literature and Complaint*, chs 3–4.

churchmen were 'stronger in your owne parliament house then your silfe'.[117] Shortly before the new parliament assembled, Sir Thomas More responded.[118] Principally a defence of purgatory, his *Supplication of Souls* also refuted Fish's weighing of lay and clerical forces in the two Houses.[119] In the Lords, More objected, the king himself was pre-eminent, and might summon new peers if he wished to rebalance the composition of the House. Spiritual lords did not get their way in defiance of the wishes of temporal lords, even where the laws of the Church and of other countries (the *ius commune*) supported their position. Thus, in the statute of Merton, lay lords had refused to permit the legitimation of children born before their parents' marriage.[120]

The lower House, Fish had claimed, was packed with lawyers, who were all (except the king's counsel) retained by the clergy. More set the record straight: many lawyers were not MPs, and the king's counsel was not present in the Commons (but rather, he left implicit, attendant upon the Lords). It was, however, More's own prior experience in the lower House that belied Fish's essential claim:

> And surely yf he had bene in the comen house as some of vs haue bene: he shuld haue sene the spyrytualte nat gladly spoken for. And we lytell dout but that ye remember actes and statutes passyd at sondry parlyamentes / suche and in such wyse & some of them so late / as your self may se that eyther ye clergy ys not the stronger parte in the kynges parlyement / or elles haue no mynd to stryue.[121]

Through their vigorous and effective criticism of the Church, previous parliaments thus contradicted the idea that the clergy dominated proceedings. A little later, another anticlerical treatise, assuming prematurely that the clergy (with More's assistance) had defeated the *Supplication of Beggars*, repeated Fish's charge: 'in the parlament / The chefe of the clergye are resident / In a maruelous great multitude. / Whos fearce displeasure is so terrible / That I iudge it were not possible / Any cause against them to conclude.'[122]

As the Reformation parliament progressed, this contention became increasingly difficult to sustain. The revolutionary character of that parliament was apparent at the time and remains obvious now. Nevertheless, this article has sought to suggest why the unprecedented nature of the Reformation parliament, especially in its early sessions, has been overstated. First, contemporaries exaggerated for partisan effect: critics of the *status quo* hailed a royal epiphany, while defenders decried a heretical catastrophe. Specifically, the claim that a torrent of pent-up anticlerical feeling was loosed may have its roots in the polemic magnifying the repressive effect of ecclesiastical law, especially concerning heresy. Second, this apparent discontinuity must be, in part, the optical distortion of fragmentary sources. Therefore, Haigh's positivist reasoning necessarily underestimates the incidence and strength of anticlerical feeling in parliament. At the risk of erring in

[117] More, *Letter to Bugenhagen*, 417.

[118] More, *Letter to Bugenhagen*, pp. lxv–lxvi.

[119] More, *Letter to Bugenhagen*, 139–41.

[120] 20 Hen. III, c. 9. This decision was held up as a demonstration of the common law's singularity: John Fortescue, *De Laudibus Legum Anglie*, ed. S.B. Chrimes (Cambridge, 1942), 93–101.

[121] More, *Letter to Bugenhagen*, 141.

[122] *A Proper Dyaloge betwene a Gentillman and an Husbandman*, ed. D.H. Parker (Toronto, 1996), 139–40.

the opposite direction – of overinterpreting, rather than underinterpreting, the surviving sources – the following reconstruction is proposed.

Lay belief that Church reform needed to transcend clerical self-interest balanced historic respect for ecclesiastical independence. As the representative assembly of the whole realm, parliament was a natural venue in which to pursue so important an objective. There, clerical shortcomings were criticized and legislative solutions advanced. Attempts at reform acquired a cumulative significance when they ran up against the apparent intransigence of churchmen: 'ye wyll nat ioyne with the temporall men in counsels and parlyamentes as ye were wonte to do / but ye kepe your conuocacyons and counsels by your selfes', complained an imaginary MP to his counterpart.[123] Because they were invoked to defend practices that undermined the commonweal, the Church's liberties themselves could become the subject of debate. Thus, the questioning of religious privileges, ecclesiastical jurisdiction, and clerical abuses, was not uncommon in early Tudor parliaments. Christopher St German's blueprint of 1531 for the legislative reform of the Church by parliament gave coherence to these views.[124]

This reconstruction does not compare the strength of anticlerical feeling in the late 15th and early 16th centuries with other periods, as Haigh's article did. In a recent revision of his views, Haigh has proposed that 'anticlericalism was a constant, and that what varied was clerical sensitivity to criticism'; this, he maintained, was particularly acute among the self-important graduate ministry of the Elizabethan Church.[125] Yet, instead of seeing anticlericalism as fixed and clerical attitudes as fluctuating, we might rather conceive of *inter*dependent variables. The Reformation's humbling of the clergy and protestantism's redefining of their role as more didactic than sacramental surely altered lay views and thereby helped to induce the status-conscious anxiety of Elizabethan churchmen. Similarly, in the Henrician period, the episcopate's policy of repression and reform Haigh himself described as a response to 'what they saw as a hydra-headed lay challenge'.[126] Such clerical apprehensions, this article suggests, were well founded, better perhaps than Haigh's slightly sceptical tone implies. Challenges to ecclesiastical jurisdiction, both by the crown (as part of the reassertion of its supremacy) and by its subjects (possibly encouraged by the royal example), seem to distinguish the early Tudor years. If so, then the equipoise between religious and secular authority may have been a casualty of the 'new monarchy'.

[123] *A Dyaloge betwene one Clemente a Clerke of the Conuocacyon, and one Bernarde a Burges of the Parlyament* (nd), sig. A6v. The authorship and date of this work are discussed in Richard Rex, 'New Additions on Christopher St German: Law, Politics and Propaganda in the 1530s', *Journal of Ecclesiastical History*, lix (2008), 281–2, 287–91, 299–300.

[124] Christopher St German, *Doctor and Student*, ed. T.F.T. Plucknett and J.L. Barton (Selden Society, xci, 1974), 315–40; J.A. Guy, *Christopher St German on Chancery and Statute* (Selden Society, supplementary ser., vi, 1985), 127–35.

[125] Christopher Haigh, 'The Clergy and Parish Discipline in England, 1570–1640', in *The Impact of the European Reformation: Princes, Clergy and People*, ed. Bridget Heal and O.P. Grell (Aldershot, 2008), 125.

[126] Haigh, *English Reformations*, 86.

Staging the Settlement: Shekhar Kapur and the Parliament of 1559*

DAVID DEAN

This article offers an assessment of Shekhar Kapur's depiction of the parliamentary making of the Elizabethan settlement in his 1998 film, *Elizabeth*. The settlement has always been a controversial subject, as indeed have Kapur's cinematic stagings of Elizabethan history. After surveying historians' accounts of the settlement, the author subjects the film's settlement sequence to a careful analysis, reading it as cinema as well as history, and argues that, despite a significant number of historical inaccuracies, the film captures much of value as a filmic representation of the past.

Keywords: historical representation; Elizabeth I; Elizabethan settlement; film and history; Shekhar Kapur

1

'We have a wise and religious queen, and one too who is favourably and propitiously disposed towards us.' So wrote the protestant, John Jewel, recently-appointed bishop of Salisbury, to the reformer, Henry Bullinger, shortly after the parliament of 1559 ended.[1] As Norman Jones has remarked, this was the parliament that 'defined the religion of England and its relationship to the state' and it did so through the two statutes of supremacy and uniformity.[2] The Act of Supremacy made Elizabeth supreme governor in matters both temporal and spiritual and it undid the work of her half-sister, Mary, who had made catholicism the official religion of the realm. The Act of Uniformity returned England to the faith of Elizabeth's half-brother, Edward, prescribing a decidedly protestant Common Prayer Book to be used in church services. The collective achievement of the Acts of Supremacy and Uniformity became known as 'the Elizabethan Settlement'. However, what actually happened in the parliament, before and after the Easter recess, have always been a matter of debate, discussion and dispute.

The parliament opened on 25 January 1559 with the traditional service in Westminster Abbey. If the conduct of that service was going to provide a clue as to the degree of the queen's commitment to protestantism, it proved to be ambiguous. Certainly,

* I would like to thank Elizabeth Ferguson, Norman Jones, Natalie Mears, Elizabeth Paradis, Deborah Gorham and the members of her graduate seminar on women, gender, and sexuality for their comments on this article.

[1] *The Zurich Letters, Comprising the Correspondence of Several English Bishops and others with some of the Helvetian Reformers, during the early part of the Reign of Queen Elizabeth. Translated from Authenticated Copies of the Autographs Preserved in the Archives of Zurich*, ed. H. Robinson (2 vols, Parker Society, Cambridge, 1842–5), i, 33.

[2] Norman Jones, *The Birth of the Elizabethan Age: England in the 1560s* (Oxford, 1993), 20.

when the abbot of Westminster met her with his monks carrying lighted torches, the queen famously dismissed them with the words: 'Away with those torches, for we see very well.'[3] The sermon was preached by the divine, Richard Cox, soon to become bishop of Ely, who poured scorn on monasticism and praised the queen's inclination to rid the English Church of monasteries, relics and images. On the other hand, she apparently accepted catholic elements, such as the use of holy water and incense during the service.[4] On 9 February, the government's Bill of Supremacy was introduced in the Commons, but was eventually replaced by a new bill, now including a clause providing for a uniform religious practice, first read on 21 February. Once this reached the Lords, it was heavily debated and much amended; even so, it faced considerable opposition and all the lords spiritual, the earl of Shrewsbury, and Viscount Montagu voted against it. Returned, much altered, to the Commons, it was approved on 22 March and was ready for the royal assent. Yet two days later, instead of coming to an end, parliament broke for Easter. When the MPs and the Lords reassembled after the break, a new bill for supremacy was introduced in the Commons; it finally passed the Lords on 26 April despite the opposition of all the spiritual peers present and Viscount Montagu. Meanwhile, a separate measure for a uniform church service had also been introduced in the Commons and it passed the Lords on 28 April by only three votes.[5] Elizabeth and her protestant advisors had succeeded and, at the closing of parliament on 8 May 1559, in the presence of the queen, Lord Keeper Nicholas Bacon urged the assembled Lords and Commons to work hard to ensure the 'observacion of one uniforme order in religion according to the lawes now established'.[6]

It was Sir John Neale's contention that the settlement was achieved largely through the efforts of a well-organised protestant lobby, many of them returned exiles from Geneva. These men, active especially in the Commons, forced a change of mind on the queen shortly before, and during, the Easter break. Preferring cautious religious change to dramatic alteration, Neale argued that Elizabeth originally planned to stop with the Act of Supremacy and was ready to make arrangements for the closing of parliament. She had already decided to leave religious uniformity for another day. However, Elizabeth changed her mind and decided to push on after Easter and secure support for the Act of Uniformity. This decision, in part an explanation of Jewell's joy at the end of the parliament, decidedly shifted England from the catholic to the protestant camp in Europe's wars of religion, earlier than the queen had intended.

Neale's view held sway for three decades until the early 1980s, when the narrative was substantially revised. Elizabeth's alleged hesitancy was challenged by Winthrop S. Hudson who traced the important influence of the Cambridge protestants; he argued that Elizabeth was committed to protestant uniformity from her accession and offered an alternative reading to the parliamentary proceedings.[7] Norman Jones subjected Neale's account of the parliament to detailed scrutiny and also found it wanting. Jones argued

---

[3] J.E. Neale, *Elizabeth I and Her Parliaments, 1559–1581* (1953), 41–2.

[4] Jennifer Loach, *Parliament under the Tudors* (Oxford, 1991), 97.

[5] Norman Jones, *Faith by Statute: Parliament and the Settlement of Religion, 1559* (1982), 138–55. Speeches by catholic peers opposing these bills survive: *Proceedings in the Parliaments of Elizabeth I*, ed. T.E Hartley (3 vols, Leicester, 1981–95), i, 7–32.

[6] *Proceedings*, ed. Hartley, 49.

[7] Winthrop S. Hudson, *The Cambridge Connection and the Elizabethan Settlement* (Durham, NC, 1980).

that there was little evidence for a change of heart on the part of the queen. Rather, Elizabeth was certain of the course she wished to pursue, she worked closely with her advisors, compromised where compromise was necessary, and remained firm when opposition was raised. The so-called puritan exiles from Geneva played little part; rather, the settlement was the product of some careful planning, astute leadership, and good fortune:

> The creation of the Settlement was not a simple process. It was a difficult political manoeuvre which might have ended in disaster. The Queen played her role well, handling dissenters and foreign enemies with great care, compromising with all sides, and doing the possible without demanding the impossible. . . . Perhaps the greatest miracle of the entire episode was that Elizabeth obtained what she sought without either abandoning most of it or causing a civil war. After considering the welter of political problems surrounding the change in religion, one cannot help but admire the political sagacity and sheer luck that brought the reformed faith back to England.[8]

Historians have generally accepted these revisionist interpretations, even if a few have found themselves more inclined towards chance and circumstance than successful political strategy, or have chosen to stress catholic intransigence over the supremacy in forcing Elizabeth to depend more on her more radical churchmen and councillors than her undoubted commitment to achieving religious uniformity from the start.[9]

At the heart of these disagreements is the question of the queen's role in the settlement, the degree of influence and control others had on her, and, of course, the complexities of parliamentary management. For Neale, it was the determined wilfulness of radical protestants that forced the queen's hand. For others, the queen also had to be convinced, but she was persuaded that protestant uniformity had to be established quickly because of the determination of uncompromising catholic bishops and peers to resist even the royal supremacy, at any cost. For Jones and Hudson, it was the determination of Elizabeth and her advisors to push through reforms in the face of that determined opposition which required a rethinking of strategy over the Easter recess, that was ultimately successful. This led to the introduction of legislation whose terms would garner sufficient support to overcome the catholic bishops and peers.

One key event during the recess was Elizabeth's decision to stage that favourite 16th-century fixture in public spectacle: a religious colloquy or debate between those of opposing viewpoints. On 31 March, in the choir of Westminster Abbey, nine divines who supported the reformed faith squared off against an identical number of catholics, including five bishops and the abbot of Westminster. It came to an abrupt end on 3 April when the catholics objected to the process, and their refusal to continue was a propaganda triumph for those supporting the protestant cause, who made the most of the opportunity to publicise catholic intransigence. Two particularly difficult bishops, John White of Winchester and Thomas Watson of Lincoln, were imprisoned, and so were no longer able to participate in the parliamentary debates that followed after the Easter recess. In this process, Jones, Hudson and others have singled out the queen's

---

[8] Jones, *Faith by Statute*, 189.

[9] Loach, *Parliament under the Tudors*, 97–101; see also T.E. Hartley, *Elizabeth's Parliaments: Queen, Lords and Commons, 1559–1601* (Manchester, 1992).

secretary, William Cecil, as the key player, the supreme parliamentary strategist and manager, with others such as Bacon and the queen's favourite, Robert Dudley, playing significant supporting roles. But it was to Cecil that the queen owed most and this view was shared by some contemporaries. In 1574, the protestant reformer, Thomas Sampson, thinking that his days on earth were numbered following a series of strokes, wrote to Cecil, now Lord Burghley, urging him to continue the reform process and not to forget the role that he, Cecil, had played in the making of the settlement: 'what your authority, credit, and doing then was, you know, God knows, and there are witnesses of it'.[10] Sampson should have known for he was part of the government's strategy to promote reform, delivering the authorised sermon at Paul's Cross shortly before the Westminster disputation began.[11]

The parliament of 1559 thus has all the makings of good theatre and it is no surprise that when Indian director, Shekhar Kapur, came to direct the film, *Elizabeth*, in 1998, he saw an opportunity for staging one of the most significant episodes of the reign. Religious division may have been one of the issues that attracted Kapur to the project in the first place, and not only because of the intriguing topic of the European wars of religion and the struggles of a young female monarch in overcoming religious division in the country she had just inherited. Kapur's celebrated earlier film, *Bandit Queen*, was a study in female power and authority in the context of deep misogyny. Moreover, entrenched beliefs and convictions, historical divisions and hatreds, contrary rituals and customs, were sharpened in India during the 1990s with the rise of the Hindu nationalist Bharatiya Janata Party. Elizabethan England is no foil for contemporary India in the film, with catholics and protestants playing substitute for muslims and hindus (or hindus and muslims), or the tensions between England and Spain standing in for those between India and Pakistan (or Pakistan and India), but it remains possible that, for at least some of those involved in the production, their observations, knowledge and experience of religious conflict in the 21st century played a role in shaping their interpretation of that which took place in England 400 years before. In writing history in film, Kapur and screenplay writer, Michael Hirst, made a number of choices which did considerable violence to the known, and accepted, historical record and avoided stories that were potentially more compelling, but I would argue that they also constructed a historical narrative that is, in part, both justifiable and persuasive, though certainly not in the sum of its parts.

2

Historians of historical feature film have long identified ways in which film–makers are forced by their chosen medium to create narratives that necessarily change and alter the known historical record. Over 30 years ago, Pierre Sorlin noted that the most common

---

[10] John Strype, *Annals of the Reformation and Establishment of Religion, and other Various Occurrences in the Church of England during Queen Elizabeth's Happy Reign: Together with an Appendix of Original Papers of State, Records, and Letters* (4 vols in 7, Oxford, 1824), i, pt 1, 119; Alec Ryrie, 'Sampson, Thomas (c.1517–1589)', *ODNB*.

[11] Hudson, *The Cambridge Connection*, 122.

approach of historians choosing to examine historical feature film was to locate the film in the political, social and cultural context of the time in which it was made, and perhaps also in the historiography of the day.[12] Fifteen years later, Thomas Prasch acknowledged a greater range of possible engagement, seeing historical feature films as addressing the distance, presence and meaning of history. One cannot but reflect that, even today, most historians remain content to engage with the problem of historical distance; while acknowledging the presentism of film, they devote most of their efforts to assessing a film's historical accuracy and, therefore, its validity and worth.[13]

Such analyses inevitably highlight the numerous 'sins' of the film-maker, all of which are, needless to say, inevitable. There is the sin of compression, where events that took place over a long period of time are truncated to fit into the near-compulsory time frame allotted by producers and the market.[14] Then there is the sin of omission where, given both time frame and the conditions of film narrative, stories are ignored because they might confuse, complicate or distract. There is the sin of alteration, where events are changed, characters transformed or transplanted, where things that historians agree are known and certain are rendered differently, alternatively, incorrectly. Finally – and this list is by no means exhaustive or complete – there is the cardinal sin of invention, where the film-maker proves that the film bears only some, little or no relation to persons living or dead and extends the well-known disclaimer to past events.[15] If one digs a little deeper, of course, there are secondary sins associated with the film medium, such as the sin of metaphor, where the languages of film are allowed to intrude on the historical, using signs rather than argument to create meaning, particularly through the use of metonymy and synecdoche, or where the genre of the historical feature film requires the film-maker to address conventions such as romance or spectacle, or to reference earlier films in some way.[16]

When it comes to *Elizabeth* these sins are quite evident. Time is severely compressed, with events of the 1570s and 1580s propelled into the beginning of the reign, thus ensuring that the deep struggle between catholic and protestant is there from the start. Important events that would disturb the narrative are omitted; for example, the romance narrative of Dudley and Elizabeth cannot be complicated by the death of Amy Robsart. Events are altered and reordered (for example, the invasion of Scotland takes place before the settlement), and things that historians are in general agreement about are ignored or distorted; for example, William Cecil (later Lord Burghley) becomes a far less important advisor to the queen than does Sir Francis Walsingham. There are curiosities and inventions in terms of costume and music, and inaccuracies of place and setting. The catalogue is long and has been compiled enthusiastically by academic historians not to

[12] Pierre Sorlin, *The Film in History: Restaging the Past* (Oxford, 1980), 3–37.

[13] Thomas Prasch, 'Film Reviews. Introduction', *American Historical Review*, c (1995), 1190–3.

[14] For a fascinating examination of the problem in terms of televised history, see Geoff Bowie (director), *The Universal Clock: The Resistance of Peter Watkins* (National Film Board of Canada, 2001).

[15] See Natalie Zemon Davis, ' "Any Resemblance to Persons Living or Dead": Film and the Challenge of Authenticity', *Yale Review*, lxxxvi (1986–7), 457–82.

[16] Leger Grindon, *Shadows on the Past: Studies in Historical Fiction Film* (Philadelphia, PA, 1994), 1–26; Robert A. Rosenstone, *Visions of the Past: The Challenge of Film to Our Idea of History* (Cambridge, MA, 1995), 1–79; Robert A. Rosenstone, *History on Film/Film on History* (2nd edn, Harlow, 2012), esp. 1–34.

mention history buffs and movie critics.[17] Not surprisingly, they are all present in the film's staging of the making of the Elizabethan settlement in parliament. However, in analysing this staging, it will be instructive to go beyond the conventional approach and acknowledge not only the influences of the present and historical inaccuracies, but to also pay attention to the way the settlement is written in film.[18]

3

Staging the Elizabethan settlement begins almost an hour into the film, when, at 52 minutes: 13 seconds we watch the duke of Norfolk dressing for the 1559 parliament; he anticipates the downfall 'of that heretic girl'. It ends at 58:38 when we observe Sir Francis Walsingham climbing up the steps from a crypt beneath the Parliament Chamber where he has had Stephen Gardiner and other catholic bishops imprisoned, to ensure the passage of the Acts of Uniformity and Supremacy. In six minutes and 25 seconds the audience sees Elizabeth overcome parliamentary opposition to succeed in establishing, as she puts it, 'a single church of England with a common prayer book and a common purpose'.[19]

Even this briefest of descriptions reveals enough errors to please any historian with the conviction that historical feature films are untrustworthy. Most obviously, neither of the two great opponents in the sequence, Walsingham and Gardiner, was present in the making of the Elizabethan settlement. Gardiner, one of the leading catholic bishops and councillors under Henry VIII and Mary, had died over four years earlier, in 1555. The only link from reality to the character in the film is an exceedingly tenuous one: Gardiner was bishop of Winchester and it was his successor in that post, John White, who was obstreperous enough to merit imprisonment and missed the proceedings after Easter. Walsingham, at least, *was* a witness to the events of 1559, for he was MP for Bossiney, but it would not be until a decade later that he became a figure in government circles: only in 1573 did he become principal secretary, a leading advisor to the queen, which is the position he clearly holds in the film.

Compared with this resituating of Gardiner and Walsingham – the one living longer than he did (and Terence Rigby does, at least, look suitably aged and decrepit in the film, complete with one dodgy eye), the other securing influence much earlier than he did (and Geoffrey Rush does play him as being in his forties rather than his actual late twenties) – the film's portrayal of the great catholic peer, Thomas Howard, 4th duke of Norfolk, is more subtle in its shifting from the historical evidence. Norfolk was at least

---

[17] See the commentaries by Rosemary Sweet, 'Elizabeth', *American Historical Review*, civ (1999), 297–8; Carole Levin, 'Elizabeth: Romantic Film Heroine or Sixteenth-Century Queen?', *Perspectives on History* (April 1999); and C. Haigh, 'Kapur's Elizabeth', in *Tudors and Stuarts on Film*, ed. S. Doran and T. Freeman (Basingstoke, 2009), 122–34. Andrew Higson offers a detailed examination of the film in *English Heritage, English Cinema: Costume Drama since 1980* (Oxford, 2003), 194–256, while Eric Josef Carlson considers the film's pedagogical usefulness in 'Teaching Elizabeth Tudor with Movies', *Sixteenth Century Journal*, xxxviii (2007), 419–28.

[18] See William Guynn, *Writing History on Film* (Abingdon, 2006), and Marnie Hughes-Warrington, *History Goes to the Movies: Studying History on Film* (Abingdon, 2007).

[19] Shekhar Kapur (director), *Elizabeth* (Polygram, 1998), 54:18. All subsequent references to the film will be cited in text.

alive and well in 1559; indeed, he played an important ceremonial role in the parliament through his office of earl marshal. His age is also more or less right in Christopher Eccleston's portrayal; Norfolk was born in 1536. However, in the film he is a vigorous and energetic opponent of Elizabeth's from the moment of her accession, in contrast to historians who are unanimous in their judgment that Norfolk, while a catholic, had little difficulty in switching allegiance from Mary Tudor to Elizabeth on the latter's accession to the throne in 1558. It was only much later, in the late 1560s with the rebellion of the northern earls and then the Ridolfi plot, that Norfolk was revealed as a conspirator against the queen and, even then, historians have generally seen him as a somewhat feeble character, manipulated by those around him at best, or as weak, unintelligent and feckless at worst.[20] Certainly, Norfolk did not oppose either the Act of Supremacy or the Act of Uniformity in 1559, let alone orchestrate opposition; indeed, he was made knight of the Garter during the parliament. If he had qualms, these did not transfer into action. As Michael Graves has suggested, Norfolk almost certainly 'remained loyal to the new church' although his later conduct 'raised doubts about his religious loyalties'.[21]

Norfolk's fellow conspirator in the film, Thomas Radcliffe, 3rd earl of Sussex (played by Jamie Foreman) took a similar stance in 1559, although indications are that he would have had no difficulty and no hesitation in supporting the queen, the royal supremacy and the Act of Uniformity. Having been Mary Tudor's lord deputy in Ireland, Elizabeth showed her confidence in him by giving him a new commission as lord lieutenant in Ireland a few months after the parliament ended. His loyalty led to his becoming lord president of the north, leading the crown's forces against the northern rebels, and he died as lord chamberlain, one of the most trusted of court offices involving personal service to the queen. His character in the film is a serious distortion, indeed a complete reversal, of his evident political stance.[22]

This combination of chronological playfulness and confused affiliations can be explained, but not justified, by the film-makers' impulse to offer audiences an England riven by religious conflict, where religious differences are clear and allegiances certain. It is a world in which one is either with the catholics or with the protestants. There is not much of a middle ground, little hesitancy, little generosity, and certainly no compromise. There are no catholics who are able to agree with the supremacy, but unwilling to support a prayer book on the Edwardian model, however modified; and there are no protestants who were content with those same modifications which mentioned the body and blood of Christ as a means of easing the queen's catholic subjects into the new theology. All is black and white or, in the film, darkness and light. The film's *mise-en-scene* and its montage both work towards this ideological end.

In the film this is achieved in visual shorthand that is both obvious and effective. Elizabeth is constantly bathed in light and her hair, soft and flowing at the beginning of the film, bound and contained at its end, serves as a metaphor for her evolution from princess to divine right virgin queen. In the settlement sequence this is achieved by a mirroring, literally, of Elizabeth and her adversary, Norfolk. It opens with a shot showing Norfolk standing in front of a mirror, his mistress (Lettice Howard, played by

---

[20] Michael A.R. Graves, 'Howard, Thomas, fourth duke of Norfolk (1538–1572)', *ODNB*.

[21] Michael A.R. Graves, 'Howard, Thomas, fourth duke of Norfolk (1538–1572)', *ODNB*.

[22] Wallace T. MacCaffrey, 'Radcliffe, Thomas, third earl of Sussex (1526/7–1583)', *ODNB*.

Amanda Ryan) soon joining him.[23] He is getting dressed for the parliament, a servant delivering first a chain of office or of the Garter (which seems to adorn several peers in the film, too many of course to be historically accurate) and then the ducal cap. As this shot closes, we hear a voiceover of Elizabeth as she practises her speech to the parliament. We then cut to a shot of Elizabeth standing before us in a loose undergarment (more modestly attired than Norfolk's mistress), her unruly hair pinned as she seeks to find the right words. We look at her full on as if we are, or at least are behind and looking through, the mirror which she is apparently facing. In contrast to Norfolk and his mistress, she and her surroundings are bathed in light; her gown is pure white, his unrelentingly black.

For the parliamentary historian, the (filmic) necessity to show Elizabeth and those who opposed her in contrasting lightness and darkness results in a number of missed opportunities. First, of course, is the fact that no one is wearing their parliamentary robes. Norfolk dresses in black, so, too, do all the peers and bishops (even their mitres are black) who we see parting the ways for their anointed sovereign. This is no sea of red as, indeed, it should have been: red robes, trimmed in ermine, each peer's robes differentiated by single, double or triple bars, are what each would have worn. This is what we see when we look at herald Robert Glover's coloured depiction of the Lords chamber, with the queen present and the Commons assembled below the railing at the opposite end, not to mention surviving portraits and material evidence.[24] Instead, the bishops and peers all look rather like hatted versions of Glover's clerks sitting or kneeling at the woolsacks in the middle of the Lords chamber. Nor is the queen wearing her parliamentary robes although, at least, there is a nod in the right direction as she is dressed all in red, though in a costume more suitable to riding in a royal park. Yet in the stark, and evidently hostile, Parliament Chamber, she still is bathed in light, highlighting the whiteness of her face and hands, and the white of her bodice above the startling red of her gown.

Second, what of the chamber itself? Rather than reconstructing the house of lords, Kapur opted to shoot the entire scene of the 1559 parliament in the chapter house of Durham Cathedral. Thus, as the sequence of the queen entering the chamber begins, we see the light streaming through stained glass windows that sit above an arc of medieval arches; she must take several Romanesque-decorated steps to get to her throne. This visual shorthand offers audiences a clear narrative, and one which was evident from the film's beginning (we first encounter Elizabeth dancing in a sunlit bucolic world in stark contrast to the lightless gloom of Mary's court): this is an enlightened monarch struggling against medieval world views and parliament will be the battleground. In this house of lords, however, there are no woolsacks, no judges, no legal officers and no scribbling clerks, but a later shot into the chamber reveals some authentic elements. Guards are present (dressed, as they would not have been, in full armour) and there are

[23] Perhaps the film-makers chose 'Lettice Howard' as the name of this fictional character to suggest further moral degradation (incest). The name is a curious fusion of two of Dudley's (later earl of Leicester) lovers: Lady Douglas Howard and Lettice Knollys, wife to Walter Devereux, Viscount Hereford. In the film an 'Isabel Knollys' is, indeed, Dudley's lover.

[24] David Dean, 'Image and Ritual in the Tudor Parliaments', in *Tudor Political Culture*, ed. Dale Hoak (Cambridge, 1995), 243–71; see also Alasdair Hawkyard and Maria Hayward, 'The Dressing and Trimming of the Parliament Chamber, 1509–1558', *Parliamentary History*, xxix (2010), 229–37.

members of the lower House standing behind a low stone wall to witness events. Yet none of the chamber's fixtures depicted by Glover, or known in other accounts, are present: there are no tapestries and no cushion cossets the royal regalia. Moreover, the seating is, of course, arranged to emphasize confrontation between Elizabeth and the man that called her 'that heretic girl': Norfolk does not stand close to the queen where, as earl marshal, he must have done at the opening of parliament; rather, he sits scowling beside Sussex on a cross bench facing the queen, rows of bishops and peers ranked on either side between them.

As Elizabeth fights to find the right words, the right tone, the right gestures and facial expressions (shown in rapidly-edited shots beginning at 52:28) Kapur chooses a form of montage that is commonplace in historical feature film: compressing time and place through a sequence of shots alternating between one time and place to another; the first, chronologically speaking, preceding the second. In this instance, we move from Elizabeth standing in front of the mirror to what was soon to come: her entrance into the Parliament Chamber where she would deliver the speech she had been practising. Here, too, there is a strong play on light and dark. In the series of interrupted shots that make up the entrance to parliament sequence, the audience becomes Elizabeth herself: we move slowly into the ranks of massed bishops and peers who part slowly, even reluctantly, as we enter, dividing to our left and right until, finally, there are no more human obstructions and we can walk up the steps to the throne. The montage sequence ends with a strong fixed shot of the throne from above and, at this point, Elizabeth enters the frame and sits (at 53.33–53:44).

In this full minute of carefully-edited shots, Kapur and Hirst drive home the key words of the queen's speech and the opposition it will engender. Elizabeth rehearses carefully, her words conflating the impulses behind the acts of supremacy and uniformity. Cate Blanchet plays the role convincingly through emotions, gestures, and words, and the sequence is edited with quick, abrupt shots to enhance her portrayal. The montage begins with alternating shots of her at the mirror and the tracking shot of her (us) entering the chamber, then shifts to a rapid succession of close-ups of Elizabeth as she tries to find the right words. The sequence culminates with a slower-paced montage:

[52:37]

Elizabeth: I am your sovereign. I have been placed here. Ahem. I – God has placed me here. [serious face]

I am your anointed sovereign. I'm your Queen, and like my father I mean to rule. [insistent face]

There is one thing higher than royalty my lords and that [muffled voice to self] is religion. [head in hands]

I pass this – I pass this act of unif . . . – I ask you to pass – I ask you to pass this act of uniformity. [smiling]

It's not for myself, it's for my people [waves hands dismissively]

[whispers] they're my people. [hands cover face]

My lords there is one God.

We have a common – There is one God – AARGH! [hands cover eyes]

This is for my people. [tears in eyes] My people are my care – [to self] my only care.

[53.27]

The sequence ends with Elizabeth's next line, a moment of undisputed historical accuracy: 'The truth be my lords, your votes are nothing without my consent' [53:28–53:30]. We now enter the debate in the chamber proper.

The camera angles, which show us the debate in the chamber, include three shots that lay out the spatial and discursive contest we are going to witness:

Shot One: a long distance shot from the benches to the queen's right: it highlights the light falling on her among the ranks of darkly-dressed peers; on occasion, Kapur uses a medium-close shot from the same perspective [53:46, 53:51].

Shot Two: a wide angle shot over Cecil's head looking out at the peers from a position to the queen's left framed on the left by a stone statue of the royal lion of England, crowned and bearing a shield. On occasion, there is a shot from the same perspective, but a little closer [53:49].

Shot Three: a medium distance shot of the packed chamber from a position to Elizabeth's right; Norfolk and his ally Sussex near centre, soldiers guarding the doors, and MPs standing behind the low wall [53:56].

The opposition that has already been established between Elizabeth and Norfolk is driven home by a rapid montage of these shots interspersed with close-ups of the protagonists. One of the most used medium close-up shots is one of the queen framed by three bishops in which, eventually, she alone is in focus [53:57, 54:45]. Another features Norfolk alone, or Norfolk and Sussex [54:07, 55:24], and a third is a close-up of Walsingham once he has entered the chamber, a sunbeam finding him [55:09]. To convey the disagreement and opposition of some, and the transition from concern to amusement and admiring support of others, Kapur inserts some close-ups of bishops and lay peers from various angles [for example, at 54:15, 54:16, 54:39, 56:42, this last being Lord Robert Dudley's sole appearance as witness to the making of the settlement].

Kapur then [56:08] introduces a full-frontal shot (in contrast to close-ups of her taken from above) to signal that the queen is gaining self-confidence and is beginning to win the debate. Her taking control is also articulated by means of the camera pulling away from the throne, drawing the viewer backwards through the seated bishops as she jokes playfully about marriage [56:17–56:35]. The debate ends with a middle range shot of the queen in the chamber: she sighs, moves her hands resignedly and looks to her left [57:38–57:43] and we move to a full-frontal shot of Cecil, with his staff, calling for division. As the timing references indicate, this is a remarkable compression: a complex debate which took place over several weeks is reduced to just over four minutes.

Once Elizabeth sits, she begins her speech [shot one] with the words: 'If there is no uniformity of religious belief here [shot two] then [shot one closer] there can only be fragmentation [shot three] dispute and quarrel [close-up of Elizabeth through bishops].' This rapid editing continues as Elizabeth proceeds to put forward the case for uniformity. A close descriptive analysis of word and image illustrates that Kapur's intent is to emphasize confrontation and conflict, but always returning to the central role played by the queen herself:

[54:02]

[close-up overhead shot of Elizabeth]

Surely my lords it is better to have a single Church of England

[close-up of Norfolk turning to Sussex]

[cut to shot two]

[cut to closer shot of Elizabeth through the bishops]

[cut to frontal shot of Cecil, looking nervously around the chamber]

[cut to close-up of opposing peers]

[cut to close-up of opposing bishops]

[cut to shot one]

A single Church of England

[close-up overhead of Elizabeth]

with a common prayer book

and – and –

[continued close-up overhead of Elizabeth, surveying her listeners a little impatiently]

[cut to (closer version of) shot one]

and a common purpose

[cut to shot two]

[close-up overhead of Elizabeth]

Now, I ask you to pass this act of uniformity

[close-up of bearded bishop closing his eyes and shaking his head no]

not

[close-up of Norfolk, looking a little nervous]

not for myself

[shot of Walsingham entering the chamber]

but for my people

[medium shot of Elizabeth through bishops out of focus; she pauses, looks around and raises her finger]

who are my only care.

[54:50]

In this sequence, the filmed narrative is quite clear: Elizabeth is alone in her wilfulness and willingness to push for uniformity. England, represented by the lion statue, is, of course, with her, and so, too, is Cecil, although his presence as an ally is obviously only supportive and rather ineffectual. It is only when Walsingham enters the chamber (and we later are asked to accept that he has arrived late because he has seen to the imprisonment of Gardiner and five other opponents in the crypt below) that Elizabeth has an admiring and firm supporter. He regards her immediately with familiarity and, like her, he is bathed in a convenient sunbeam.

Walsingham's arrival seems to spark new confidence in the queen, for she responds to the bearded bishop's response to her words, 'Madam, by this act you force us to relinquish our allegiance to the Holy Father' [54:52–54:57], with humour and a degree of coquettishness: 'How can I force you your grace? [she laughs] I am a woman!' As she says this, the audience is treated to another shot of Walsingham, now showing admiration, and a second shot of five peers who also seem to be appreciative [55:09–55:13]. The queen's charm, wit and confidence seem to be winning votes. She seizes the opportunity to reveal her intent ('I have no desire to make windows into men's souls') and make a vital point ('I simply ask can any man in truth serve two masters and be faithful to both?') [55:15–55:28]. When a bishop responds that 'this is heresy!', she retorts: 'No your grace this is common sense . . . which is a most English virtue' [55:29–55:40]. Kapur cuts to a shot of an admiring Walsingham amid murmurs of approval and appreciation from others. Her achievement worries Norfolk who turns to Sussex and asks the whereabouts of Gardiner and the others [55:44]. We then witness (according to the film) Walsingham's work: the film cuts to a darkened cellar and the audience witnesses an exchange between Gardiner and the imprisoned bishops. Gardiner reassures them that 'The bishops will pass no measure which severs us from Rome', but as he says this we hear, as do they, the debate raging above them. The contrast between Gardiner's declaration and the reality above is revealed starkly in one shot: a full-frontal of Elizabeth (the first we have seen in the entire scene) looking exceedingly confident [56:08].

Much of the dialogue is, of course, an invention, but there is one moment in which historical accuracy loses out to perceived historical authenticity. There is, of course, no evidence from her own extant writings, which are considerable, that Elizabeth wrote the words 'I have no desire to make windows into men's souls.' Something of the sort may well have been said by her, and it receives a place in the *Oxford Dictionary of Quotations*, but, as that venerable reference work notes, it is an attribution that comes from a letter written by Sir Francis Bacon.[25] Nevertheless, as powerful as the public's knowing that Elizabeth claimed to live and die a virgin (the construction of which identity is the major theme and narrative of the film), is the public's knowing that Elizabeth said certain things of which this protestation about letting individuals decide their faith according to their own conscience is, perhaps, the most prominent. Indeed, it is essentially explained at the end of the sequence, as we shall see.

With one sentence during her mirror sequence, which blends into the chamber scene, Kapur and Hirst have thus introduced the audience to the idea of the royal supremacy. In four more sentences we now know that the queen urges religious uniformity, and why. Now, in less than a minute [56:08–57:03], they incorporate the troubled issue of the queen's marriage into the debate. Two bishops urge her to marry; she responds with approval but asks the key question: 'Aye, but marry who your grace? Will you give me some suggestion? For some say France, and others Spain, and some cannot abide

[25] *The Oxford Dictionary of Quotations*, ed. Angela Partington (Oxford, 1996), 274.

foreigners at all! So I'm not sure how best to please you unless I marry one of each!' Her response is greeted with delight by many in the chamber. When a young peer complains that she is making 'fun of the sanctity of marriage', she retorts that he is not one to lecture her on the subject since he has been twice divorced and is now on his third wife. Those around him laugh uproariously.

This sequence, like the earlier ones, is captured in rapid montage that drives home the energy and delight of the exchange. But it ends seriously. The camera closes in on her, a shot from below in contrast to the earlier close-ups from above, and it stays on her as she sits back on her throne, lowers her eyes, raises them again and then speaks firmly, her authority affirmed by a slow tracking shot, again unique to this scene. And while we have heard murmurs of approval and disapproval, now we hear the slow strains of heroic music as Elizabeth says: 'Each of you must vote according to your conscience. But remember this. In your hands, upon this moment [music begins] lies the future happiness of my people and the peace of this realm. Let that be upon your conscience also' [57:03–57:36]. The house divides on Cecil's instructions.

We learn of the passage of the Elizabethan settlement not by a counting of the votes in the Lords or being shown Bacon's final speech before the queen on the last day of parliament, but through a final moment of confrontation between Walsingham and Gardiner. Immediately after Cecil orders a division, we are placed in the crypt, looking up towards the sound of jangling keys and the opening of a door as light floods in and Walsingham descends. The camera then cuts back and forth between Walsingham and Gardiner. To the latter's demand: 'I would know on what authority you have kept us locked up here', Walsingham replies: 'Your graces must forgive me. But you are now free to go.' Gardiner's insistent 'I am sure this infernal work hath not saved your bastard Queen', earns the reply: 'Her Majesty has won the argument.' And Gardiner's question: 'By what count?', receives the answer: 'By five your grace. Five', at which point the camera, from Walsingham's perspective, reveals six bishops standing in the crypt in addition to Gardiner. As Walsingham climbs up the steps into the light, Gardiner curses him: 'You will be damned for this – and I pray God your wretched soul will burn in hell!' [58:35].

In cinematic terms, this is a brilliant moment; sadly, it is, of course, historically inaccurate. This final confrontation never took place, and the passage of the settlement did not depend on a close vote with success for the regime achieved only because the right number of bishops was imprisoned. There were, in fact, seven bishops and the abbot of Westminster absent from the crucial vote on uniformity but only two (White and Watson) because of imprisonment; two were ill, one too old, one had not yet been consecrated and so received no summons, while only one (the bishop of Bath and Wells) may, like the abbot, have been too intimidated to attend.[26]

More largely, the key parliamentary debates did not take place in the queen's presence, and certainly did not take place with her as participant. The meanderings and complexities of bill procedure are entirely absent, the lobbying in the Commons that took place completely ignored. The script barely echoes any of the extant speeches and reports of debate that occurred. The time frame is so truncated that the audience has no

---

[26] Hudson, *The Cambridge Connection*, 123 n. 28.

sense of the settlement as needing careful negotiation, care and compromise. Cecil's key role in convincing the queen and in managing the parliament is entirely absent.

Yet as an historical narrative, there are numerous correspondences between the film and the event as agreed upon by historians; at least, those who have revised Neale's interpretation. The queen is certain from the start; she needs no convincing by a puritan minority, and she is firmly in control, showing signs of independence from her key advisor (albeit erroneously Walsingham and not Cecil) that they can only admire. If the numbers are wrong, and were inconsequential in terms of the vote, there is no denying that two ardently catholic bishops were imprisoned and two others perhaps intimidated to stay away. The three interrelated central issues that have dominated historians' analysis of the settlement – supremacy, uniformity and marriage – are all presented, and engagingly so. Although the film depicts only the Lords, and is simply wrong in having debate take place when the queen is not only present but is also the main participant, the film, nevertheless, succeeds in representing the dynamics of parliamentary debate and the theatre of parliament. Rhetorical strategies (pleading and cajoling, pretence and conviction, honesty and devilish advocacy), emotions (anger, bemusement, sincerity, laughter), facial expressions and gestures, all make compelling viewing and, of course, we find traces of each in the many reports of debates, diaries and journals that have survived for the reign, if not specifically for 1559.

Moreover, there is, of course, a larger agenda for Kapur and Hirst, and that is to offer a dynamic and engaging depiction of female monarchy at a moment of crisis. In contrast to Neale's portrayal of an indecisive and uncertain young woman, Kapur's Elizabeth is her own actor, devising and shaping her own speech, growing in confidence as the debate progresses (albeit especially after Walsingham had entered the chamber), drawing on a range of discursive and bodily strategies – alternating moments of seriousness, amusement, coyness, flirtation – to cajole and convince. In this, drawing inspiration perhaps from later speeches such as those at Tilbury or the 'Golden Speech' in her last parliament, director, screenwriter, and actor, offer audiences an arguably brilliant short-hand introduction to the world of gendered politics in mid–16th-century England.[27]

4

If Kapur's staging of the Elizabethan settlement contains many historical inaccuracies, there is a case to be made for its achieving a degree of authenticity, however modest. This is not the place to argue this theoretical proposition more fully, either for this film or for other historical feature films, but it should be noted that, over the past decade or so, an increasing number of historians have been engaging with film, and other forms of popular or public history, such as re-enactments, theatre productions, or animators in museums, in ways that bring into sharp focus issues such as the relationship between

---

[27] See Judith M. Richards, 'Mary Tudor as "Sole Quene"?: Gendering Tudor Monarchy', *Historical Journal*, xl (1997), 895–924; Carole Levin, *The Heart and Stomach of a King: Elizabeth I and the Politics of Sex and Power* (Philadelphia, PA, 1994); A.N. McLaren, *Political Culture in the Reign of Elizabeth I* (Cambridge, 1999); Natalie Mears, *Queenship and Political Discourse in the Elizabethan Realms* (Cambridge, 2005), among many other works.

accuracy and authenticity, historical distance, narrative, and performance.[28] There are, of course, historians who will always choose to limit themselves to showing how the historical film merely uses the past as a vehicle to analyse the present (of course it does, and so, too, does much historical writing in more conventional forms) or to play the undeniably enjoyable game of error-spotting to make the (ultimately self-fulfilling) argument that films are an unreliable and unhelpful medium for engaging with the past. Not to go further and engage with film narrative is to surrender the filmed past to film-makers and remain content to complain about the desultory and damaging effects of dramatic licence.[29]

Kapur's *Elizabeth* may not be a very satisfactory staging of the complexities of the parliament of 1559 and, no doubt, many of us have cringed on receiving an under-graduate essay insisting that the queen won the day by allying herself with ardent Walsingham rather than bumbling Cecil, and by imprisoning Gardiner and the requisite number of bishops to defeat the Norfolk-Sussex camp. The film would have been a better film had Cecil been given his due, had Norfolk been portrayed as the loyal catholic he was, had all the doubts and hesitations and confusions of the 1559 parliament been depicted. However, if the film enabled viewers to understand that a young queen faced considerable and determined opposition, that gender politics was at the heart of the matter, that the supremacy and uniformity were associated in the minds of con-temporaries with the issues of marriage and succession, and, yes, that parliament was an important institution in which these issues had to be managed and debated, then is that such a mean achievement?

Moreover, if we return to the varying historical interpretations discussed at the beginning of this article, Kapur's account seems to capture some of what historians have been saying recently about the settlement. It was, to quote from Jones, 'not a simple process', it was 'a difficult political manoeuvre which might have ended in disaster'; the queen 'played her role well' and 'obtained what she sought without either abandoning most of it or causing a civil war'. Michael Graves concluded that, in 1559, 'Elizabeth had scored an impressive parliamentary success over entrenched Catholics in the Lords', and that is not a bad summary of Kapur's staging of the Elizabethan settlement.[30]

---

[28] Mark Salber Phillips, 'Distance and Historical Representation', *History Workshop Journal*, lvii (2004), 123–41; David Dean, 'Getting it Right: An Historian Among the Actors', *Bulletin of the Canadian Historical Association*, xxxiv (2008), 33–4; Charlotte M. Canning and Thomas Postlewait, *Representing the Past: Essays in Performance Historiography* (Iowa City, IA, 2010); *Enacting History*, ed. Scott Magelssen and Rhona Justice-Malloy (Tuscaloosa, AL, 2011); *Filming and Performing Renaissance History*, ed. Mark Thornton Burnett and Adrian Streete (Basingstoke, 2011); see also the works by Rosenstone, Guynn, and Warrington-Hughes cited earlier.

[29] See Peter Verstraten, *Film Narratology* (Toronto, ON, 2009).

[30] Michael A.R. Graves, *Elizabethan Parliaments 1559–1601* (2nd edn, Harlow, 1996), 27.

William Cecil, Lord Burghley, and Managing with the Men-of-Business

NORMAN JONES

Michael Graves taught us to think of parliamentary management done through the parliamentary 'men-of-business', gentlemen with close ties to powerful men in the privy council. This article asks how 'men-of-business' were managed by Elizabeth's head manager, Lord Burghley. Choosing justices of the peace was a complex, fraught activity, and one which Lord Burghley did with a great deal of care. However, despite his best efforts to have only men of probity and proper religious inclinations, he was hampered by local concerns. Managing the men-of-business meant careful awareness of their places, their connections, and their independence. Burghley was managing shared governance, each magistrate within his degree, for common causes, which is what made it a common weal. It was a system that required management, rather than fiats, but it had to be managed with a gentle touch. What Burghley and the men-of-business were running was a semi-bureaucratised late feudal monarchy, taking the form of a 'monarchical commonwealth'. Mutual need kept the local elites working with the crown's managers.

Keywords: Lord Burghley; management; justices of the peace; parliament; bishops; law; magistrates

Over the course of his distinguished career, Michael Graves taught us a great deal about Tudor parliaments. His doctoral dissertation turned, after many trials, into his book, *The House of Lords in the Parliaments of Edward VI and Mary I: An Institutional Study* (1981). In his introduction, Graves made a comment that echoed down his later work:

> Politicking also meant parliamentary management, not designed to head off or stifle opposition but usually to ensure efficient productive parliaments in which speedy transaction of official business was a first priority. In order to fulfill that objective, the privy council had to cope successfully with competing priorities. Members of the governing class had projects of their own to promote. Some of them were of a general nature, designed to benefit the commonweal, but usually they were intended to advance the interests of their proposers.[1]

His exploration of the Lords made him suspicious of J.E. Neale's assumptions about the evolution of Elizabethan parliaments, with its emphasis on the house of commons, and it prompted him to ask about how the Commons, too, was managed. In 1983 he published an extremely influential article, 'The Management of the Elizabethan House

---

[1] Michael A.R. Graves, *The House of Lords in the Parliaments of Edward VI and Mary I: An Institutional Study* (Cambridge, 1981), 3.

of Commons: The Council's Men-of-Business', tackling the question and pointedly undermining Neale's argument about the existence of a 'Puritan Choir' of opposition in the early Elizabethan parliaments.[2]

Neale had presumed the members of this 'choir' to be puritan radicals who resisted Elizabeth's religious policy. Graves showed them, for the most part, to be clients of the privy council. Built upon careful study of these men, especially of Sir Thomas Norton, of whom Graves eventually wrote a biography,[3] they turned out to be 'active loyalists' who were loyal to the queen and bound to prominent councillors or their allies by bonds of clientage. Moreover, they appear to be resisting because they could be employed by the councillors to say things they themselves dared not voice, such as calling for the execution of Mary, queen of Scots.[4]

Ironically, Graves's work on Elizabethan parliaments did not tackle the question of managing the house of lords. Moreover, we can now know a great deal more about men active in parliament, thanks to the work of the searchable form of the History of Parliament Trust volumes, and the completion of T.E. Hartley's three volumes of *Proceedings in the Parliaments of Elizabeth I*.[5] The purpose of the article, then, is to broaden Graves's conception of parliamentary management, to ask how William Cecil, Lord Burghley, worked with the parliamentary classes.

Recent work on the state in early modern England has emphasized the role played by semi-independent local authorities and local people who used the state as a tool to solve particular local issues. Patrick Collinson remarked that these local governors were not simply subjects of the crown. They were citizens of a commonwealth that functioned only because of their sense of civic duty. To express this, he coined the description of Tudor England as a 'monarchical republic' in which traditions of popular participation sat somewhat uneasily alongside the sovereign authority of the crown. He illustrated this with the 1584 story of the Bond of Association, which sought to create an emergency government in case the queen suddenly died.[6]

Steve Hindle has argued forcefully that law was a lever in the hands of people who sought protection, increasing the power of the state from the grass roots up. As he says, early modern English governance was not arcane or remote. It was a process in which subjects were intimately involved and one which they learned to manipulate, and even change, in their own interest. Michael Braddick and John Walters have argued in a similar fashion. They downplay the institutions of the state, stressing, instead, the importance of the network of local officeholders who were instrumental in creating and evolving the ways in which the crown's central agencies worked. These agencies were set in a hierarchy that might appear to be distinct, but they were experienced as part of

---

[2] Michael A.R. Graves, 'The Management of the Elizabethan House of Commons: The Council's Men-of-Business', *Parliamentary History*, ii (1983), 11–38.

[3] Michael A.R. Graves, *Thomas Norton: The Parliament Man* (Oxford, 1994).

[4] Michael A.R. Graves, 'Managing Elizabethan Parliaments', in *The Parliaments of Elizabethan England*, ed. David M. Dean and Norman L. Jones (Oxford, 1990), 55.

[5] The searchable biographies of all members of the Elizabethan house of commons are available at *http://www.historyofparliamentonline.org/research/members/members-1558-1603* (accessed 19 October 2014); *Proceedings in the Parliaments of Elizabeth I*, ed. T.E Hartley (3 vols, Leicester, 1981–95).

[6] Patrick Collinson, '*De Republica Anglorum* or History with the Politics put Back' and 'The Monarchical Republic of Queen Elizabeth I', in Patrick Collinson, *Elizabethan Essays* (1994), 1–30, 31–58.

an organic local order. Together they created the basis for the early modern 'power grid'. Individuals' placing on this three-dimensional grid was determined by the number of hierarchies in which they participated and the degree to which their ranking within those separate hierarchies was mutually reinforcing.[7] My own work convinces me that Hindle and Braddick are correct in seeing the importance of local power grids, but it also prompts me to ask how Elizabeth and Burghley worked with the people in these power grids, to create royal government.

Although it was greatly expanded by the Tudors, the remit of royal government was very narrow. Its primary job was to keep the king's peace within the realm while defending it from external enemies. What rudimentary bureaucracy it had was designed to enforce the law and collect revenue, which is why the royal courts loomed so large in the national mind. It should not be forgotten that England was, after the Norman conquest, a proprietary state technically owned by the monarch – even if the great nobles did not like to be reminded of it. This created a particular sort of relation between the crown and those who held property. Here we must quote Sir Thomas Smith, that touchstone of all discussions of the Tudor constitution:

> For no man holds land simply free in England, but he or she that holds the Crown of England: all others holde their land in fee, that is upon a faith or trust, and some service to be done. . . . That is, in trust and confidence, that he shall be true to the Lorde of whom he holds it, pay such rents, doe such service, and observe such conditions as was annexed to the first donation. Thus all save the Prince be indeed not *viri domini*, but rather *fiduciary domini*, and *possessors*.[8]

As Smith says, owing service in return for the land [or corporate charter] held from the monarch created the core relationship between the crown and the magisterial classes. It also created the points of leverage and contact between them. Landlords owed service as governors and soldiers at the order of the monarch And the monarch, in good feudal fashion, demanded that service, as well as rents, fees and duties. As Smith is careful to point out, this was a contractual arrangement, in which the stakeholders worked together.

In our era of 'monarchical republicanism', it is good to be reminded that Smith himself translated the Latin '*res publica*' as 'common wealth', a term that catches the nature of government in the common cause better than 'republic', that implies more participation than he would have allowed. Smith defines it as a form of social contract founded on mutual benefit: 'A society or common doing of a multitude of freemen collected together and united by common accord and covenants among themselves, for the conservation of themselves as well in peace as in war.'[9] Smith probably would have us notice that he says they are 'freemen' who come together in their common interest,

---

[7] Steven Hindle, 'County Government in England', in *A Companion to Tudor Britain*, ed. Robert Tittler and Norman Jones (Oxford, 2004), 98–115; Michael Braddick and John Walter, 'Grids of Power: Order, Hierarchy and Subordination', in *Negotiating Power in Early Modern Society: Order, Hierarchy and Subordination in Britain and Ireland*, ed. Michael J. Braddick and John Walter (Cambridge, 2001), 38–9.

[8] Thomas Smith, *De repvblica anglorvm: The maner of gouernement or policie of the realme of England* (1584), 111–12.

[9] Smith, *De repvblica anglorvm*, 10.

rather than the people. For, as Elyot insists in his *The boke named the gouernour,* and Smith confirmed, the common people did not participate in government.[10] In short, England was a common weal, in which the social orders were created by God and without them there would be the chaos of a republic.[11]

If we ask about the management of the Elizabethan state as it was done, we must recognize the conception of status and duty shared by the magisterial classes. It was their sense of owed service and joint responsibility that made it work, giving the central state what leverage it had over the localities.

Steve Hindle has nicely summarized the miracle of Tudor government. Observing that the Elizabethan state had only about 1,200 paid officials, he comments:

> Much of Tudor governance was, perforce, carried out by amateurs who volunteered their service out of a combination of desire for national or local recognition of their honour and prestige and of an ethos of public duty which was derived partly from the tradition of classical republicanism mediated through the humanist curricula of grammar schools and universities and partly from indigenous habits of political participation in the institutions of manor, parish and county.[12]

The role of the crown was to use its authority as the greatest landowner and the legitimator of local power to maintain the reciprocal obligations built on feudal contracts, legal rulings, and, increasingly, statute law. All of these were recognized by the larger community as legitimately binding, in part because they were derived from, and recognized by, divine precedent and appropriate consultation. In its self-conception, the Elizabethan government was less a monarchical republic than a feudal, federal monarchy whose use of parliament was the ultimate expression of both the monarch's inability to rule without the support of the powerful, and of the powerful people's need of binding arbitration for their own good. This made parliament only one point of management and the men who sat in parliament were co-managers of the commonwealth.

The governance of Elizabethan England took place in an informal world in which place, personal connection, trust, honour and expertise were granted authority that never appeared on an organisation chart. Largely informal, it depended heavily on the will, knowledge and motivation of a few hundred gentlemen and nobles for its effectiveness. It was shaped by law and custom, but the understanding of these on the part of the ruling class determined what could actually be accomplished.

In modern social science jargon, the Elizabethan state depended upon 'social knowledge'. This is defined as common understanding and practice that is a result of the connections between the individual members of society, resident in no single one of them. It was a form of knowledge acquired in childhood by imitation, which makes it very hard to document, but it is, none the less, real.

Consequently, in any discussion of Elizabethan government, we must recognize that it was effected through overlapping formal and informal networks, networks that were based on the ruling community's sense of its duty and purpose. Most importantly, it

[10] Thomas Elyot, *The boke named the gouernour* (1531), sig. Ai v–Aii.
[11] Elyot, *The boke named the gouernour,* Aii v.
[12] Hindle, 'County Government in England', 98.

must be recognized that the act of governing, and of political leadership, was personal. Successful rule in the pre-bureaucratic, pre-statist systems required individuals to bear their shares of the common responsibility.

William Cecil gives us a fine picture of how this informality worked by invoking owed service. In June 1569, Cecil was pondering how to defend the realm from dangerous invaders and how to prevent a civil war like those raging in France and Flanders. The resulting document was entitled 'A necessary consideration of the perillous state of this tyme'. Heavily corrected and interlined in Cecil's own spidery hand, it presents a stark sketch of the weakness of the crown. Written just before the Revolt of the Northern Earls, it is eloquent in its expectations of the magisterial classes.

His propositions were twofold. First, that all nations who accepted the authority of the bishop of Rome felt it was their duty in conscience to persecute 'with all violence' the recusants in their midst. It followed that the same states that persecuted their recusant citizens would attack their neighbours who did not recognize papal authority. Second, England was their greatest enemy, and so their natural target. No monarchy in Christendom was a greater loss to Rome, or a better model for reformation, than England, with its good laws. Hated by Spain and France, England had, through the lack of persecution of its enemies, nourished seditions, so that it was seen to be weak. These propositions lead him to argue for an aggressive aid to foreign protestants, and prepa-ration for defence at home: 'And herein the first and principal mean to prevent these perils with the assistance of Her Majesty', he says, must 'altogether use the speedy force of her own assured good subject', by boosting their readiness 'to avoid and shift out of the borders of this whole land the miserable spectacle and captivity of slaughter . . . [of] which the . . . reports . . . do come from all foreign parts in France, Flanders, Spain and . . . do bring sufficient terror to all wise and sensible persons'.[13]

His solution to these threats rested on the voluntary creation, led by nobles, bishops, knights and the leading men in each locality, of a bond of association. Those who took the oath to defend the queen would contribute money to a trusted person in every shire, who would keep it to use for the defence of the realm whenever the queen or her council called for them to do so. These leading men would invite lesser men – merchants, clothiers, farmers, householders, mayors and their ilk – to subscribe and contribute, too. Those who agreed to sign and pay were to be secretly noted in a book, along with those who refused. The refusals were to be categorised into two kinds: recusants of conscience and recusants who simply did not have the means to contribute.[14]

In short, when England faced such a crisis, the queen could call upon every gentle-man to do his duty and make a voluntary contribution. There is no call to build an army, raise taxes, or do any of the other things we might think a state could do when faced with such danger. Instead, we have the assumption that the nobles and gentlemen will see to the organisation of the defence if asked.

Strikingly, after the northern rebellion had been suppressed, Cecil drafted a thank-you note for the queen to send to certain gentlemen of Northumberland. She had heard of

[13] TNA, SP12/51, ff. 9–13.
[14] TNA, SP12/51, ff. 9–13.

their good and faithful service from the lord warden, the governor of Berwick, and the earl of Sussex. She expressed her appreciation and asked for their continued fidelity.[15] Set against the background of the trials and retaliations being carried out on their neighbours who had rebelled, this is a telling gesture.

The use of the word 'fidelity' in the letter to the Northumbrians reminds us of Smith's observation that every man holds his land 'in trust and confidence, that he shall be true to the Lorde' who gave it, and it also requires us to notice the concept of 'trust'. The rhetoric of governance invoked trust and friendship all of the time. Thousands of orders from the crown were addressed to 'right trusty and well beloved' subjects. More strikingly, letters from the privy council to local commissioners were signed by the councillors 'Your Loving Friends', changing direct orders into friendly requests. The privy council's trust in its friends to carry out its orders was sometimes abused, but the pretence of trust and friendship was maintained.[16]

Tudor political culture was displayed in several rhetorical streams. These streams had their sources in feudal honour, the common law, Christian morality, and humanist values. In a world in which there was limited direct coercion, these values, like that of trust, had to be announced and reinforced frequently by all of the actors, from the queen down to school teachers, homilists, catechists and mothers.

Perhaps the easiest way to see these overlapping rhetorics is to look at politics as Tudor people did, as being about individual morality, not political values. It is striking to anyone doing intellectual history that, in the early 17th century, the ways in which Europeans analysed human behaviours and people's relation to the state changed radically. By the 1620s, there was a sharp decline in moral theology as an analytical tool and a burst of thinking that replaced the analysis of individual responsibility to God with arguments emphasizing economic rationality and reason of state. These Baconian ways of thinking ignored metaphysics in favour of observable patterns. I demonstrated this in my work on usury law, noting that the law of God 'in conscience' was explicitly separated from the law of the state by statute in 1624. In those days, a new generation, the founding generation of English economists, was thinking about economic relations in terms of relative demand, interest rates, and capital flows. It had divorced morality from action. As Sir Robert Filmer argued in his *Questio quoblibetica*, written in the 1620s, usury was as lawful as any other contract, unless reasons of state required it to be regulated. When Sir William Cecil had analysed the same question, in the 1570s, he had reached a very different conclusion, driven by a scholastic analysis of usury that depended upon Biblical, theological, and classical arguments. Usury, in his mind, was a sin that God expected the state to prevent. Individuals, as greedy and stiff-necked

[15] HMC, *Salisbury MSS*, i, 574.

[16] A superb example of this ironic call on trust and friendship is the 1591 letter from the privy council to 'our loving frendes the Sheriffe and Justices of peace of the county of Norff', in which they are rebuked for dereliction of duty. It has been eight months, the loving councillors say, since the justices received their order to investigate purveyances in the county. 'Whereas we greatelye Marvell, consideringe the usuall Complaintes made in parliament we doe therefore againe will & require you in her Mat's name, that presentlie you doe proceade to the diligent execucon & perfourmaunce of the full effecte of the same our former letters.' They sign it 'Your Loving Friends': *The Official Papers of Sir Nathaniel Bacon of Stiffkey, Norfolk as Justice of the Peace 1580–1620*, ed. H.W. Saunders (Camden, 3rd ser., xxvi, 1915), 64–5.

sinners, needed to be protected from their own evil lest the wrath of God fall on them and on the state.[17]

It is this setting of good and bad action in the context of individual virtue, in accord with that individual's place in God's creation, which shapes Elizabethan understanding of governance. Their conception of politics was that it was a series of individual actions that ought to be guided and judged by the *virtu* of those actions. God and society had expectations for those to whom much power and authority had been given. Scripture, custom and history taught them how to use that power. A providential God would reward and punish the use and misuse of it – and punishment and reward flowed from God to the people if the governors of the people were virtuous. If they were not, the paradigm of Sodom and Gomorrah was invoked, along with examples from Greek and Roman history. Narratives of martyrdom carried the same message – obedience pleased God.

This conception of politics was caught neatly by an anecdote related by Sir Francis Bacon. He remembered: 'When any great officer, ecclesiastical or civil, was to be made, the queen would inquire after the piety, integrity, learning of the man. And when she was satisfied in these qualifications, she would consider of his personage. And upon such an occasion she pleased once to say to me, "Bacon, how can the magistrate maintain his authority when the man is despised?" '[18]

This is one reason William Cecil was obsessed with genealogy as a form of history. He saw breeding as an indication of both station and virtue – and family histories could tell you much about behaviour, as well as who had to listen to whom. For historians like Cecil, who personally wrote out copies of long genealogies, government rested on birth, birth order determined authority and the right to give orders, and the working of providence was evident in the rise and falls of families and the states they ran.[19]

Conceiving governance in terms of those who have the right to govern rather than in terms of reason of state meant that the state could not be separated from the people born to run it. He read widely in the genealogies of royal families, as well as working them out for himself and having them painted on the walls of his house. This was not simply evidence of his desire to climb the social tree – although he undoubtedly did aspire for his family to rise, as their merit deserved. It was about understanding how God had arranged the world and the place of people in that arrangement.

Reading his favourite author, Cicero, reinforced this tendency to see politics as the expression of individual virtue. *De officiis* or *Contra Verrem* or *De Re Publica* all taught him that the individual had duties to the commonwealth, and that the individual could choose the path of virtue. Senecan stoicism taught the same thing, and so did the Bible. And so, of course, did the histories he read. This quest for personal virtue was summed up by his brother-in-law's personal motto, *mediocria firma*, the golden mean that kept a man doing his duty well. It is probably not an accident that William Cecil often reminds

[17] Norman Jones, *God and the Moneylenders: Usury and Law in Early Modern England* (Oxford, 1989); Norman Jones, 'William Cecil and the Making of Economic Policy in the 1560s', in *The Commonwealth of Tudor England*, ed. P. Fideler and T. Mayer (1992), 169–93; Robert Filmer, *Questio Quodlibetica A discourse whether it may be lawful to take use for money* (1678).

[18] Francis Bacon, 'Certain Apothegms of the Lord Bacon's', *The Works of Francis Bacon*, ed. James Spedding, Robert Leslie Ellis and Douglas Denon Heath (15 vols, 1900), i, 123.

[19] Anthony Grafton, *What was History? The Art of History in Early Modern Europe* (Cambridge, 2007), 162.

one of Cato the Censor, with his stern sense of duty, virtue, and tradition. The examples of famous Greeks and Romans were freely used as templates for modelling and understanding action. Sir Thomas Smith, in fact, made the comparisons explicit, using Roman history as a foil for England.

Consequently, the governor's first question was 'Who', not 'What'. The ideology of the person, though it was a worry if he was a catholic, was seldom a consideration. His status and standing were the deciding factors, unless he openly refused to obey. Elizabeth's respect for Mary, queen of Scots' rank is an example of this, as is Burghley's 'bloody question', with its insistence that obedience to the queen, rather than religious belief, was the appropriate test. But it does not mean that ideology was ignored. Elizabeth's privy council tried to make ideological distinctions among the key people in local government, the justices of the peace. Thrice they surveyed them, and each time little was done about what they learned. In this process we can glimpse the problem presented by a formal attempt to manage local government.

In 1564, the privy council asked the bishops to investigate the attitude of their local justices of the peace towards the settlement of religion. The result was lists that categorised local gentlemen as 'favourers', 'neutrals', and 'non-favourers', giving us a picture of just how catholic or protestant the bishops believed the front line of law enforcement to be. Famously, however, the privy council did not act against most of the men on the list. Although known to oppose the queen's religion, many continued to serve on the local benches.

In 1569, JPs were expected to take the oath of supremacy, and there was an attempt to weed catholics out of the Inns of Court. However, as the case of Edmund Plowden illustrates, men continued to serve if they gave their bond for good behaviour.

Again, in the fall of 1587, during the Armada crisis, the privy council bade the bishops to give an account of the JPs within their dioceses. The results were instructive, though not in the sense the council wanted.[20] The system of governance did not readily permit them to weed out catholics, since catholics with the right standing could hardly be excluded from the judicial bench. It was very difficult for them to escape their way of perceiving authority as accorded by birth and position.

The bishops were clear about the problem. They could not promote favourers of religion who did not have the birth and status for appointment. Scory of Hereford confessed that he would like to see bureaucrats like his chancellor appointed, considering 'there is so little choice of such as be favourable to this religion'.[21] Bishop Robert Horne at Winchester thought the solution was converting the existing members and young aristocrats. The young earl of Southampton and young William Lord Sands 'might be now in their youth so trained in religion that hereafter when they come to their authority and rule they should not hinder the same'.[22]

[20] John Strype, *Annals of the Reformation and Establishment of Religion, and other Various Occurrences in the Church of England during Queen Elizabeth's Happy Reign: Together with an Appendix of Original Papers of State, Records, and Letters* (4 vols in 7, Oxford, 1824), iii, pt 2, 448–76.

[21] Mary Bateson, 'Collection of original letters from the bishops to the privy council, 1564, with returns of the justices of the peace and others classified according to their religious convictions', in *Camden Misc.* ix (Camden, new ser., liii, 1895), 17.

[22] Bateson, 'Collection of original letters', 54.

It appears that it was Horne's suggestion that the council chose to follow. 'Once a family entered the ranks of the magisterial gentry, the central government had a very powerful incentive not to offend unnecessarily the natural rulers of the localities', says Ron Fritze, so, as justices died or retired, the crown tended to appoint younger-than-usual men to the commissions of the peace. It indicates, he says, that the degree to which the central government could enforce the Reformation was limited by the extent to which the natural rulers of a given county community shared the religious inclinations of a given regime.[23]

In 1587, attempts to rearrange the judicial bench provoked the earl of Derby to make a personal trip to court to complain. To Derby, the religious 'unsoundness of divers of his consil' did not matter. His honour and status were offended by meddling with the men he had recommended.[24] His local power ensured that he had to be taken into account by Burghley.

Derby's honour was important because it was honour, and its cousin conscience, that kept people governing. The gentlemen who were expected to run local government were very aware that lineage and service made one gentle, and it was this sensibility that created the interface of government. Service was expected as a duty, but honour had to be maintained.[25] As Richard Cust has put it: 'Honour can be said to mediate between the aspirations of the individual and the judgement of society. It therefore provides a means of exploring the values and norms of a society, and also the ways in which individuals compete to sustain or increase their status and power within that society.'[26] To make Cust's description concrete, look at the gates which Dr Caius built for his college in the 1570s. New students entered the college through the Gate of Humility, while studying in the college they would pass through the Gate of Virtue every day, and finally, when they left to receive their degrees, they departed through the Gate of Honour. Students rose from abasement to honour through virtue.

The Gate of Honour, for the magisterial classes, was primarily guarded by the queen, making honour an important managerial tool. Handing out honours, withholding honours, and dishonouring were forms of influence.

The magistracy was in a neo-Platonic universe in which honour and duty, derived from lineage and office, flowed both toward and away from the centre. They may have had duties to their betters and their queen, but they also had duties to their families and localities that made their responses much more a matter of self-interest than is sometimes admitted. Concepts of honour, obedience, lineage and service certainly motivated people, but honour, and slight, was in the eyes of the beholder, just as when to serve and how enthusiastically was a calculation that related to values that were more localised

[23] Ronald H. Fritze and William B. Robison, 'Age and Magistracy – An Ambiguous Connection? The Situation of the Justices of the Peace of Hampshire and Surrey, 1485–1570', *Lamar Journal of the Humanities*, xx (1994), 47–8.

[24] Strype, *Annals*, iii, pt 2, 489–90.

[25] Felicity Heal and Clive Holmes, *The Gentry in England and Wales 1500–1700* (Stanford, CA, 1994), 24–33.

[26] Richard Cust, 'Honour and Politics in Early Stuart England: The Case of Beaumont v. Hastings', *Past & Present*, No. 149 (1995), 58–9.

than general. Honour was a 'discourse tool' that could be used to justify behaviour.[27] But it carried a multitude of meanings, making it hard to use.

Mervyn James has noted that, by the early 17th century, the 'moralisation' of politics had occurred. Tudor order was not possible without the collaboration of the majority of the governing class. Ergo it needed to be freely accepted, assimilated and given governing force. The process creating this was comprehensively expressed in the synthesis of honour, humanistic wisdom and protestant religion in the Sidney circle at Elizabeth's court – which means that the Elizabethan ruling class was fusing these concepts into a tool of management.[28] It was this fusion that allowed the emergence of what Naunton called the *Togati*, the professional bureaucrats, like Burghley, whose honour and power derived from service rather than lineage.[29]

In a society in which honour was very important, the invitation to serve was evidence of status. It conferred honour along with work. By the same token, to be skipped over or displaced was a dishonour that brought shame and embarrassment. On the local level, honour, an abstract concept, turned into power and responsibility. Honour demanded that one serve, but, *noblesse oblige*, one had to use the power given for the desired ends or it might be withdrawn. Certainly, your peers would be aware of your behaviour in positions of honour and might shame you. This may be why the many, many commissions issued by the crown were built of careful layers of prestige and connection. Local commissioners did most of the work, but it was done under the eyes of the great men of the region and the state who were also appointed. For example, all commissions for the peace contained members who represented the local hierarchies, the regionally powerful, and the servants of the crown.

H.S. Cockburn's edition of the assize records makes this clear. The entry for each assize begins with a list of all the members of the commission of the peace who had the right to attend. Cockburn makes a distinction in these lists between the 'honorary' JPs, who were not expected to attend, and the country magistrates who were (and who were sometimes fined if they did not). It is apparent that, in this sense, 'honorary' should be read as 'men of honour' whose names lent honour and authority to those associated with them. The acts of the county magistracy are thus given greater weight by being linked to all levels of the hierarchy, giving them joint responsibility for the assize. When Lord Treasurer Burghley's name appeared on every commission of the peace, it was not to honour him, it was to honour those associated with him – and to give him standing to interfere. For example, at the Hertford Assize of 4 March 1573, there were 38 justices of the peace on the list; 18 actually appeared. The most senior justice present was Sir Ralph Sadler. A major land owner in the county, he was also chancellor of the duchy of Lancaster and a member of the privy council. In him the interests of the county and the crown came together as he and

[27] William Palmer, 'Scenes from Provincial Life: History, Honor, and Meaning in the Tudor North', *Renaissance Quarterly*, liii (2000), 448.

[28] Mervyn James, *English Politics and the Concept of Honour 1485–1640, Past & Present* Supplements, iii (1978), 2.

[29] Robert Naunton, *Fragmenta Regalia, or, Observations on Queen Elizabeth, Her Times & Favorites*, ed. John S. Cerovski (Washington, DC, 1985), 48.

Justice John Southcote of the queen's bench (a JP in Hertfordshire as well as the presiding justice) conducted the gaol delivery.[30]

Burghley's presence on the commission of the peace in every county underscores the importance of the law as a point of leverage and interaction between the local governors and the crown. The English mingling of all the ruling classes in the commissions was a unique and important method of governance. In France, for instance, men of great birth were not expected to provide local justice, leaving that to mere men of law. As Lord Keeper Bacon said in 1617, the commission of the peace 'knits government elsewhere with the government of corporations, and puts them together'. This, he said, created a commonwealth so strong that you could not make a better one with a level.[31]

This knitting together, a product of feudal rights and Tudor management, is visible in all sorts of commissions issued by the privy council, as the central and the local shared responsibility. The formula that required all the commissioners, or any two or three of them, to conduct a piece of business, kept the window open for central engagement while making it clear that the locals could get on with the business at hand. At the same time, the great men who served on the council expected to take a hand in local business. After all, it was local power that prepared them for, and proved their value for, service to the queen. It was also local power that made it possible to extend the power of the crown into the localities. That is why it was important for privy council members to maintain and expand their particular areas of influence. For instance, Burghley systematically accumulated local offices. He was steward and recorder of Stamford, the town nearest his country seat in Lincolnshire. He was also steward of King's Lynn and Yarmouth, recorder of Boston, surveyor of royal lands in Lincolnshire, keeper of Rockingham Forest and Cliffe Park, *custos rotulorum* of Lincolnshire and Northamptonshire, and steward of numerous royal estates in the area. In London he was steward, escheator, bailiff, and clerk of the manor of Westminster, where he also had a home. He became lord lieutenant of Lincolnshire in 1587 and of Hertfordshire and Essex in the following year.

Burghley did not hold these jobs *in commendam*. He arbitrated local disputes, and sat on the commission of sewers concerned with fen drainage. He was as important a figure in his own region as he was at court. He was, from 1559, an active chancellor of Cambridge University, steward of Trinity College lands, and steward to the bishoprics of Lichfield and Coventry, St David's, and Winchester.[32]

Of course, Burghley was not alone in playing an active role on multiple levels, bridging national and local government. We see the same with other powerful people. William Fleetwood, recorder of London, and a parliamentary man of business, was a good friend of Burghley's, as well as other privy councillors.

Recorder Fleetwood, a freeman of the Guild of the Merchant Taylors, worked closely with every lord mayor of London and all the aldermen, and kept up a hectic legal pace. In the last week of September and the first week of October 1575, he

---

[30] *Calendar of Assize Records: Hertfordshire Indictments, Elizabeth I*, ed. J.S. Cockburn (11 vols, 1975–85), vii, 1.

[31] Francis Bacon, 'The Lord Chancellor's Speech in the Starchamber 13 Februarii 1617', available at *http://www.uofaweb.ualberta.ca/historyandclassics/pdfs/496-BACON-SPEECHES.pdf* (accessed 29 Nov. 2008).

[32] 'William Cecil, Lord Burghley', *ODNB*.

participated in 19 legal events. He reported all of them in a letter to Burghley that ended with his hope to see him and his family socially at the end of the week.[33]

In this period, Fleetwood was in contact with all of the governors of London, the barons of the exchequer, the justices of Surrey, Buckinghamshire, Southwark and London, and a long list of others, high and low, including sewer and river commissioners, and bawds, counterfeiters, and ale vendors. A map of Fleetwood's 'social grid' would show that he, like most others of the magisterial class, had a complex, mingled, set of informal, as well as formal, connections. Moreover, Fleetwood was, like most of them, a creator of law as well as a lawyer, since he was a very active member of parliament until his death in 1594.

It was through these contacts, from the highest to the lowest, that the social knowledge of informal government passed. Burghley understood this so well that he carefully tracked locations and relationships of the magisterial classes. He grasped that power was related to genealogy and geography. His anonymous biographer asked rhetorically: 'what nobleman or gentleman and their dwellings, matches and pedigrees, did he not know?' He acquired this knowledge by keeping pedigree charts, among other things.[34]

These connections were multiplied by Burghley's networks, which ranged from patron and client to father-in-law and brother-in-law, with friendships and business relationships mixed in to varying degrees. Burghley, as a rising man, was building a dynasty, but at the same time he was building affinities of various kinds, all of which were useful on many levels. He married his children well. His eldest son, Thomas, married the daughter of Lord Latimer, giving him family ties to the earls of Northumberland, Westmorland and of Rutland. His daughter, Anne, married Edward de Vere, 17th earl of Oxford. He had granted himself the wardship of young de Vere and used it to arrange the wedding. His other daughter, Elizabeth, married William Wentworth, eldest son of Lord Wentworth of Nettlestead. Robert Cecil married Elizabeth, daughter of William Brooke, Lord Cobham, a perfect match with another leading administrator's family.

All of this expansion of his kin network gave him opportunities to mix, mingle and command. His son Thomas's entry into the Percy family gave the Cecils an important tie to power in the north, and Burghley had probably hoped that his marriage of Anne to the earl of Oxford would do the same in the south, although the marriage was so bad that it is likely that being the father-in-law of the earl of Oxford became a burden.

But did family connection, by blood or marriage, engender loyalty along with children? Could familial relations be used as a lever to provoke actions? The answer to this is yes, probably. It undoubtedly did provoke desired actions, but not directly. Like patronage, family ties were much larger than any particular instance, so that one seldom sees a 'do it my way' sort of order from an esteemed relative. However, family did fit into the broader model of honour, in that membership in the right family made you honourable, and nomination by an honourable person made you worthy.

---

[33] A full transcription was printed by William Murdin in *A Collection of State Papers, Relating to Affairs in the Reign of Queen Elizabeth for the Years 1571–1596* (1759), 259. A partial transcription is at HMC, *Salisbury MSS*, ii, entry 327. The two transcriptions disagree about the date: Murdin says it is 1 Oct. 1573, and HMC, *Salisbury MSS* puts it at 2 Oct. 1575.

[34] Arthur Collins, *The Life of the Great Statesman William Cecil Lord Burghley* (1732), 65–7.

For example, Burghley's nephew, Henry Cheke, comes to mind. Cecil had married Mary Cheke in 1541. She died early in 1544, but he remained connected to the Cheke family for the rest of his life. Mary's brother, Sir John, once William Cecil's tutor, had died in Mary's reign, leaving a son, Henry. When Henry was aged 15 years, in 1563, he wrote his Uncle William a letter in Greek asking for his patronage. As a result, Cecil oversaw his education at Cambridge.

Five years later, the University Senate sought to win favour with its chancellor by offering Henry an MA. They praised him for being like his late father, Sir John, in learning, piety, and purity of life, and justified their generosity by pointing out that they had recent precedents among the Howard and Seymour families for elected youths of 20 years old. They earnestly sought Cecil's approbation. Then, assuming Cecil's silence was consent, the Senate acted a week later, offering young Henry his MA and a seat in the Senate. Henry had the good sense to write to his uncle, William, and ask his permission before taking the degree. It is clear from the ornate, italic Latin of these letters that the university thought it would please Cecil by honouring the memory of his old tutor and brother-in-law. Young Henry claimed to have nothing to do with his promotion, which is likely.[35]

Eventually, Henry was made secretary to the Council of the North. Over the years, he wrote Cecil many letters, always asking for more patronage. His uncle generally supported him, though never as much as Henry hoped.[36] If we look at this story one way, it is clear that family ties were important and that Cecil saw it as duty to support young Cheke, giving him an education and some patronage. If we look at it another way, we can see the Senate of Cambridge University seeking to please their chancellor by honouring his relative with a gratuitous MA. In neither case was there a direct *quid pro quo*, but Henry invoked his social capital and Cambridge hoped to create future social capital.

Marriage could create important alliances and move money, so they frequently played a part in regional politics. In 1564, Sir William Cecil advised the earl of Bedford, departing for his post as governor of Berwick, 'Do what you can, to make the Gentlemen accord amongst themselves; and to extinguish old factions, either by some device of marrying, or by redemption of titles of land, such like incumbrances, which commonly the seeds of discord [sow].'[37] As master of the Court of Wards from 1561, Cecil often acted on this observation, disposing of heirs in marriage with a clear sense of the effects of marriages on politics.

The complicated case of Barbara Gamage, a very rich heiress from Glamorgan, shows how the struggle for a girl's hand could be made a matter of national, as well as local, politics. To make a complicated story simple, the young lady lost her father in 1584. Even before his death, the suitors had been circling. After it, she was taken under the protection of her uncle or cousin, Sir Edward Stradling, who was at once besieged by suits on behalf of Robert Sidney, stepson of the earl of Leicester, and Edward Croft, the son of Sir James Croft and a Herbert on his matrilineal side. They both wanted her

[35] BL, Lansdowne MS 10, ff. 157, 169, 171.

[36] John Strype, *The Life of the Learned Sir John Cheke* (Oxford, 1821), 140–1; BL, Lansdowne MS 7, f. 56; TNA, SP12/39, f. 115; SP12/48, f. 52; SP12/49, f. 165; SP12/69, f. 15; SP12/74, f. 124.

[37] BL, Harleian MS 6990, f. 3v.

fortune. Sir James Croft got the privy council to intervene and give the girl into the custody of the sheriff, a Herbert and kin of the Crofts. On the other side, Lord Burghley intervened as master of the wards because, although she was of age, she had not yet sued for livery of her lands. Burghley ordered the girl to be transferred to Sir Edward Carne. Meanwhile, Barbara's cousins, Sir Walter Raleigh and Lord Howard of Effingham, became enraged on her behalf, Raleigh demanding to be recognized as her kin, insisting that she not 'be bought and sold in Wales without her Majesty's privity and consent or advise of my Lord Chamberlain [Howard] and myself'. Just to confuse matters, Sir Francis Walsingham became involved. He gave Barbara back to Stradling, who very quickly married her to Robert Sidney. The pursuit of Barbara Gamage had embroiled the governing families of Glamorgan and Herefordshire in a bitter dispute that threatened their ability to co-operate in government.[38]

People often married their children to their friends' children, for friendship formed another bond, as did the civil niceties of the small societies to which the magistracy belonged, whether they were towns, colleges, inns, guilds, or commissions of the peace. It was in these relationships that social knowledge was cemented, as multiple generations interacted personally. One of the lessons they taught was that the maintenance of friendly relations made honour flow and made life easier. This was well known to the authors of courtesy books, but it was seldom explained as a political skill. In 1622, John Reynolds published a translation of Eustace de Refuge's 1615 *Treatise on the Court* that made it explicit.

De Refuge, a contemporary of Robert Cecil, was a successful and highly-placed ambassador and judge under Henri IV and Louis XIII, thanks to personal skill and a very good marriage. Late in his life, de Refuge distilled what he knew about politics into his *Treatise*, which is hailed by its most recent translator as 'the early modern management classic on organizational behaviour'.[39] John Reynolds translated it, at the prompting of Sir Edward Sackville, soon to be the 4th earl of Dorset, who had discovered it during his exile on the Continent following a duel in which he killed a Scotsman. Perhaps Sackville recognized the truth of de Refuge's argument, though he did not seem able to take it to heart. Reynolds presented it to the future Charles I as a manual for those involved in the court 'that virtue might not be robbed of her desserts, and honour by vice, but that merit and reward might still march hand in hand'.[40]

The first book of the *Treatise* is dedicated to civility, which he subdivides into affability, graceful speech, and appropriate apparel. All of these are about encouraging access and trust. A courtier who speaks judiciously and pleasantly 'will speedily engender a hope that they may easily have access to us, and converse with us as often as they please'.[41] This makes inferiors comfortable in opening up their thoughts, as it were, to a friend.

[38] Penry Williams, *The Council in the Marches of Wales under Elizabeth I* (Cardiff, 1958), 242–6, 229–39.

[39] Eustache de Refuge, *Treatise on the Court: The Early Modern Management Classic on Organizational Behaviour*, ed. and trans. J. Chris Cooper (Boca Raton, FL, 2008). Cooper does not translate the first book of the *Treatise*, focusing only on how to manage the 'chief executive officer' prince.

[40] *A treatise of the court or Instructions for courtiers: Digested into two books. Written in French by the noble, and learned iuris-consull Monsr Denys de Refuges, Councellor of Estate, and many tymes ambassador (in foraigne parts) for ye two last French kings his masters*, trans. John Reynolds (1617), sig. (a) v.

[41] *A treatise of the court*, trans. Reynolds, 9.

Of course, these affable conversations must be conducted with decency and gravity, without coarse or inappropriate humour, as befits the rank and condition of the speaker and his audience:

> But as the respect and honour a great man sheweth us, is not onely agreeable and pleasing to us in respect of his person: but also because his countenance and favour purchaseth us more credit in those who are present: right to his disrespect and disdaine, doth not onely anger us because of himselfe but it is insupportable in respect of the base esteeme that others make of us, to see us so sleighted and neglected of him.[42]

This echoes what Sir William Cecil told the earl of Bedford: 'let it not appear, you use any man, with singular affection, above the rest, and yet you may use (indeed) as you see cause, men either of wisdom, or credit'.[43]

De Refuge instructs in the use of jokes, flattery, and other skills of the courtier, but the point of his first book is that political success lies in skilful relations with other people. In particular, the effective courtier knows how to perform good offices for others. Favours are the:

> cement of human society, and the fetters and manacles (says an ancient) wherewith we may inchaine and captivate others, especially at Court, where the interest and performance thereof is the twist, or cord, that conjoins and combines so many people, one to another: yea, although for the most part, they are drawne thereunto with different and contrarie affections.[44]

He solemnly warns, however, that you should not expect direct *quid pro quo* for good offices, doing some good deeds without any expectation, and 'take heed that he not suddenly demand of him a recompense, for feare that being discovered, to desire and crave the like, he make it apparent he did it purposely for the same end'.[45]

If enchained by a favour, he says, we must seek every opportunity to repay the debt, but this is to be done carefully, since we do not want it to appear that our friend did it only to gain an advantage. The timing of the repayment is of key importance. We should be neither embarrassingly quick to do it, nor impolitely tardy. We must seek opportunities to return it, yet we must do it without flattery or ostentation. We must avoid the appearance of motives that dishonour ourselves, or our benefactors.[46]

This *Treatise* makes plain the *politesse* that was practised, or was supposed to be practised, among people of rank as a normal part of the negotiation of power. Recent scholarship on gift giving in honour cultures supports de Refuge's point. The archives are full of correspondence about favours sought and given, along with gifts sent and received. A quick search on State Papers Online alone produces 36 hits for the word 'buck', reminding us that deer and other foods were the common currency of favour. For example, in 1587, Julius Caesar, once Burghley's ward who had become the city of

---

[42] *A treatise of the court*, trans. Reynolds, 10.

[43] BL, Harleian MS 6990, f. 2.

[44] *A treatise of the court*, trans. Reynolds, 20.

[45] *A treatise of the court*, trans. Reynolds, 22.

[46] *A treatise of the court*, trans. Reynolds, 26.

London's civil lawyer and was soon to be the sole judge in the court of the admiralty, petitioned Burghley for a deer. Caesar needed it for entertaining a company in London the following Monday.[47] Caesar's ability to call upon Burghley for such a gift, in rather grovelling terms, indicates his inferior status; Burghley's willingness to give confirms his superior generosity. Both recognized that their mutual bond was confirmed and continued by the gift.[48]

Of course, the most important good deeds that could be done for others was the extension of patronage by giving offices that were either in a person's grant or which the patron could get other patrons to provide. Often, the provision of these appointments was like Caesar's request for a deer – extended to recognize and maintain a relationship, rather than as a direct act of governance. Burghley recognized this when, in his letter denying the existence of a *regnum ceciliana*, he invited William Herle to consider 'how and uppon whom for these late yeres all maner of offices good and bad, spyrituall and temporall have ben bestowed, [to whom] the persons benefitted do belong and whom they do follow'.[49] 'To whom they belong' and 'whom they follow' are telling phrases.

All of these 'courtesies' were about maintaining working relations with those below and above you, wherever you were in the hierarchy. They were conducted person-to-person, and they were about showing respect, deference, trust and honour, as appropriate, in order to keep the machinery of government and self-advancement working well.

The government run by Elizabeth and Burghley can best be described as a late-feudal, customary system that was gradually growing more formal. It recognized that families of power and influence should, and could, look after their own locales, depending on the monarch to enhance their authority, arbitrate their disputes and organise their defence. Together with their fellow magistrates, the locally powerful worked with the crown to keep the peace and defend the nation, when they felt like it, if they got around to it. This localisation of power hobbled the crown, because Elizabeth and her council had to motivate, mollify and reward the appropriate powerful people. In a system with such limited coercive power, the use of the informal networks of influence was the key to the success of men like Burghley. Deference, honour, patronage, family connection and professional acquaintance had to be used to maintain and extend the crown's influence.

Working with the 'Men-of-Business' was about managing the interactions of the local elites, using honour, favour, and connection to create consensual co-operation. It was not despotic rule, because it depended upon the local leaders to enforce their common decisions. It was not a republic, in anything like the classical definition of the word, because it recognized the monarch's ownership.[50] Burghley was managing shared governance, each magistrate within his degree, for common causes, which is what made it

---

[47] BL, Lansdowne MS 54, f. 168: 1 Aug. 1587.

[48] Felicity Heal, 'Food Gifts, the Household and the Politics of Exchange in Early Modern England', *Past & Present*, No. 199 (2008), 41–70.

[49] TNA, SP12/181/42, ff. 153r–156v: Lord Burghley to William Herle [Mar. 1589].

[50] 'Republic: A state in which the supreme power rests in the people and their elected representatives or officers, as opposed to one governed by a king or similar ruler; a commonwealth', *Oxford English Dictionary*.

a common weal. It was a system that required management, rather than fiats, but it had to be managed with a gentle touch. What Burghley and the Men-of-Business were running was a semi-bureaucratised late-feudal monarchy, taking the form of a 'monarchical commonwealth'.

By the time Elizabeth died, the system was weakening, but, for Elizabeth, Burghley and others of their generation, it was obvious how to govern. They had the social knowledge to work with the magisterial classes for the common good.

Foreign Policy and the Parliament of 1576

GLYN PARRY

This article brings together scattered, but important, new evidence about foreign policy debates in and around the reconvened parliament of early 1576. It demonstrates that co-operative parliamentary management did not exclude principled political differences from the Commons, but nor were members of the Commons trying to 'seize the initiative' when they initiated foreign policy discussion. The queen and her privy council, for a variety of reasons, had initially sought parliamentary support for a foreign policy guided by religious solidarity rather than dynastic legitimacy, but when they belatedly abandoned this plan they underestimated the strength of the expectations they had raised. Some zealous protestant members of the Commons felt encouraged to believe that parliament would act as the great council of the realm, to be consulted over important matters of state, and especially whether Elizabeth should accept the recently-offered sovereignty of Holland and Zealand. The retreat from this position began with the arrival of Champagney, envoy of the Spanish viceroy in the Netherlands, Requesens. Champagney exploited the gap between Elizabeth's position and the committed protestants on her council, and especially Burghley's internal debate between his protestant idealism and his economic and strategic realism. Burghley's eventual withdrawal from the proposed arrangement to enlist virulently anti-catholic Commons' members in support of the ambitious foreign policy bitterly disappointed large sections of popular protestant opinion in the 'public sphere', who virulently attacked both Burghley and Elizabeth. This enabled conservatives to mount increasingly effective responses against both radical protestantism and its dangerous propensity for foreign entanglements.

Keywords: parliament of 1576; foreign policy; conciliar management failure; ideological debates; 'public sphere'; imperial ambitions

The affairs of this country change from hour to hour, and there is a continual inconsistency, but it is not to be wondered at, as they all depend upon events elsewhere. (Antonio de Guaras to the duke of Alba, 28 October 1576)[1]

Despite their historical importance, the Elizabethan parliaments are sparsely documented. Therefore, every fragment of information about them deserves close examination, especially when the fragments describing parliamentary debates in 1576 demonstrate how political differences could interrupt the co-operative infrastructure maintenance that Michael Graves, with Geoffrey Elton, so magisterially described.[2]

---

[1] *CSP Span., 1568–79*, p. 438.
[2] G.R. Elton, *The Parliament of England, 1559–1581* (Cambridge, 1986).

Elton emphasized parliament's lack of independent power to influence policy, particularly the political irrelevance of the house of commons compared with court or privy council. He argued that the Commons only mattered politically when the crown and nobility chose to use it to publicise, and gauge reactions to, policies.[3] This emphasis on institutional co-operation has tended to obscure his acknowledgement that touchy, self-important 'men of strong views on major issues' sat in parliament, not least because that acknowledgement concluded a typically pungent analysis of Thomas Norton's friendly advice to Christopher Hatton in 1572 on how to manage such men in order to facilitate the council's legislative programme.[4] The fact that Elton's encomium of conciliar management introduced a section of *The Parliament of England 1559–1581* devoted to 'politics' suggests the strict limits he imposed on the ideological content of parliamentary activity. But the fact that, in 1576, Norton and his patron, Hatton, found themselves at ideological odds over the Commons' right to express opinions on foreign policy without Elizabeth's invitation, suggests that co-operative parliamentary management did not exclude principled political debate from the Commons, even for Norton, whose role as a quintessential intermediary between council and Commons, Michael Graves so assiduously delineated.[5]

Elton pointed out that Elizabeth imposed new restrictions on the Commons' freedom of speech by developing a doctrine that they could discuss matters of state only on her initiative.[6] Thus, the attempt by members of the Commons to initiate foreign policy debate in 1576 might be interpreted as a constitutionally-significant response to her innovation, reviving the Henrician parliament's precedent of debating great affairs as the great council of the realm, if conciliar managers had not used their authority instantly to suppress this initiative. However, Elizabeth herself acknowledged that members of the Commons 'are councelors . . . during the parliament' if less prestigious than her 'standing councelers'.[7] The dispute originated less in constitutional theories than in ideological differences over whether England's long-term strategic interests would be better protected by a foreign policy guided by religious solidarity, or by dynastic legitimacy. The importance of these differences is not diminished by the efficient suppression of their manifestation in the Commons. In raising the issue, supporters of an ardently protestant foreign policy demonstrated their allegiance to an international protestant *res publica*, rather than obey debating restrictions imposed by a queen increasingly reluctant to accept the implications that ideological politics held for dynastic legitimacy. They were

[3] Elton, *Parliament*, 377–8.

[4] Elton, *Parliament*, 321–9, quotation at 328.

[5] Michael A.R. Graves, 'Thomas Norton the Parliament Man: An Elizabethan M.P., 1559–1581', *Historical Journal*, xxiii (1980), 17–35; Michael A.R. Graves, 'The Management of the Elizabethan House of Commons: The Council's Men-of-Business', *Parliamentary History*, ii (1983), 11–38; Michael A.R. Graves, 'The Common Lawyers and the Privy Council's Parliamentary Men-of-Business, 1584–1601', *Parliamentary History*, viii (1989), 189–215; Michael A.R. Graves, *Thomas Norton: The Parliament Man* (Oxford, 1994). Graves minimised the ideological tensions between Norton and his conciliar patrons, but Patrick Collinson, 'Puritans, Men of Business and Elizabethan Parliaments', *Parliamentary History*, vii (1988), 187–211, and Patrick Collinson, 'The Elizabethan Exclusion Crisis and the Elizabethan Polity', *Proceedings of the British Academy*, lxxxiv (1994), 51–92, restore the ideological character to parliament denied by Graves and Elton.

[6] Elton, *Parliament*, 343.

[7] Elizabeth's words through the lord keeper, 10 Apr. 1593, in *Proceedings in the Parliaments of Elizabeth I*, ed. T.E. Hartley (3 vols, Leicester, 1981–95), iii, 172.

also responding to a political vacuum created when both queen and council abandoned an earlier plan to use parliament to gather wide public support for just such an ideological foreign policy.

For months, court and council had been divided over whether Elizabeth should accept the sovereignty of Holland and Zealand, offered once more in late 1575, and thus open war with Spain. That decision was to have been remitted to the parliament of 1576, where decisions theoretically reserved for the royal prerogative had to accommodate political and fiscal reality. Closely examining this encounter between theory and reality enables us to see this parliament, and particularly the house of commons, operating as the great council of the realm, where the political nation could be consulted over important matters of state.[8] Examining how the Commons performed this traditional function in 1576 shifts our focus back to debates over political principles, without raising sterile speculations about constitutional innovations. It also clarifies the political independence of those members of the Commons who normally collaborated with the privy council in enacting its legislative programme, when we see them acting as temporary councillors to the monarch. Yet the limitations on their freedom of action, imposed by the realities of Elizabethan politics, emphasizes that occasional demonstrations of initiative did not amount to 'seizing the initiative' in the long term. Finally, by looking at the background to discussion of national issues in the Commons, we can glimpse wider public debate over foreign policy in 1576, epitomising how the Dutch revolt had raised the ideological temperature of English politics, and also raised issues about the nature of an enlarged Tudor state in a 'monarchical republic'.

Elizabeth and her privy council planned to bring foreign policy issues to parliament precisely because neither council nor court could decide whether accepting the sovereignty of Holland and Zealand would best protect England's economic, strategic and religious interests in the current situation of the Netherlands' revolt. For a decade, Dutch resistance to Philip II's policies of fiscal and religious centralisation had raised profound questions about English interests, without receiving a consistent response. Elizabeth's desire to see the restoration of the *status quo ante*, reconciling the provinces to Philip's obedience with their ancient liberties restored, demilitarised and free from French interference, while economically sensible, seemed increasingly unrealistic. Her nostalgia for the traditional Anglo-Burgundian relationship, cemented by the marketing of English woollen cloth through Antwerp, failed to appreciate the increasing political and religious polarisation of the Netherlands provoked by Philip II's determination to impose catholic orthodoxy on provinces already alienated by his encroachments upon their self-government.[9] She also overlooked the concern of some of her leading councillors with preserving the international protestant *res publica* against catholic assaults.

---

[8] G.R. Elton, 'Tudor Government: The Points of Contact: Parliament', in G.R. Elton, *Studies in Tudor and Stuart Politics and Government* (4 vols, Cambridge, 1974–92), iii, 9, emphasizes this function of the Henrician parliaments, and G.R. Elton, 'Parliament in the Sixteenth Century: Functions and Fortunes', in Elton, *Studies in Tudor and Stuart Politics*, iii, 160, denies any major conflict between crown and Commons in 1576.

[9] Geoffrey Parker, *The Dutch Revolt* (1977), 84–90; Geoffrey Parker, *The Grand Strategy of Philip II* (New Haven, CT, 1998), and Geoffrey Parker, 'The Place of Tudor England in the Messianic Vision of Philip II of Spain', *Transactions of the Royal Historical Society*, xii (2002), 167–221.

For some councillors, if they could persuade Elizabeth to overcome her respect for dynastic legitimacy, accepting the sovereignty of Holland and Zealand raised a further question: would the result be an enlarged imperial monarchy or a federal protestant state? Religious ideology, therefore, complicated their strategic calculations when responding to the offer of sovereignty. William Cecil had favoured the interests of protestantism over dynastic legitimacy when successfully undermining Mary Stuart's rule in Scotland from 1559, making that kingdom an English dependency in order to protect Elizabeth and the English Reformation against international catholicism.[10] Yet he had never persuaded Elizabeth to accept the *imperium* of even an insular protestant British empire.[11] Moreover, he had defeated Mary and her Guise relatives when Philip II still sought Elizabeth's goodwill to counterbalance French power, and when Spain's strategic interests could accommodate England weakening French influence. From the late 1560s, however, Cecil's apocalyptic protestantism encouraged darker expectations, especially a *rapprochement* between France and Spain, assumed after their meeting at Bayonne in 1565 to be plotting an international catholic conspiracy against protestantism. The first fruits of this alliance appeared in the Ridolfi plot, directed against both Elizabeth and Cecil; by 1576, Cecil's calculations over openly supporting protestant rebellion in Holland and Zealand had to acknowledge much greater risks than he had faced in Scotland.[12] His fear that the conclusion of peace in France would release the catholic Guise to support the Spanish, dragging in Henri III by offering to advance French royal interests in the Netherlands, explains Cecil's concern with negotiations to end the latest French civil war during the winter and spring of 1575–6. His cautious response to Holland and Zealand's offers reflects his apprehension that peace in France could unite the forces of international catholicism against an over-extended England.

The earl of Leicester's initial reluctance to accept the proffered sovereignty succumbed to the attractions of an idealised protestant knight errantry that would allow him greater freedom of action within a federal state. Eventually, Elizabeth's inability to control her nobility, once over the horizon, would contribute to his pursuit of an independent *imperium* in the Netherlands in 1585, but even the prospect of a traditional military role could inspire an unlikely, but powerful, alliance between Leicester and the earl of Sussex in early 1576, which pushed the matter towards parliament.[13] Councillors marginalised by Burghley and Leicester could, nevertheless, play a spoiling role. Despite Burghley's criticism, Sir James Croft retained Elizabeth's ear because of his personal loyalty under Mary, and because her favourite, Christopher Hatton, supported Croft's defence of the ancient Burgundian alliance as essential to England's financial future. Hatton and Croft would combine against discussion of unwelcome issues in the Commons. They could count on catholic courtiers, who enjoyed privileged access to

---

[10] John Guy, *My Heart is My Own: The Life of Mary Queen of Scots* (2004), 107–17; Stephen Alford, *The Early Elizabethan Polity: William Cecil and the British Succession Crisis, 1558–1569* (Cambridge, 1998); Glyn Parry, 'The Monarchical Republic and Magic: William Cecil and The Exclusion of Mary Queen of Scots', *Reformation: The Journal of the Tyndale Society*, xvii (2012), 29–47.

[11] Jane E.A. Dawson, 'William Cecil and the British Dimension of Early Elizabethan Foreign Policy', *History*, lxxiv (1989), 196–216; Roger A. Mason, 'Scotland, Elizabethan England and the Idea of Britain', *Transactions of the Royal Historical Society*, xiv (2004), 279–93.

[12] Guy, *Mary Queen of Scots*, 461–6.

[13] Paul E.J. Hammer, *Elizabeth's Wars: War, Government, and Society in Tudor England, 1544–1604* (Basingstoke, 2003), 2–4; Richard Tuck, *Philosophy and Government, 1572–1651* (Cambridge, 1993), 157, 261.

the privy chamber and opposed supporting protestant rebels as a stain on Elizabeth's honour, which also threatened to repeat earlier military disasters when England had intervened in religious wars in Europe. These differences within the court played out in the parliament of 1576, but matters finally came to a head there because the council failed to keep its implicit bargains over Holland and Zealand with those virulently anti-catholic members of the Commons who normally co-operated with the council in establishing a protestant state.[14]

For several years, events in the Netherlands had been posing difficult questions for English protestants about the nature and extent of their state. Dutch attempts to build a grand coalition against Spanish forces had foundered when the massacre of St Bartholomew in August 1572 removed Huguenot support and left them exposed to Spanish revenge with only England's uncertain aid.[15] This forced them to venture beyond their usual offer of a naval union to prevent the flow of vital supplies to the Spanish. They now suggested that Elizabeth take Flushing or Middleburg as staples for wool exports in return for English help.[16] By December, Dutch desperation and sympathetic noises from her more protestant councillors encouraged them to send an embassy reiterating previous requests that Elizabeth would take into her protection 'the whole country of Holland and Zelland with theyr bodyes and goodes to be entyerly at her disposition', together with four cautionary towns. Elizabeth publicly dismissed them as rebels, despite their claim, which they would reiterate in 1576, that they owed 'nether dewtye, nor homage at all to the K[ing] of Spa[ine] as K[ing] of Spa[yne], nor yet to the Lords of Brabant and Holland, longer then they mainteyned unto them theire auncient rytes and lybertyes without innovation or breake in the leaste jotte'.[17]

This careful contractual justification seemed no more comprehensible to Elizabeth in June 1573, when continuing military decline forced William of Orange into unofficial, verbal offers of Dutch sovereignty.[18] After several fruitless requests received equivocal answers, in October 1575 Spanish victories forced the Dutch to renew pressure on Elizabeth to accept their sovereignty, by threatening to hand themselves over to the duke of Anjou, newly escaped from Henri III's court.[19] Orange secretly protested his devotion to England, but subsequent negotiations foundered, partly because the Dutch encouraged domestic French peace negotiations, which formed an important part of

---

[14] Graves, *Thomas Norton*, 306–9, emphasizes Norton's relative comfort with the Elizabethan Church's ability to reform itself.

[15] Parker, *Dutch Revolt*, 123–42.

[16] Thomas Cotton argued that controlling the only useful ports on that coast would make 'Her Majestie, the only commander of the narrow seas': Cotton to Burghley, from Flushing, 23 Aug. 1572; BL, Cotton MS, Galba C. IV, ff. 251–2.

[17] BL, Harleian MS 1582, ff. 202r–203r: William Herle recalling this embassy and its arguments to Burghley, 11 June 1573. The Spanish agent, de Guaras, described it to Alba, 4 Jan. 1573: Joseph M. Kervyn De Lettenhove, *Relations Politiques des Pays-Bas et de L'Angleterre sous la Regne de Philippe II* (11 vols, Brussels, 1882–1900), vi, 616–8, and to Zayas, 7 Jan. 1573: *CSP Span., 1568–79*, p. 455.

[18] Herle, on 11 June 1573, transmitted Orange's verbal offer of 'the enteire possession of Holland and Zelland, which was the earnest desyre of the States of the land so to present her with all': BL, Harleian MS 1582, ff. 203r–v.

[19] Edward Chester informed Burghley, on 6 Oct. 1575, that Holland and Zealand were resolved to reject Philip II's authority: Hatfield House, Salisbury MS, CP 160/81; and they did so on 13 October: Parker, *Dutch Revolt*, 146. Anjou escaped Henri III's court on 15 September: *CSP Ven., 1558–80*, pp. 537–8.

English calculations.[20] Those calculations usually sought the *status quo ante*, sometimes through the non-confrontational expedient of an international protestant defensive league; more rarely through the confrontational, open-ended and, therefore, expensive options of protecting the Dutch militarily, or even accepting their sovereignty. Depending on international politics, courtly and conciliar policy disputes, and the timing of events, Elizabeth flirted with one or more of these policies at any moment.

Elizabeth and her council, especially Burghley, assumed that openly protecting the Dutch or accepting their sovereignty implied more than an intimidating war with Spain. English intervention might persuade 'the French king if he can master and subdue them of the religion in Fraunce, . . . to ioyne with the King of Spayne against us'.[21] Therefore, politics in and outside the 1576 parliament operated in counterpoint with English perceptions of conditions in France, where, or so some claimed, even a patched-up peace would free the bigoted catholic, Henri III, to join a catholic league, assumed to have secretly existed since the Franco-Spanish *entente* at Bayonne in 1565. Opponents of Netherlands' intervention exploited such fears, arguing that the Huguenots might assist Henri against England to protect French interests in the Low Countries.[22] Therefore, following Anjou's escape, English politicians anxiously watched from late November as peace negotiations in France crawled along into the following spring, a peace which would raise the costs of accepting Dutch sovereignty beyond the possible benefits. Another factor influencing parliamentary manœuvres was trade with Spain and its possessions, which left English merchants and merchandise 'subiect to . . . seasure' by Philip II.[23] Consequently, Elizabeth's increasingly threadbare policy of restoring the *status quo ante* to guarantee English economic and political interests also required her to prevent both a Spanish absolute conquest and French domination of the Netherlands. The ideological cleavage between the *politique* Elizabeth and the more convinced protestants on her council ensured that their collective responses to these problems remained conflicted and incoherent.

At the end of October, queen and council managed to unite in sending John Hastings to the Dutch merely, as Burghley put it, 'to dissuade them from Fraunce', therefore allowing the Dutch to assume that Elizabeth would accept their sovereignty.[24] Yet Walsingham, wearily realistic about Elizabeth's 'politic' procrastination, believed that only decisive action could save the Dutch, and 'assured them from the begynneng' that their ambassadors wasted their time. Leicester and Sussex also initially dismissed their offer. However, Hastings's optimistic assessment of Dutch resources and the process of discussion lent substance to the perennial English fantasy of a revived continental empire, especially since the French seemed unable to conclude peace. The two earls increasingly perceived this as freeing them from restrictive courtiership to enjoy tradi-

---

[20] Lettenhove, *Relations Politiques*, viii, 10, 15.

[21] BL, Harleian MS 285, ff. 23v–24r: 'Instructions for John Hastings' sent 'to the Prince of Orange', 29 Oct. 1575. The mirror image also applied: when the Huguenots of Guienne, Gascony, and Languedoc 'offered to declare themselves in the service of this Queen', her acceptance depended on Spanish acquiescence: *CSP Span., 1568–79*, p. 449: Guaras to Alba, 15 Dec. 1572.

[22] See below, pp. 85–6.

[23] BL, Harleian MS 285, f. 24r, and see below, pp. 70, 80.

[24] Lettenhove, *Relations Politiques*, viii, 128: Burghley's memorandum of 20 Jan. 1576.

tional military leadership. For Leicester, there may have been the added attraction of creating an avowedly protestant last world empire.[25]

For once, Burghley found himself outmanœuvred. Appalled by the idea of France controlling the Netherlands, he cynically encouraged Dutch belief in Elizabeth's willingness to accept their proposals, but then found himself overwhelmed in council by Leicester's alliance with Sussex, and pushed towards a real engagement with the Dutch which he feared might unite France and Spain against England. Convinced that Elizabeth's security depended upon protecting her British *imperium*, and seared by bitter memories of the disastrous Newhaven expedition he had advocated in 1563, by the time parliament resumed, Burghley ironically found himself contemplating a dangerous and expensive intervention in Europe. His response would bring upon both him and Elizabeth the opprobrium of godly protestant opinion concerned about Dutch survival and the wider protestant cause.[26]

We can probably blame Elizabeth and Burghley for her emissary, John Hastings, exceeding his written instructions and inviting a Dutch embassy 'to present theme sellves, their lives, goodes and contry to Her Majestie's soveraynty and protectyon'.[27] Hastings's instructions encouraged this invitation: to assess whether Dutch resources could sustain a long war, and what benefits Elizabeth might receive 'by reteyning those countries in our protection'.[28] The Dutch had long insisted that their mercantile resources would enhance Elizabeth's security, making her 'mistres and commander of the whole seas and of the grettest navye in Christendom'. Now she apparently took them at their word, since this furthered her old policy of keeping her options open. This theme of naval power reappeared in propaganda designed to influence parliament in February, as did the larger question of whether divine justice would allow Elizabeth 'to take the possession of any of those countries wherto we have not made any title'.[29] Despite recent frustrating experience of Elizabeth's temporising, and Walsingham's warnings, their peril compelled the Dutch to send envoys, led by Paul Buys and Philippe de St Marnix, sieur de St Aldegonde, responding to what they later insisted had been Elizabeth's invitations.[30] Another consideration was probably Philip II's unilateral rescheduling of loan repayments in September, which fatally undermined his viceroy Requesens's successful reconquest.[31] With both sides exhausted, English assistance might tip the balance.

Even so, initially Orange only offered a naval union, to close the narrow seas to Spanish supplies, in return for loans.[32] The English responded by offering vague

[25] Glyn Parry, *The Arch-Conjuror of England: John Dee* (New Haven, CT, 2011), 103–26; G.R. Elton, 'England and the Continent in the Sixteenth Century', in Elton, *Studies in Tudor and Stuart Politics*, ii, 306, on earlier imperial ambitions.

[26] TNA, SP70/137, ff. 220r–221v: William Herle to Burghley, 14 Mar. 1576; Dawson, 'William Cecil and the British Dimension', 196–216.

[27] TNA, SP70/137, ff. 205r–210v, at 205r: William Herle to Burghley, 11 Mar. 1576.

[28] BL, Harleian MS 285, f. 24v.

[29] TNA, SP70/137, ff. 205r–210v: Herle to Burghley, 11 Mar. 1576; BL, Harleian MS 285, ff. 23v–24r, and see *Certein Letters*, below, p. 75.

[30] TNA, SP70/137, ff. 205r–210v: Herle to Burghley, 11 Mar. 1576.

[31] BL, Cotton MS, Galba C. V, f. 208, and see Parker, *Dutch Revolt*, 169–70.

[32] BL, Cotton MS, Galba C. VI. i, ff. 18–19.

protection, but on 20 November, Hastings conveyed Dutch determination 'to make Her rather ladie than Protectrix of alle', with substantial revenues.[33] Orange now emphasized the need for decisiveness, again hinting that an imminent French peace offered him other options.[34] On 26 November, Buys and St Aldegonde received their letters of credence, although they only arrived at the English court with Hastings and a written offer of sovereignty on 3 January, because Orange wanted to strengthen his negotiating hand by mediating a truce in France, which his representatives only patched up in late December.[35] Meanwhile, interested parties drew their own conclusions. With the Antwerp money-market disturbed by war and Philip's bankruptcy, Elizabeth's credit rating soared at Cologne, where financiers offered large sums at 5%, betting her absorption of Holland and Zealand would tip the balance against Spain.[36] Partisans like William Herle believed such wealth would 'make her the grettest prynce that had bin in Englande of mani yeres', while Hastings foresaw events in 1576 in an even larger, apocalyptic context. The French might take Artois and Flanders; a protestant alliance in Germany, Denmark and Sweden would guarantee Elizabeth's *imperium* in Holland and Zealand, extending protection over Amsterdam, Utrecht and Overijsel. More importantly, this would confirm her as 'soverayne of the sea' and able to 'advaunce the glory of God and the kingdome of his sonne Jesu-Christ and to make ende of this pernicious difference in all Christendome, which is in Almayne touching the Supper' as well as to wrest the Indies from Spain.[37]

Such apocalyptic expectations would have oppressed even honest negotiations, but the personal agendas on both sides compounded the problems. Buys let slip that he considered St Aldegonde too pro-French.[38] According to Buys, at an early interview Elizabeth promised, 'in the word of a prince, to dele breeffly and sincerely with theme', knowing that she would cause more damage 'by prolonging of theme, than she cowd do them good' by deferring their 'juste and honorable' cause.[39] Yet courtiers less committed to the Dutch noted how the disturbing implications of these discussions 'maketh her very melancholy, and . . . greatly out of quiet'.[40] By delegating

[33] TNA, SP70/136, f. 48, in *CSP Foreign, 1575–7*, pp. 183–4.

[34] TNA, SP70/136, f. 56, in *CSP Foreign, 1575–7*, p. 187. Herle claimed to have softened the original peremptory draft of these offers: Lettenhove, *Relations Politiques*, viii, 425.

[35] TNA, SP70/136, f. 69, in *CSP Foreign, 1575–7*, no. 469; Lettenhove, *Relations Politiques*, viii, 98; *CSP Ven., 1558–80*, p. 541: the Venetian ambassador from Paris, 19 Dec. 1575. BL, Harleian MS 285, ff. 32r–36v: Hastings to Burghley, 26 Dec. 1576; *CSP Foreign, 1575–7*, no. 519: Dale to Sir Thomas Smith and Walsingham, 25 Dec. 1575, reporting uncertainty over whether peace had been made – the Huguenots thought not.

[36] *CSP Foreign, 1575–7*, no. 444: Edward Castelyn to Walsingham, 6 Nov. 1575; no. 511: Rowland Foxe to Walsingham, from Cologne, 22 Dec. 1575. Philip had been paying 15%–20% before his unilateral reduction of interest payments; Elizabeth paid 12% on the Genoese treasure seized in 1568: BL, Cotton MS, Galba C. V, ff. 252–3.

[37] BL, Harleian MS 285, f. 36r.

[38] TNA, SP70/139, f. 39: Edward Chester to Burghley, 20 July 1576.

[39] TNA, SP70/137, ff. 205r–209v, fuller than *CSP Foreign, 1575–7*, no. 663, and TNA, SP70/137, ff. 245r–246v: Herle to Burghley, 20 Mar. 1576, on relying on assurances in 'the invyolable word of a prince'. The first interview occurred on 7 January, the second lasted an hour on 9 January, with Leicester, Sussex, Burghley, Walsingham and Hastings present: Lettenhove, *Relations Politiques*, viii, 98.

[40] Edmund Lodge, *Illustrations of British History, Biography and Manners* (3 vols, 1838), ii, 59–61: Henry Talbot to the earl of Shrewsbury, 4 Jan. 1576.

consultation to a divided council, Elizabeth postponed difficult decisions, particularly when Henri III and Anjou's ambassadors were inviting her to arbitrate in their peace negotiations and hinting at a revived French match. From 10 January, the full council interrogated the Dutch envoys twice daily on numerous worries preoccupying even supportive councillors. The Dutch reiterated the familiar arguments: 'the grownde and justyce of our cawse'; increasing Elizabeth's power and wealth; the strategic advantages of a strong buffer state against Spain; strengthening alliances with northern European powers; controlling crucial trade routes, enabling her to dictate to her enemies.

However, prompted by Burghley, on 12 January the council descended to detailed inventories of Dutch resources – military strength, supplies, revenues, costs, towns and fortifications, trade, naval and land forces, and military intelligence. Burghley still claimed difficulty in grasping how contract theory enabled the Dutch to renounce their obedience to Philip 'as duke or earle of the lowe countries', and demanded to know what prevented them seeking peace through the constitutional process they had already exhausted. He also, typically, wanted historical precedents for successful renunciations of rulers. Though he claimed that Elizabeth was 'no waye interested by title in the said countrey', the choice between protection and sovereignty remained open; it depended on the extent of Dutch resources. Opposition also surfaced in a petition from English merchants trading with Spain, which Burghley noted for council discussion that day.[41]

St Aldegonde supplied historical justifications for renouncing Philip's authority, and on 15 January, the council acknowledged their right 'both to defend themselves as they have done and to seeke ayde otherwise' to be 'delivered of the yoke and bondage of the Spaniardes'.[42] Yet the council realized that the huge financial and political costs involved required parliamentary consent and 'the goodwill of the Estates of the realm', whose lives and money would be at risk. The vulnerable Spanish trade gave councillors pause, for Philip would seize English goods in his territories 'as at this time theire is great aboundance', a point Burghley would reiterate after lobbying by affected merchants. Therefore, the council had to echo Elizabeth's renewed offer of a peace conference to demonstrate Philip's intransigence and excuse intervention. However, their response included a new line from those councillors committed to an avowedly protestant policy. Elizabeth might prefer negotiated peace, but the council had to consider the longer-term interests of the protestant *res publica*, and the danger posed not merely to Elizabeth but to 'her coheires' by the 'strang and prowd' Spanish possessing 'soe riche a countrye, and that so neare a neighbour as the lowe countries'. The

---

[41] TNA, SP70/137, ff. 14–15r, longer than *CSP Foreign, 1575–7*, pp. 226–7, and compare Lettenhove, *Relations Politiques*, viii, 254–5, for Herle's accurate recollection in March of Burghley's demands; TNA, SP12/107/17. That day, Edward Bacon believed that Elizabeth would accept the offer, though contrary to modern assumptions about subsidies being automatically approved, he reported 'somme suspect it a devise for a subsidie', perhaps Sir Nicholas Bacon's dismissive interpretation?: *The Papers of Nathaniel Bacon of Stiffkey*, ed. A. Hassell Smith, Gillian M. Baker and R.W. Kenny (5 vols, Norwich, 1979–2000), i, 182: Edward Bacon to Nathaniel Bacon, 12 Jan. 1576.

[42] TNA, SP70/137, ff. 25–26v. The French ambassador complained of being neglected by Walsingham for several days before 14 January, so preoccupied was the Council: *CSP Foreign, 1575–7*, no. 571.

enduring strategic interests of England meant that Elizabeth could not allow the Spanish to conquer her ancient allies.[43]

The next day, the council's opinion paper, drafted by Burghley, started from this strategic consideration. It rehearsed the powerful reasons why Elizabeth's desire for peace negotiations was unrealistic, and why parliament had to support an aggressively protestant foreign policy. Philip, Burghley emphasized, would invade England from a conquered Netherlands, raising taxes for immense naval and land forces while strangling English trade and destroying English finances. He would impose catholicism, as he does 'by putting Hir Majesty's subjects to death in his countryes for the same', an obsession we shall encounter again. This proved a coherent Popish Plot to undermine England through Mary, queen of Scots, catholic exiles, and their numerous, wealthy fifth column. Therefore 'to avoyde the perill hereof, it wer good, before his power be made mightie, to stey the same'.

Here the balance of the mixed messages shifted towards aggression. Ostensibly, the council shared Elizabeth's desire for the Dutch 'to enjoye theire maner of lawful liberties, and the Kinge his auncient forme of government'; the difference lay in the means to this end. The paper nodded to a peace treaty, but emphasized 'ayding them with force' immediately, because every day 'their power shall decay and his encrease'. This has the vigorous, impetuous ring of Leicester and Sussex's knight-errantry, rather than Burghley's careful balancing of arguments, and may reflect their temporary dominance of council discussion. This tone, especially, appears in their plan to use a ceasefire proposal to publicise Spanish perfidy, for they knew that Requesens needed Philip's consent before complying. That could secure parliamentary financing for intervention, by demonstrating Spanish bellicosity to 'some of the rychest' English merchants trading to Spain and the Netherlands, and 'imparting the weightenes hereof to the chefest of this next parliament'.[44] Leicester's tactical alliance with Sussex may explain why, as Herle later claimed, the council referred the issue to parliament, 'the cawses being so weighty and generall'. According to Herle, Elizabeth, to delay Dutch negotiations with the French, even acquiesced to a parliamentary debate because 'to have the generall consent of the reallm therunto, and their generall aydes withall' would 'forteffye the actyon throwly'.[45] Parliament did, indeed, debate both the Spanish and Netherlands' trades alongside the sovereignty of Holland and Zealand, though the council eventually drew back.

For the Dutch and their English supporters, parliamentary consultation had obvious advantages. The Dutch could trust the enduring consensus of the English political elite more than Elizabeth's temporary word, while supportive councillors needed public

[43] BL, Cotton MS, Galba C. V, ff. 62r–65r, accurately in Lettenhove, *Relations Politiques*, viii, 118–20, briefly in *CSP Foreign, 1575–7*, pp. 229–30, no. 574, which (no. 577) shows the council simultaneously dealing with the commissioners for Spanish causes over seizures and reprisals. Simon Adams, 'Elizabeth I and the Sovereignty of the Netherlands 1576–1585', *Transactions of the Royal Historical Society*, xiv (2004), 309–19, claims, at 314, that Elizabeth refused the Dutch offer on 15 January, but that does not explain the continuing conciliar debate about the options – Elizabeth may have decided, the council had not.

[44] BL, Cotton MS, Galba C. V, ff. 67–71, Burghley's original draft at ff. 84–7.

[45] TNA, SP70/137, ff. 205r–210v; *CSP Foreign, 1575–7*, pp. 265–7: William Herle's recollection to Burghley, 11 Mar. 1576, of these events, doubtless with Buys and St Aldegonde at his elbow. The privy council reminded Orange in June that, from the first, 'it was plainly tould them that Hir Majestie would not endure that the Frenche should have anie footynge there': *CSP Foreign, 1575–7*, no. 819; TNA, SP70/138, ff. 193–200r: 19 June 1576.

opinion to back such a vast enterprise. An anonymous paper, connected to a group of convinced English and Dutch protestants, held that 'the accepting of the soveraintye wilbe more acceptable to the generalitye of this realme, both gentlemen and marchants, who with theyr bodyes and purses shall sustayne the quarrell'.[46] The group repeated the paper's arguments in pro-Dutch propaganda aimed at English public opinion. It addressed the central issue, Elizabeth's claim to the Netherlands, dismissing the Spanish Habsburgs as 'the pretended heyres of the howse of Burgondye'. It also tapped into the vein of apocalyptic prophecy running just below the skin of ardent protestantism, insisting that 'the death of the King of Spayne is every day loked for'.[47]

Perhaps over-confident, following the council's response of 16 January, the Dutch asked Elizabeth to proclaim herself their sovereign if Requesens refused a ceasefire. Burghley replied on 20 January that this dishonourably prejudged his response, and endangered English merchants and merchandise in Spain, Brabant and Flanders 'to be shipped home now this spryngtyme'. Without sufficient warning, they must forego great payments due from Spain, Antwerp and Bruges, paralysing England's economy. The lord treasurer's grasp of economic realities, however, conflicted with his protestant fears about a popish plot. The Dutch played on this, complaining that Elizabeth's delaying tactics to hinder their French negotiations had ruined their defences, exposing England to Spanish revenge and forced conversion to catholicism, 'according to the decrets of the Counsell of Trent'. Burghley could only concede that Orange might solicit strictly-limited French help. Clearly, Burghley had run out of alternatives, because he now accepted that, if Philip finally rejected peace, then Elizabeth and the French must impose a settlement. He also explicitly acknowledged the Dutch contractual right to reject Philip's authority. This effectively abandoned the *status quo ante* and, instead, foresaw the alternative nightmare that 'the contry wilbe possessed by the French'. Faced with this prospect, even Burghley reluctantly concluded that, though unable to defend 'all Holland', Elizabeth might accept the island of Walcheren, including Middelburg and Flushing, subsidised by the Dutch. In return, she would take 'the title of defence of the whole States of the countreys' until Philip restored their liberties.[48] Though still short of assuming absolute sovereignty, Burghley's concession shows that the committed prot-estants in council and court had won the policy struggle, and expected a united protestant *res publica* to rubber stamp this proposal in parliament. To complete their triumph, Elizabeth broke off marriage negotiations with Anjou until peace had returned to France, but began prolonged arbitration between the Huguenots and Henri III, which temporarily kept France out of the Netherlands.[49]

Rumours that Elizabeth would accept the sovereignty of Holland and Zealand had been enthralling Europe for months. To dissuade her from intervening, Requesens despatched a special envoy, Frederick Perrenot, baron de Champagney. He arrived in London on 27 January, delayed by pirates and bad weather. Philip II's bigoted agent in London, Guaras, had already concluded that Elizabeth and the council had decided on

---

[46] TNA, SP70/137, ff. 73r–74r, briefly calendared in *CSP Foreign, 1575–7*, no. 599.

[47] TNA, SP70/137, f. 73v. In March, zealous Daniel Rogers repeated predictions circulating since 1574 that Philip would die before mid 1576: Lettenhove, *Relations Politiques*, viii, 236.

[48] BL, Cotton MS, Galba C. V, ff. 72r–75v. The next day, he drafted an explanation for the Spanish of her decision to aid the Dutch that blamed threatened French intervention: *CSP Foreign, 1575–7*, no. 578.

[49] *CSP Ven., 1558–80*, p. 546.

open confrontation.[50] However, Champagney was superbly equipped to deal with the complicated intrigues at Elizabeth's court – a Netherlands patriot, he was a sophisticated nobleman, highly intelligent, perceptive, charming and articulate. Requesens had antagonised Elizabeth's council by grumbling about her ministers, but Champagney immediately sought out the reluctant Burghley, whose opinion mattered most. Unlike Guaras, Champagney believed that the council was still debating the Dutch offers.[51] At their first interview, Burghley rehearsed his newly-acquired arguments about Dutch contractual rights, and the threat of French intervention once they concluded domestic peace. Champagney emphasized French religious divisions and warned that English interference in the Netherlands, on whatever pretext, would rebound on Elizabeth, even hinting at a succession crisis with Mary Stuart waiting in the wings.[52] Honour satisfied, both sides withdrew.

The Dutch still conferred frequently with Elizabeth and the council, and openly acquired men and munitions. Therefore, she received Champagney coolly on 5 February, though as an accomplished courtier he hardly needed Hatton's advice to speak softly to the queen. Elizabeth insisted that she would use force to prevent Spain ruling absolutely in the Netherlands. However, Champagney noted her indignation against the Dutch pirates and especially seditious calvinism, and that she still insisted on restoring the *status quo ante*. Immediately after this interview, Champagney began exploiting the gap he saw between Elizabeth's position and Leicester's preparations for the coming parliament. He sought alliances with English courtiers who would stymie parliamentary support for accepting Holland and Zealand's sovereignty. He attempted to cultivate Sir James Croft, perennial spokesman for the Burgundian alliance, though at first non-committal in view of Leicester's current dominance. Hatton, whom Champagney had met in Antwerp, seemingly appreciated his argument about the risks of war in Elizabeth's alleged policy, especially for '*tous ceulx qui dépendent de sa personne*'. As her favourite and one who spoke '*avec ung langaige que m'ha semblé de catholicque*', Hatton also emphasized the religious chasm between Elizabeth and the Dutch.[53]

From these unpromising beginnings, Champagney cultivated Hatton and Croft to drive a wedge between Elizabeth and Leicester's policy. As Elizabeth's favourite, Hatton gave Champagney indirect influence over her opinion. Privy councillors and noblemen possessed some independent authority, freeing them to manipulate Elizabeth's thinking for their own ends, but Hatton's lack of political office and total dependence on her goodwill made it more dangerous for him to distort political intelligence or to thwart Elizabeth's policies.[54] During the parliament, Hatton's activities as a back-stairs conduit of alternative advice worked brilliantly for both Champagney and Elizabeth, whose initial coolness showed how the English had misunderstood his mission. Champagney, a *politique* catholic, preached moderation and clemency, and shared Elizabeth's desire for a Spanish ceasefire with Holland and Zealand, the removal of Spanish troops and

---

[50] *CSP Span., 1568–79*, p. 522.

[51] TNA, SP12/107/28.

[52] Lettenhove, *Relations Politiques*, viii, 138–43.

[53] Lettenhove, *Relations Politiques*, viii, 157–62; *CSP Span., 1568–79*, pp. 522, 529.

[54] Walsingham suggested to Burghley, on 6 Oct. 1575, that Elizabeth should be tricked into sending royal navy ships into the narrow seas, ostensibly against pirates but really to rescue Anjou from Henri III's captivity: TNA, SP12/105/51.

restoration of his country's ancient constitutions.[55] Like Elizabeth, his lack of religious zeal allowed him to be politically flexible, and facilitated his relationship with the crypto-catholic Hatton. Where Hatton had to be circumspect in his support, Croft, as a councillor, could openly support the ancient Burgundian alliance, and, perhaps, shared Champagney's religious moderation. Champagney already knew catholic noblemen like the earl of Arundel, who could use their traditional rights to counsel the monarch against antagonising Philip.

More importantly for what followed during the parliament, Champagney fed Croft and Arundel with arguments they used in papers to Elizabeth, appealing to her to conserve Philip's friendship and avoid supporting rebels.[56] Champagney also benefited from events in France and on the narrow seas that gave Burghley sufficient reason to reverse his earlier support for military adventures. Once Burghley had second thoughts, in the first week of February, his loyal brother-in-law, Sir Nicholas Bacon, could be relied upon for support in council, as Arundel informed Champagney.[57]

Until then, the conciliar majority appeared to favour the Dutch, whose arguments also resonated with public opinion in London. By the end of January, Champagney found that '*Les tavernes, la boursse, les rues*' talked of nothing but the forthcoming parliament's role in extending Elizabeth's sovereignty. Worse still, the English public clearly accepted the Dutch contractual right to replace Philip with Elizabeth. This implied that parliament would underwrite her acceptance of their sovereignty, particularly because Champagney suspected Elizabeth of plotting with the French to carve up the Netherlands under the guise of her marriage negotiations with Anjou.[58]

The Dutch and their English courtly allies also used print to persuade public and parliamentary opinion to accept either alternative: a dynastic extension of Elizabeth's *imperium* or the creation of a contractual federal state. When parliament resumed on 8 February, after being prorogued for almost four years, an incensed Guaras reported that St Aldegonde had devised a genealogy alleging that the house of Burgundy and their Habsburg successors had usurped in Holland and Zealand, which really belonged to Elizabeth. Three days later, Champagney believed this genealogy would be printed. This probably supported the council paper which dismissed 'the pretended heyres of the howse of Burgondye', though it has disappeared.[59] Using such genealogical arguments pandered to the English emphasis on inherited rights, rather than civil law notions of contractual sovereignty, which Elizabeth refused to countenance. But it also implied an inherited right of *imperium* that echoed Burghley's previous advocacy for Elizabeth's *imperium* over the British Isles, despite his denial on 12 January that Elizabeth could claim Holland and Zealand.[60]

---

[55] Parker, *Dutch Revolt*, 163, 171.

[56] Lettenhove, *Relations Politiques*, viii, 278–9: Champagney's report to the Netherlands council of state, 17 Mar. 1576, following Requesens's death.

[57] Lettenhove, *Relations Politiques*, viii, 165.

[58] Lettenhove, *Relations Politiques*, viii, 152: Champagney to Requesens, 31 Jan. 1576.

[59] Though St Aldegonde was still compiling it on 28 February: *CSP Span., 1568–79*, p. 528, and Lettenhove, *Relations Politiques*, viii, 171.

[60] Burghley smeared Mary Stuart before the 1572 parliament with *A Detection of the Doings of Mary Queen of Scots* (1571): Guy, *Mary Queen of Scots*, 467–70.

Burghley's obsession with genealogy, the marrow of politics, meant that he already possessed the genealogical evidence, from his client, Thomas Dannett. A cousin of Mildred, Lady Burghley, and a conspirator against Mary I who fled into exile, Dannett had become implicated in John Hales's succession tract advancing the Grey claim in 1564, and needed Cecil's protection against Elizabeth's consequent anger.[61] This may explain why, in 1566, Cecil and Leicester suppressed Dannett's English translation of Philippe de Commynes's *Memoires*, given delicate English relations with the Spanish over the Netherlands. Dannett had tried to publish in the *Memoires* Elizabeth's genealogical claim to Holland and Zealand, which St Aldegonde seemingly repeated in 1576. Dannett glossed Commynes's explanation of the Burgundian inheritance through Margaret, daughter and heir of Earl William of Holland and Zealand, with an alternative genealogy which made Margaret younger sister to the childless William, which meant 'the Queenes Maiestie being descended of Philippa the said William's eldest sister, is right heir of all these countries', since she descended from Philippa's husband, Edward III.[62] Burghley would hesitate over using this argument, when justifying Elizabeth's intervention in the Netherlands in 1585, but in 1576 he may have accepted this dynastic *imperium* before drawing back from the growing risks in accepting the Dutch offers.[63]

In contrast, more obscure writers, perhaps connected to Leicester and the Dutch envoys, used the press to orchestrate support for a protestant federal, contractual state. On 8 February, Guaras also reported that 'a pernicious book is published to persuade the people of the justice of their cause, containing only the most unheard of falsehood and wickedness'.[64] This was *Certein Letters wherin is set forth a Discourse of the Peace that was attempted and sought to have bin put in effecte by the Lords and States of Holland and Zelande in the year of oure Lorde 1574*, intended to demonstrate Spanish duplicity.[65] It supported the council's plan to garner political and financial support for the absorption of Holland and Zealand, because 'this Parliament can lack no help of consent and sinewes, that this Realme can give'. It also connected this opportunity with the larger struggle against the post-Tridentine Popish Plot.[66] Since it reiterated some of St Aldegonde's and Buys's arguments to the privy council in January about 'the grownde and justyce of our cawse, of the grettnes and commodyty that sholld ensue therby to Her Majesty, of the necessity that might move her to embrace it, of the facility in keping of it, of the fryndes and

---

[61] M. Levine, *The Early Elizabethan Succession Question 1558–1568* (Stanford, CA, 1966), 72–9. Dannett advanced Burghley's business in the Commons in 1572 and, with Thomas Norton, hounded Norfolk to execution and spoke against Mary, queen of Scots: *Proceedings*, ed. Hartley, i, 261, 295–8, 394.

[62] *The Historie of Philip De Commines Knight, Lord of Argenton*, trans. T. Dannett (1596). Henry E. Huntington Library, San Marino, CA, MS EL 1045, f. 87v, makes the same genealogical adjustment to Commynes (c.1591) but avoids the polemical conclusion. St Aldegonde's treatise citing medieval precedents for the provinces' right to enforce their contracts with their lords mentioned Edward III's marriage with Philippa, but drew no conclusions: printed in Lettenhove, *Relations Politiques*, viii, 113–18. TNA, SP12/248, f. 65, lists amongst Burghley's books 'at the Court' at his death, both *Memoires de Philippe Commynes* and Dannett's *Historie of Philip De Comines*.

[63] Parry, *The Arch-Conjuror*, 142.

[64] *CSP Span.*, *1568–79*, p. 523.

[65] *Certein Letters wherin is set forth a Discourse of the Peace that was attempted and sought to have bin put in effecte by the Lords and States of Holland and Zelande in the year of oure Lorde 1574* (1576). The gap in the *Stationers' Register* at this period preserves the obscurity of its authors and backers.

[66] *Certein Letters*, sigs b7v, b5r.

traffyck that it wolld procure, and of the brydell that ytt wolld be to all her advarsaryes', it probably emanated from their circle.[67] Further, it purveyed political theories giving reversionary authority in a composite state to inferior magistrates, emphasizing Philip's broken contracts with the Netherlands' provinces, rather than 'discent in her Ma[jesty] (if the holder against his oth wil stand upon discent alone)'. Genealogy gave less security than 'election by the States upon breach of othes and pacts', and, if the Spanish resisted, 'rightfull conquest uppon iust causes, for so manifest iniuries and perils'. Elizabeth's rule would be 'a sweete and easye yoke to the people willing to receive it' according to their ancient liberties.[68] This book, like the related manuscript treatises, shows how carefully the Dutch and their English allies prepared to lobby parliament, because their unusual, and previously-unnoticed, campaign had to compete with intense lobbying from domestic interest groups, anxious to promote or defeat legislation after the long pro-rogation since 1572.

Since it mentions Champagney's presence, _Certein Letters_ dates from the beginning of February, carefully timed to coincide with parliament's planned resumption, although in the event that was postponed for over a week. The council's daily negotiations with the Dutch possibly slowed their preparations, but the delay may also indicate divisions amongst the councillors. Differences over the constitutional nature of the combined state probably mattered less than Burghley's growing doubts, which made the council's plan unworkable.[69] Champagney's first audience with Elizabeth on 5 February possibly encouraged Burghley's hesitancy, though her vehemence in stating England's strategic interests persuaded Champagney that the council had decided on aggression.[70] Some councillors seem to have talked openly about co-opting parliamentary support. An unnamed courtier, possibly Arundel, assured Champagney on 7 February, that parlia-ment would agree to Elizabeth openly possessing the rebel towns and territories. Guaras asserted that St Aldegonde and Buys would immediately petition parliament, and 'after the causes of the action have been explained to them, all the estates will consent to leave the matter in the hands of the queen and Council'.[71]

This roughly corresponds to the conciliar plan to orchestrate parliamentary political and financial support. Guaras understandably assumed that the council had concluded on intervention. Yet continuing conciliar disagreement may explain Speaker Bell's unusual suggestion, when opening the Commons' session, that 'uppon every motion made certaine might be apointed to consider whyther the matter moved were fit to bee commytted to bill' before any debate.[72] This would enable a committee of privy

[67] TNA, SP70/137, f. 208r: Herle to Burghley, 11 Mar. 1576, effectively summarizing _Certein Letters_, passim.

[68] _Certein Letters_, sigs a2r–a3v, b7r. It then emphasized the Netherlands' power and resources, and the benefits for England in uniting with the Dutch navy – all arguments possibly raised in the Commons on 6 March; see below, p. 84.

[69] Champagney, on 31 January, reported rumours that parliament would have been prorogued further if not so imminent, but it was postponed for eight days: Lettenhove, _Relations Politiques_, viii, 152; confirmed by _CSP Ven., 1558–80_, p. 545, which mentions a prorogation in the week before 8 February.

[70] _CSP Span., 1568–79_, p. 522: Guaras to Zayas, 6 Feb. 1576.

[71] Lettenhove, _Relations Politiques_, viii, 163. _CSP Span., 1568–79_, pp. 522–3, two despatches of 6 and 8 February, the former expecting parliament to resume a week later – another sign of the council's indecisive-ness, or Guaras's poor intelligence?

[72] _Proceedings_, ed. Hartley, i, 476.

councillors to intercept a Dutch petition, finally decide their response, draft a suitable bill, and control debate when reporting back to the House. Preparing such a fail-safe device suggests that the council still dithered over its Netherlands policy. Perhaps Peter Wentworth's speech to the Commons that first morning, complaining that royal and conciliar control stifled free debate, while it rehearsed long-held personal obsessions, also partly reflected general unease amongst zealous protestants at the council's overcaution and indecision.[73]

For no Dutch petition appeared. Guaras attributed this to Champagney's persuasiveness, but, apart from Elizabeth's reluctance, Burghley's growing realization of the economic and military consequences of openly aiding Holland and Zealand increasingly divided the council. Leicester and Sussex responded by trying to force the seriously ill Nicholas Bacon into retirement, silencing Burghley's consistent backer in council.[74] During these opening days of parliament, the council held long consultations with an increasingly distracted Elizabeth. The committed councillors seemingly persuaded her to offer public protection to Holland and Zealand, a decision she almost immediately reversed. At an audience on 12 February, Champagney, again, reminded Elizabeth of the consequences of joining the rebels, and she repeated the threat to English interests posed by both French and Spanish domination of the Netherlands.[75] By then, Guaras could only inform Philip that 'matters here are constantly changing', though he now believed that Elizabeth would not send forces to the Netherlands, despite the large unofficial flows of men and munitions. He dismissed as deceptive time-wasting, Elizabeth's suggested embassy to Philip, intended to justify her intervention in defence of his patrimony and English interests, though it epitomised her habitual playing for time, which would ultimately destroy Dutch hopes.[76]

In these circumstances, a Dutch parliamentary petition threatened to provoke the quick resolution that she and Burghley now wished to avoid, which explains its non-appearance. Champagney kept up the pressure by warning Leicester about the consequences of assisting the rebels, which he knew would cause friction when Leicester duly reported to the queen. On 14 February, Elizabeth commanded Champagney to rehash the whole matter again with Burghley, Leicester and Sussex. By now, Elizabeth had renewed her league with France against Spain, which meant, as Guaras pointed out, further postponement of decision making, which 'will depend mainly upon the outcome of the dissensions in France'.[77] The news that Henry of Navarre had escaped from Henri III's court seemed to herald another outbreak of hostilities, which might yet enable England to secure the sovereignty of Holland and Zealand while the French were distracted.[78]

---

[73] Text in *Proceedings*, ed. Hartley, i, 425–34.

[74] Lettenhove, *Relations Politiques*, viii, 165: Champagney to Requesens, 9 Feb. 1576. Thus removing Bacon from the Woolsack and nominal control of the Lords, though his influence over their proceedings can be overestimated.

[75] TNA, SP70/137, ff. 89r–v, in *CSP Foreign, 1575–7*, p. 243.

[76] *CSP Span., 1568–79*, pp. 524–5: Guaras to Zayas, 11 Feb. 1576.

[77] Lettenhove, *Relations Politiques*, viii, 174–80; *CSP Span., 1568–79*, p. 525: Guaras to Zayas, 18 Feb. 1576.

[78] *CSP Span., 1568–79*, p. 525: Guaras to Zayas, 18 Feb. 1576; *CSP Foreign, 1575–7*, no. 623: Dale to Walsingham, Paris, 21 Feb. 1576.

This fluid context sheds new light on Sir Walter Mildmay's speech for the subsidy on
10 February, which has been seen as innovative, because the council took parliament
into its confidence about the need for money to meet future threats.[79] However, raising
taxes for both ordinary and extraordinary expenses had long become ritualised, and
Mildmay's speech is remarkable chiefly as an expression of the council's continuing
indecision over war with Spain.[80] Its superficially logical structure merely alluded to
what members knew from public discussion over the sovereignty of Holland and
Zealand. Mildmay justified expenditure that might be undertaken against Spain in the
Netherlands with broad hints, beginning by recalling the Roman Spanish yoke under
Mary, and how Elizabeth had created security by expensive, but successful, military
interventions, chiefly in Scotland. Alluding to the Popish Plot behind the 1569 northern
rebellion, he then warned that 'the tayle of thoes stormes which are so bitter and so
boystrous in other countryes may reach us also before they be ended', because the
Netherlands' crisis implied threats from the Spanish, 'the adversaryes of our religion,
both for our profession, and for that also this realme is a mercifull sanctuary for such
poore Christians as fly hither for succour'. Only preparation for external war would
provide internal security. In the context of the public Dutch mission, the message was
obvious. Finally, he emphasized that the subsidy would reflect the subjects' gratitude,
without having to mention that it increased Elizabeth's flexibility in responding to a very
fluid situation, including maintaining 'forces by land and by sea, to answere any thing
that shalbe attempted against her and us' by 'the privy or open malice of enemyes'.[81]
The situation of February 1576 thus enabled Mildmay to confirm the international
popish plot against the protestant realm as a shared article of faith with the Commons.[82]
It also chimed with Philip Sidney's contemporary protestant redefinition of Ciceronian
prudence as a virtuous offensive vigilance.[83] With the Subsidy Bill proceeding with its
usual undebated rapidity, ardent protestants in the Commons could focus once more on
the prospective Dutch petition.

Disappointment awaited them. We can trace the privy council's shift away from their
plan to harness parliamentary support, by following an obscure draft bill 'that the
Queen's Majesty may entreat the Subjects of foreign Princes in such sort, as they shall
entreat the Subjects of this Realm'. This previously-neglected bill received its first
reading on 21 February, and its second on 24 February, when duly committed.[84] The
topic had recently exercised the council when it authorised private reprisals against
foreign seizures of goods, particularly by Spain. On one level, the bill tried to remove

[79] W. MacCaffrey, 'Parliament and Foreign Policy', in *The Parliaments of Elizabethan England*, ed. D.M.
Dean and N.L. Jones (Oxford, 1990), 78–9, criticized by T.E. Hartley, *Elizabeth's Parliaments: Queen, Lords and
Commons, 1559–1601* (Manchester, 1992), 40, which, however, overlooks the context.

[80] J.D. Alsop, 'Parliament and Taxation', in *Parliaments of Elizabethan England*, ed. Dean and Jones, 91–116.
See further, R.W. Hoyle, 'Crown, Parliament and Taxation in Sixteenth-Century England', *English Historical
Review*, cix (1994), 1174–96. The subsidy committee's bill repeated that of 1571: Elton, *Parliament*, 167, which
ignores Mildmay's speech, revealing tight conciliar control, for only four non-conciliar members survived
from 1571: Alsop, 'Parliament and Taxation', 107 n. 50.

[81] *Proceedings*, ed. Hartley, i, 440–4.

[82] Mildmay's subsidy speeches in 1581, 1585, 1587 and 1589, hardly altered from this prototype: Alsop,
'Parliament and Taxation', 104.

[83] B. Worden, *The Sound of Virtue: Philip Sidney's 'Arcadia' and Elizabethan Politics* (New Haven, CT, 1996).

[84] *CJ*, i, 107, 108. Elton, *Parliament*, 239, mentions it in passing.

the persistent objection to Elizabeth's acceptance of the sovereignty of Holland and Zealand, that 'the great wealth of our subiectes' in merchandise in Spain was vulnerable to Philip's reprisals.[85] Thomas Cromwell's belief that the bill enabled Elizabeth to reciprocate 'when any forreyne prince dealeth with her subiectes or their goodes by way of arest or restrain of their coming in', suggests that it also addressed the current moral panic about the inquisition persecuting English protestant merchants in Spain. The Anglo-Dutch group behind *Certein Letters* had exploited this popular anxiety, complaining that 'in Spaine it self, her Ma[jesty's] subiects are daily taken and imprisoned, manacled tormented and exquisitely murdered in contempte of her Majesties honour, and the safe freedom of mutual trafique', neatly blending religious and economic complaints.[86] The bill, clearly a government measure, went to a committee dominated by 'All the Privy Council, being of this House', a privilege reserved for the subsidy and politically important bills with prerogative implications, or potential for quarrels with the Lords.[87] As usual in this session, Christopher Hatton, already developing his interest in Netherlands' policies, was named after the councillors.

Analysis of the other committee members increases the impression of special treatment, and indicates the bill's real purpose – to provide against economic warfare with Spain when anticipated hostilities broke out. Government lawyers experienced in drafting bills were automatically nominated, notably Thomas Wilson, master of requests, currently on an embassy in France. Others, however, included William Fleetwood, recorder of London and Burghley's loyal supporter, experienced in Iberian economic warfare through his work in the court of admiralty.[88] Fleetwood's London colleague and perennial facilitator of council business in the Commons, Thomas Norton, who strongly desired Elizabeth to take the sovereignty of Holland and Zealand, also appears.[89] Francis Alford, a civil lawyer and Marian exile, would repeatedly urge intervention in the Netherlands in 1587, and that Elizabeth should accept their sovereignty.[90] Another lawyer appointee, but more radical religious reformer and opponent of catholicism, was Robert Snagge.[91] Others included James Dalton, as active a collaborator with Burghley as anyone, and Robert Newdigate, who sometimes over-zealously assisted the privy

---

[85] BL, Harleian MS 285, ff. 23v–24r: 'Instructions for John Hastings to be sent into Holland', 29 Oct. 1575, and see above, pp. 67, 70–2, for later reiterations.

[86] Thomas Cromwell's journal, in *Proceedings*, ed. Hartley, i, 481, 483; *Certein Letters*, sig. b6r. In 1575, Sir Henry Cobham's embassy to Philip II attempted a diplomatic solution to this problem: W. MacCaffrey, *Queen Elizabeth and the Making of Policy, 1572–1588* (Princeton, NJ, 1981), 199–200, and in Jan. 1577: *CSP Ven., 1558–80*, no. 666.

[87] Ten committees in all, including bills confirming letters patent (*CJ*, i, 108), fraudulent conveyances by northern rebels (*CJ*, i, 108), the case of Edward Smalley, Arthur Hall's servant (*CJ*, i, 109), the petition for reforming Church discipline (*CJ*, i, 109), fines and recoveries (*CJ*, i, 111), excess of apparel, which raised prerogative issues and sparked conflict with the Lords (*CJ*, i, 113), the petition for Elizabeth to marry (*CJ*, i, 114), and the bill for Lord Stourton, another causing conflict with the Lords (*CJ*, i, 115). The privy councillors were Sir James Croft, Sir Francis Knollys, Sir Walter Mildmay, Sir Ralph Sadler, Sir Thomas Smith, and Francis Walsingham: *The History of Parliament: The House of Commons, 1558–1603*, ed. P.W. Hasler (3 vols, 1981) [hereafter cited as *HPC, 1558–1603*], i, 77.

[88] *HPC, 1558–1603*, iii, 629–31; ii, 133–8.

[89] Graves, *Thomas Norton*; *HPC, 1558–1603*, iii, 145–9.

[90] *HPC, 1558–1603*, i, 337, and *Proceedings*, ed. Hartley, ii, 300, 387–9.

[91] *HPC, 1558–1603*, iii, 408–9.

council's parliamentary programme.[92] The general impression of reliable senior members with strong council connections eager to advance a protestant foreign policy increases with the addition of minor royal servants at court and in the country. Henry Knyvet, a distant kinsman of Elizabeth and Sussex, gentleman pensioner and multiple local officeholder, also urged Elizabeth to accept the sovereignty of Holland and Zealand in 1587.[93] Sir John Thynne, closely connected to Burghley, and Thomas Colby, a Suffolk magistrate and formerly Archbishop Parker's steward, represented protestant zeal in their counties.[94] Another local facilitator of government business, Thomas St Poll, persecuted recusants in Lincolnshire and Mary, queen of Scots in the Commons avidly enough to receive the council's thanks and a knighthood. Robert Shute, recorder of Cambridge and client of Lord North, Leicester's supporter in his Netherlands' policy as in so much else, was also named.[95] Christopher Yelverton, recorder of Northampton and yet another experienced lawyer, assisted the council's parliamentary management, but still managed to please Thomas Cartwright with his zeal.[96]

These familiar, experienced committee men preceded, more significantly, merchants with direct interest in the bill. Sir Rowland Hayward, senior member for London, had Iberian interests, but more importantly, had served as commissioner for reprisals against Spanish goods when Philip seized English merchandise in 1572–3.[97] Dominick Chester of Bristol experienced this problem when trading with Portugal and France. Following the general arrest of English goods in Portugal and Spain in 1570, between 1571 and 1574 the privy council authorised Chester and others to seize Portuguese goods in England in reprisal. This produced little improvement and, in January 1575, the council impounded a Portuguese cargo at Southampton to compensate Chester.[98] John Marshe, a merchant adventurer who spoke strongly against Norfolk and Mary, queen of Scots in 1572, had extensive Spanish trading interests and instigated the Spanish Company in 1572. His great experience in the Netherlands' wool trade made him a useful informant for Burghley.[99] Philip Langley of Bristol also helped found the Spanish Company.[100] To these were joined William Selby, a monopolist of the Newcastle sea-coal trade, and John Aldrich of Norwich, another zealous protestant deeply involved in the Netherlands' wool trade.[101]

Some of these men possibly contributed to the bill's unrecorded second reading debate. The committee so heavily amended the bill on 24 February, following this

[92] *HPC, 1558–1603*, ii, 8–9; iii, 128–9.

[93] *HPC, 1558–1603*, ii, 420–3, and *Proceedings*, ed. Hartley, ii, 301.

[94] *HPC, 1558–1603*, iii, 506–7; ii, 627.

[95] *HPC, 1558–1603*, iii, 379–80.

[96] *HPC, 1558–1603*, iii, 679–81. Other appointees included the ambitious protestant lawyer, John Frenche (*HPC, 1558–1603*, ii, 158), and either Edward or John Stanhope, closely connected to Burghley, though John also enjoyed Hatton's patronage (*HPC, 1558–1603*, iii, 436–7, 438–40).

[97] *HPC, 1558–1603*, ii, 283–5.

[98] In 1573, the council acted similarly for Chester against French seizures (*HPC, 1558–1603*, i, 597–8), which overlooks the nature of this bill and puts Dominick's brother, Thomas, on this committee; see *Acts of the Privy Council of England*, ed. J.R. Dasent (42 vols, 1890–1907), viii, 4, 6, 20–1, 23, 32, 160, 178–9, 183, 268, 324, 329–30.

[99] *HPC, 1558–1603*, iii, 20–2.

[100] *HPC, 1558–1603*, ii, 438.

[101] *HPC, 1558–1603*, iii, 365; i, 333.

second reading, that it had to return as a new bill for a first reading.[102] This suggests that the committee dealt conscientiously with its contentious issues, another sign of its political importance. However, thereafter it disappears from the parliamentary record, the usual fate of bills unable to resolve conflicting interests, but in this case probably indicating a date after which the weight of council opinion shifted against uniting with Holland and Zealand. Perhaps the Spanish merchants and Burghley's clients stressed the practical difficulties in enabling the council to forestall Spanish reprisals. Not all the council's zealous protestant collaborators agreed with this retreat, as we shall see.

In line with this parliamentary withdrawal, by 26 February the Dutch representatives found themselves strenuously objecting to Elizabeth's renewed insistence on brokering their peace with Philip. Hatton confirmed this latest reversal by telling Champagney that his mission for peace and reconciliation had raised his reputation amongst some courtiers, though the deeply-divided council continued to confer with the Dutch. St Aldegonde doggedly persisted in compiling Elizabeth's Netherlands' pedigree but, as Guaras recognized, the erratic course of English policy reflected their fears about the strategic implications of events 'in France, Genoa and the Turk', especially France. By 28 February, despatches from Anjou implying a firm French peace, again transformed the strategic situation. They raised the prospect that English intervention would be opposed by a united France defending national interests, perhaps supporting Spain. Burghley had feared precisely this outcome, and this news encouraged the shift of opinion in council against extending English sovereignty.[103]

This may explain a desperate ploy by the convinced protestants in the Commons, reported by Guaras but no other source. On 27 February, the Subsidy Bill received its third Commons' reading and duly passed, but, according to the reasonably well-informed Guaras, 'they have offered the Queen the present subsidy, and much more, if she will accept the offer made by Orange'. 'Others', probably a privy councillor such as Croft, or just possibly Hatton, 'replied that the business should be left to the Queen and Council, and it was decided that parliament itself should not further deal with it'. No other source mentions this attempt to connect an enhanced subsidy with Elizabeth extending her sovereignty over Holland and Zealand. Writing on the same day, Champagney still assumed that the council would introduce the issue of Holland and Zealand into parliament soon, but, to his knowledge, parliament still debated only domestic concerns. Closing the session, Elizabeth specifically thanked members for a subsidy 'frankly offered without any perswasion or difficulty at all'. However, this alleged linkage may reflect an independent attempt by the council's business managers to resuscitate the original policy. It certainly resembles the council's tactic of February 1587, when Mildmay, Knollys and Hatton, by then a privy councillor, encouraged their collaborators in the Commons to propose a large benevolence for Elizabeth, besides the subsidy, if she would accept the sovereignty of Holland and

---

[102] *CJ*, i, 108.

[103] Hatfield House, Salisbury MS, CP 160/31; *CSP Span., 1568–79*, pp. 527–8. By encouraging Elizabeth's decision in mid-February only to marry Anjou if France was at peace, conservatives favouring a French match raised another hurdle to an aggressive policy in the Netherlands, if such a peace could be patched up: *CSP Ven., 1558–80*, p. 546. In fact, Anjou deceived Elizabeth; negotiations dragged into April.

Zealand.[104] Whatever did happen in late February 1576, the convinced protestants must have been increasingly worried that the council no longer steered a consistently protestant course through the stormy events of the following week.

Several times, Champagney failed to prise a straight answer out of Elizabeth or her council about their intentions towards Orange and the Netherlands, because the council remained deadlocked. By 28 February, the French court in Auvergne heard the rumour that Elizabeth 'has resolutely undertaken the enterprise of the Low Country' in alliance with the Huguenots and Duke Casimir of the Palatinate. That day, the privy council denied any such intention to Champagney, reiterating Elizabeth's desire for the *status quo ante*.[105] Stories from Brussels about Spanish troop mutinies increased Champagney's difficulties and encouraged those demanding military intervention. Yet, at the same time, draft instructions for Sir Henry Cobham's embassy to the Spanish viceroy, Requesens, used the threat of French absorption of the Netherlands to press for meaningful peace negotiations.[106] Some councillors had already begun canvassing a utopian grand alliance against Spain, incorporating Henri III, Anjou, the German princes and the coastal powers of the North Sea and Baltic, a clear indication that the prospect of Elizabeth incorporating Holland and Zealand had, in practical terms, disappeared. Elizabeth embroidered her own version of this fantasy for Champagney on 28 February: the restoration of the former conditions in the Netherlands leading to the general reconciliation of christendom.[107]

Apocalyptic dreams of universal reform attracted Elizabeth more than speculative international protestant alliances, though both militated against accepting the Dutch offers. Some courtiers exploited her prejudices to encourage this denial. On 2 March, John Young, master of Pembroke College, Cambridge, who would owe his elevation as bishop of Rochester in 1578 to Christopher Hatton, found himself preaching before Elizabeth at short notice, on David's humility in Psalm 131.[108] Appealing in proto-Shakespearian terms to Elizabeth's jealous prerogative control of foreign policy: 'It is a harde matter nowe a dayes for one man to play onely one mans part, for every man lyke these common players in plaies and enterludes playeth many partes', Young advised Londoners of 'vile and base condition', whose foreign policy discussions Champagney had noticed, not to meddle in 'matters of state and government . . . to[o] great for them to be conversant in'. His attempt to marginalise public opinion 'was not well taken in part of some of the hearers, where it was spoken', but his interpretation of his text also touched Elizabeth's sensitivity about the sacred status of monarchy. Since ambition clogged the meanest rulers, it should not be marvelled at in 'the best, the greatest, the

---

[104] *CSP Span.*, *1568–79*, pp. 527–8; Lettenhove, *Relations Politiques*, viii, 205; S. D'Ewes, *A Compleat Journal of the Votes, Speeches and Debates: both of the House of Lords and House of Commons throughout the whole reign of Queen Elizabeth, of glorious memory* (1693), 235; *Proceedings*, ed. Hartley, ii, 297–310, though in the end their courage failed them. See MacCaffrey, *Queen Elizabeth and the Making of Policy*, 488–9, and Hartley, *Elizabeth's Parliaments*, 43–5. No diarist recording this session for Burghley mentions this or Scott and Norton's speeches on 6 March, whether from sympathy or ignorance is unclear: see Elton, *Parliament*, 13.

[105] TNA, SP70/137, ff. 142r–v: Wilkes to Walsingham, 28 Feb. 1576; *CSP Foreign, 1575–7*, no. 636.

[106] Lettenhove, *Relations Politiques*, viii, 212, 213–5.

[107] Lettenhove, *Relations Politiques*, viii, 213, 222–3.

[108] Brett Usher, 'John Young (c.1532–1605)', *ODNB* (2004); John Young, *A Sermon preached before the Queenes Maiestie, the second of March An. 1575* [i.e., 1576] (1576). Young lacked time to write a short sermon, and three times skipped his prepared text: sigs C4v, C6r–v.

chiefest, the highest', especially under pressure from 'those, whose whole studie and endevour evermore hath bene, and is at this day, to undermine those which bee in authoritie, to invade and occupie other mens kingdoms, to wring the Scepter and Swords out of Princes handes'. Ambition 'in the hyest and most daungerous degrees of al other' explained the ruin of every 'Kingdome, Empire, or Monarchie', for the diminution of one prince lessened all monarchy.[109]

Young's arguments sought to lock a door already swinging shut, but the Dutch themselves finally turned the key. Orange barely controlled the Flushing pirates, who supported the Dutch insurgency partly to cover their depredations on both friendly and enemy shipping in the English Channel. In early March, they seized the fiancée of the Portuguese ambassador to England from a royal navy ship within sight of Dover, despising Elizabeth's safe conduct. In other circumstances, Elizabeth might have minimised this attack upon her honour, but, perhaps wearied by Dutch importunity and surrounded by catholic and pro-Spanish courtiers keen to imagine a general affront to monarchy, she chose to create a major diplomatic incident. Thus encouraged, English merchants petitioned about the Flushingers' piracy, adding to the furore. On 5 March, the council required Burghley to arrest all Flushing vessels and crews, a ban immediately extended to the whole of Zealand.[110] Champagney believed that the Dutch envoys had been placed under house arrest, perhaps because, exasperated by Elizabeth's continuing procrastination, they insouciantly responded that, as declared enemies, the Portuguese were fair prize. Even William Herle acknowledged that such intransigence exacerbated the political disaster for 'the commune cawse', while diehard supporters of the Dutch were now 'asshamed to deffend theme'.[111]

The affair disturbed relationships for another month, boosting courtly opposition to the rebels and poisoning Elizabeth's opinion of the Dutch, a change measureable by the sudden rise in Champagney's stock at court. Writing on 6 March, Guaras for once ignored the influence of international events and attributed the changed atmosphere solely to Champagney's diplomatic skills, because initially 'they received him very sourly . . . but his great talent has changed them and he is now much caressed by the Queen and Council'. That day, Champagney dined at Sir Thomas Gresham's with Sussex, Burghley and Leicester, who now claimed to be working hard for a peace settlement. Hatton also continued his princely entertainment, incensing protestant public opinion, for 'lampoons greatly libelling Hatton have been circulated', presumably by the vile and base meddlers Young had condemned in his sermon.[112]

Hatton's role in facilitating Champagney's influence with Elizabeth, and the implications of the privy council's effective retreat to a peace policy, had also become evident

---

[109] Young, *A Sermon preached*, sigs. C1v, C1r, A1v, A8v, B7r, B8r.

[110] Hatfield House, Salisbury MS, CP 160/34; Lettenhove, *Relations Politiques*, viii, 237; similar orders went to the fleet: TNA, SP12/107/52.

[111] TNA, SP70/137, f. 206v: Herle to Burghley, 11 Mar. 1576, reporting Paul Buys's claim that the lady was fair prize; complaints against the pirates were often invented 'only to allter the Quene's majestie's affectyon towardes theme'. Three months later, the privy council still pretended this offence was unprecedented 'by any prince that hath been so friendly dealt withall', although by then the seizure of the earl of Oxford, and more importantly the Merchant Adventurers' fleet, had compounded the offence: TNA, SP70/138, ff. 193r–200r, 203r–v: privy council to Orange via William Winter, 19 June 1576.

[112] *CSP Span., 1568–79*, p. 529; Lettenhove, *Relations Politiques*, viii, 248–9.

to the ardent protestants who normally facilitated conciliar business in the Commons. Hours before Champagney's semi-public triumph at Gresham's, they tried desperately to revive the original plan, despite the turn of events, which had altered conciliar opinion. Their co-operation with the council's legislative programme did not diminish their commitment to an ideological foreign policy, despite the council's backtracking. Our source this time is Champagney reporting to Requesens. His version seems plausible, given his alarm about parliamentary discussion of Holland and Zealand, the congruence between his account and the protagonists' known beliefs, and his description of the conciliar response in the Commons.

According to Champagney, on 6 March Sir Thomas Scott proposed that the Commons should petition the queen to accept the Dutch offers to extend the realm, and, underlining the ideological motivation, '*quant a quant la religion*'. Perhaps in an orchestrated move, 'Morton' (*sic.* for Norton), one of the members for London, supported this speech, as did a third member.[113] Scott, related to Leicester, dominated the Kentish magistracy, served on important committees in several parliaments and reliably assisted the council in his county and the Commons.[114] Vehemently anti-papist, he supported executing both Norfolk and Mary, queen of Scots in 1572, and was chosen to help arrest Arthur Hall in 1581.[115] His petition motion seems to be his only recorded utterance in 1576, but sounds entirely plausible from an outspoken protestant with strong court connections, though whether Leicester inspired his move is unknown. Norton's support also makes sense, since his devotion to the council and its leading figures in the Commons, Walsingham and Mildmay, was only exceeded by his rabid anti-catholicism and implausible belief that Elizabeth would stop the international catholic conspiracy. The contradictions between his assumptions and her actions crystallised in 1581, when his outspokeness against the Anjou match and its catholic implications landed him in the Tower.[116] This motion, therefore, appears to be a concerted effort by ideologically driven, experienced MPs to save their fond hopes of a religiously-based Netherlands' policy, which the council had abandoned. Perhaps they reiterated some of the Dutch arguments made to the council in January and repeated in *Certein Letters* at the resumption of this parliament. The motion may have provoked some debate, because Norton was adroit at using parliamentary tactics, timing motions to fit the mood of the House. He may even have suggested that Scott raise the issue while Sir James Croft, their obvious conciliar opponent, was taking bills to the Lords.[117]

[113] Lettenhove, *Relations Politiques*, viii, 249, more correctly in A.L.P. De Robaulx de Soumoy, *Mémoires de Frederic Perrenot Sieur de Champagney 1573–1590* (Brussels, 1860), 393. Champagney had a tin ear for English names and identified this third member as '*Alton qui est ung homme de lettre*', possibly the civilian, Francis Alford, who blamed his later disgrace on his parliamentary service, 'but I repent me not, for that I know I have done my country some good': *HPC, 1558–1603*, i, 335–8.

[114] *HPC, 1558–1603*, iii, 356–8, and see, e.g., *Acts of the Privy Council*, x, 374.

[115] *Proceedings*, ed. Hartley, i, 324, 349–50, 393–4, 532; see also L.A. Knafla, 'Sir Thomas Scott', *ODNB*.

[116] Graves, *Thomas Norton*, 119–26, 389–403.

[117] Norton's advice on parliamentary tactics: BL, Harleian MS 253, ff. 34v–35r. Croft took four bills up to the Lords that morning: D'Ewes, *Journal*, 253. Guaras's alternative sources reported on 6 March that 'those who wished to raise the question of the succession have been silenced, as also have those who wished to jeopardise the Queen of Scotland' – possibly two linked obsessions Scott and Norton included in their petition: *CSP Span., 1568–79*, p. 529.

According to Champagney, Croft immediately moved to quash this initiative. His argument would be repeated by other opponents of a protestant, anti-Spanish foreign policy, lending veracity to Champagney's account, despite his misnaming the councillor Sir 'Thomas'. Croft argued that such propositions revealed disaffection from the queen, advising her to enterprise things without any foundation or right in law. They must have forgotten, he added, how the Newhaven enterprise in 1563 had damaged Her Majesty. It seemed to him that the proposers showed great presumption in putting forward such ideas, in a place where it did not appertain to them in the slightest to deal with the issue.[118] Croft's assertion that Elizabeth had no legal claims to the Netherlands, despite the genealogical and contractual theories already widely understood in London, certainly sounds like the conservative courtiers of these months. It was an argument which Elizabeth herself deployed when it suited her. The conclusion that foreign policy belonged exclusively to her prerogative and exceeded the competence of the Commons was increasingly familiar but conflicted with parliament's historic role as the great council of the realm. It may distantly echo the privy council's original plan to use parliament as a sounding board for policy, which it would then dutifully refer to queen and council.

However, the mention of the Newhaven expedition of 1563 shrewdly reminded the House of the last time an English expeditionary force had been forced into humiliating retreat by French Huguenots and catholics, united by hatred of their ancestral enemy. It may also confirm Champagney's boast that he primed Croft with excellent arguments against intervention. It would certainly encourage Burghley's caution. He still bore the mental scars from that disastrous blunder in continental warfare and, in the new context of apparently firm peace in France, it helped to emphasize the increasing threat that the French posed to any English force sent to the Netherlands. No wonder catholics at court trotted out the same points over the next few years, whenever outright war with Spain seemed to threaten, because they certainly resonated with Elizabeth. As Burghley sourly admitted, 'Her Majestie hath with very bitter speeches reproved those that first advised her to assiste the Protestauntes in Fraunce' – especially himself.[119]

In these tumultuous days, timing was everything, and Norton and Scott's attempt to revitalise the issue in the Commons may have been stimulated by the collapse of Spanish arms in the Netherlands. Spanish bankruptcy provoked mutinies, compounded by the death of Requesens on 5 March following weeks of sickness.[120] Rumours of his death had circulated for some time, and that very day Elizabeth pointedly asked Champagney when he last heard from Requesens.[121] His death seemed to portend great changes, and the protestant zealot, Daniel Rogers, excitedly retailed prophecies of Philip's imminent death, rumours of which had been encouraging, and encouraged by, the remaining

---

[118] Lettenhove, *Relations Politiques*, viii, 249.

[119] Lettenhove, *Relations Politiques*, viii, 278–9, on Champagney's boast; TNA, SP12/108/82, p. 2.

[120] TNA, SP70/137, ff. 180r–v: Henry Mason to Burghley, Antwerp, 4 Mar. 1576; *CSP Foreign, 1575–7*, p. 260; TNA, SP70/137, ff. 189r–190v: Daniel Rogers to Burghley, Antwerp, 7 Mar. 1576, in W. Murdin, *A Collection of State Papers* (2 vols, 1740), ii, 292, and *CSP Foreign, 1575–7*, pp. 262–3.

[121] Lettenhove, *Relations Politiques*, viii, 238.

supporters of the protestant policy at court. Even the Cologne money men now bet on English success, offering Elizabeth enormous loans at a mere 5%.[122]

It could be argued, therefore, that Scott and Norton acted to seize the moment, against Elizabeth's wishes, where councillors could not, and that the clash with Croft reflected divisions within the council rather than between it and its parliamentary collaborators.[123] However, although definite news of Requesens's death and predictions of 'great mutations' in the Netherlands reached Walsingham by 9 March, the ardent protestants had missed the parliamentary tide.[124] For the next few days, groups of courtiers besieged Elizabeth, urging her not merely to protect the Dutch, but, now that effective Spanish government had collapsed, to occupy the strategic towns already offered in Holland and Zealand. Equally desperate, on 11 March, Buys demanded, via Burghley, some 'dyrect and absolut answer from Her Majesty in wryteing, grownded upon that that Mr Hastinges was sent to theme for'.[125] That same day, a conveniently-timed petition to the council complaining about the Spanish inquisition's persecution of English merchants attempted to redress the balance upset by the Flushing pirates, and to revive support for the bill lost in committee. Champagney claimed that, in response, he had sought to charm the queen, rallying his friends amongst her chief ministers.[126]

He had obvious motives for exaggerating the danger and his role in averting it. Elizabeth, in fact, saw the power vacuum following Requesens's death and the collapse of Spanish control as the chance to restore the *status quo ante* in the Netherlands, not to embrace calvinist rebels and pirates. Having initially ignored Champagney, she now overwhelmed him with repeated hospitality, as someone who could encourage the expulsion of Spanish troops.[127] Hatton and Croft exploited their triumph, perhaps beyond what their rivals could stomach. On the day that Elizabeth prorogued parliament, Champagney claimed that their control of parliamentary debates had earned her gratitude, while Leicester now smoothly implied that he had always supported peace. Two days later, Champagney reiterated that, although Croft 'is much envied, and taken for a Catholic' by some at court, like Hatton he had gained great credit amongst others 'for having spoken very effectively two or three times, things which were to the Queen's liking' in parliament.[128]

---

[122] Lettenhove, *Relations Politiques*, viii, 236, from Daniel Rogers's journal on the successful predictions of Requesens's death and prophecies that Philip would die before mid 1576, a death already rumoured in France, Portugal and England. Guaras, on 24 March, noted diabolical predictions that Philip would die before 27 June 1577, while courtiers 'constantly asserted' that he was already dead, seeking to 'continue to trouble the states': *CSP Span., 1568–79*, p. 530.

[123] Graves, 'The Management of the Elizabethan House of Commons', 30–1.

[124] Lettenhove, *Relations Politiques*, viii, 245, Champagney plaintively reporting to Requesens, on 10 March, the news of his death, received in London 'hier soir', provoking conjectures '*des grandes mutations*'.

[125] TNA, SP70/137, f. 206v: Herle's report to Burghley, 11 Mar. 1576.

[126] Lettenhove, *Relations Politiques*, viii, 257–8: Champagney to the Netherlands council of state, 12 Mar. 1576; TNA, SP15/24/70: John Foxall and Barnard Field to the privy council, 11 Mar. 1576. TNA, SP12/108/82, SP12/24/70, SP15/24/70, complaints to the privy council regarding Spanish Inquisition seizures of ships and goods.

[127] Adams, 'Sovereignty of the Netherlands', 315.

[128] Lettenhove, *Relations Politiques*, viii, 265, 278–9. So effective in quashing debate that Paul Buys claimed, on 11 March, that parliament 'hath yett passed hitherunto without ani motyon att all of their case': TNA, SP70/137, f. 208v.

Hatton, in particular, used this parliament to complete his transition from established favourite to rising politician, particularly by his prompt response to Peter Wentworth's opening address on freedom of speech.[129] However, some councillors objected to his interference in political decision making, particularly about the Netherlands. By supporting Champagney's mission to Elizabeth, he had bypassed the normal flow of information and advice, and Elizabeth felt it necessary to exclude him from any consultation for a few days after the end of parliament.[130]

Such jealousy reflected the turmoil amongst Hatton's opponents, where the prorogation of parliament brought recriminations against Burghley's apparent betrayal. Herle bluntly informed Burghley that 'amongst gentillmen and sowdyors, and amongst those of good sort that professe the relygion' it was openly asserted that 'Your Lordship hath bin the only lett and overthrowe of this Holland service, disswading Her Magesty from the enterprise'.[131] Burghley ignored this criticism for some weeks before replying in surprisingly temperate terms, trying to shift the blame to Leicester and Sussex, public supporters of 'this Holland service'. Herle knew only part of the story, for 'The conning of worldlynges is greatest in hyding ther passadges with contrary overt speches', but the best evidence 'is the towchston of ther honest lyves' – never Leicester's strong point.[132] However, as the lynchpin of the council, Burghley's opinion carried enormous weight and, with enough support, could match Leicester and Sussex. His inherent anxieties about the costs and uncertainties of continental warfare had offered Champagney some leverage, but peace in France and the collapse of Spanish power in the Netherlands probably had more effect on his thinking. The Flushing pirates gave him the ideal excuse to abandon the project of incorporating Holland and Zealand. Over the next few months, he would express public outrage against the piratical rabble, but privately he urged secret negotiations to resolve the crisis, and through Herle, assured the Dutch of his 'inward affection'.[133] As mutual reprisals between the Dutch and the English escalated, he worked to ensure the unofficial flow of money, men and munitions to the Netherlands, for him the limit of England's safe involvement.[134]

Elizabeth ended by humiliating the Dutch envoys, neither accepting their sovereignty, nor extending her protection, nor even agreeing to lend them money. The embittered godly, their once exalted hopes now dashed, responded with a series of libels distributed in City and court personally attacking Elizabeth and making 'dishonorable interpretations of her majesty's godly actions and purposes', according to the sharp proclamation issued against them.[135] Periodically, the council revived the idea of accepting Dutch sovereignty, usually to forestall the French. Yet without a parliament in

[129] Lettenhove, *Relations Politiques*, viii, 280; Champagney naïvely believed Elizabeth planned to ennoble him and appoint him to the council.

[130] Lettenhove, *Relations Politiques*, viii, 288. Ironically, Hatton's increasing political influence sometimes freed him to pursue policies closer to Leicester's, especially after losing enormously in the Spanish sack of Antwerp in Nov. 1576: Huntington Library, MS EL 6236.

[131] TNA, SP70/137, ff. 220r–v; *CSP Foreign, 1575–7*, pp. 269–70.

[132] Lettenhove, *Relations Politiques*, viii, 328–9.

[133] TNA, SP70/137, ff. 245r–246v; *CSP Foreign, 1575–7*, p. 276.

[134] Lettenhove, *Relations Politiques*, viii, 340.

[135] *Tudor Royal Proclamations*, ed. P.L. Hughes and J.F. Larkin (3 vols, New Haven, CT, 1964–9), ii, 400–1: 'Offering Rewards for Information on Libels against the Queen', Westminster, 26 Mar. 1576.

session, such manœuvres lacked the political and financial commitment to be taken seriously, as the Dutch knew. They enjoyed snubbing English envoys sent in May to distract them from French negotiations. In July, Orange curtly turned down offers to revive the whole question, though zealous English partisans insisted that Elizabeth would find all Holland 'at her devotion'.[136] In 1581, much to Leicester's chagrin, Anjou effectively assumed the sovereignty of the Netherlands, after Elizabeth claimed another fit of conscience about possessing 'that [which] apperteyns to another'.[137] However, clear-sighted politicians now assumed parliament's role in persuading public opinion to support a risky foreign policy. In November 1581, Walsingham considered it axiomatic that parliament discuss whether Elizabeth should assist Anjou in 'his enterprise of the Lowe Countryes'. For there the realm would be 'made acquainted with such reasons as doth induce her majestie' to support Anjou, 'least otherwise being not acquainted with the reasons they may enter into some hard conceptions touching the same'.[138] Where the safety and prosperity of the realm would be risked in open war with Spain, the essential role of parliament as the great council of the realm had not been diminished by the council's failure to manage its business in 1576.

That failure had been caused by the ideological differences between Elizabeth and some of her council, but especially by tensions within the council. They encompassed more than religious differences and fluctuating international power-politics. Differences over the nature of the Tudor state weakened the council's decision-making process. Burghley's focus on the British Isles as Elizabeth's dynastic *imperium* only reluctantly and hesitantly expanded to provinces where her dubious dynastic claims could not guarantee the protection of protestantism after her death. Expanding the realm into Holland and Zealand on a contractual basis would create a federal monarchy dominated by a bureaucratic and military caste with a freer hand in defending an international protestant *res publica*. Leicester's acceptance of the viceroyalty of the Netherlands in 1585, to Elizabeth's fury, reveals some of these consequences. Her dynastic refusal to claim the sovereignty that his action implied collided with the political needs of the international protestant cause and Leicester's own ambition to lead it. The result was conflict and bitter disappointment, as the ardent protestant parliamentarians experienced in 1576 when they put their allegiance to the international protestant republic before their obedience to their monarch. In co-operating with her régime, they remained aware of that ideological tension, though in showing initiative in attempting to ameliorate it they were hardly preparing to 'seize the initiative'.

At another level, the parliament of 1576 provides further evidence of the extent of Patrick Collinson's 'monarchical republic'.[139] The manuscript and print evidence

---

[136] Lettenhove, *Relations Politiques*, viii, 355–7: John Lee to Burghley; viii, 385: Beale to Walsingham, 29 May 1576; viii, 408: Daniel Rogers's renewed offer to Orange, 15 July 1576; TNA, SP70/139, ff. 39r–40r: Edward Chester to Burghley, 20 July 1576.

[137] Lodge, *Illustrations of British History*, ii, no. clxvii, 207–8: Leicester to the earl of Shrewsbury, 8 Mar. 1581.

[138] BL, Harleian MS 1582, ff. 38r–41r.

[139] Patrick Collinson, 'The Monarchical Republic of Queen Elizabeth I', in Patrick Collinson, *Elizabethans* (2003), 31–57; *The Monarchical Republic of Early Modern England: Essays in Response to Patrick Collinson*, ed. John F. McDiarmid (Aldershot, 2007).

reviewed here testifies to the matrix within which this parliament operated: a self-conscious body of protestant public opinion, anxious to debate both in and outside parliament the long-term future of an ideological English, or even European, *res publica*, while uncomfortably aware of how that contrasted with Elizabeth's short-term, even retrospective, focus. Whether that republic should be confined within the concept of a 'public sphere' is a question for another time.[140]

Yet it did provoke a conservative reaction, supported by Hatton and evident in John Young's demand that 'vile' Englishmen must not meddle in matters above their station. Hatton also patronised that more formidable conservative, John Whitgift, already marshalling arguments for an 'imperial' conception of monarchy that condemned the 'popularity' to which the protestant 'republic' appealed through the very nature of its discourse – manuscript and print pamphlets, impassioned prophecy, rumour, tavern debate, impertinent speeches and petitions in the house of commons, even magic. By the 1590s, Archbishop Whitgift's cultural counter-revolution had penetrated into some surprising areas of life.[141] Perhaps, if we seek to explain how accusations of 'faction' proliferated in Elizabeth's last decade, we need to examine this contrast between two styles of both conceiving and conducting politics.[142]

---

[140] Peter Lake, 'The Politics of Popularity and the Public Sphere: The "Monarchical Republic" of Elizabeth I Defends Itself', in *The Politics of the Public Sphere in Early Modern England*, ed. Peter Lake and Steven Pincus (Manchester, 2007), 59–94.

[141] Peter Lake, 'The Monarchical Republic of Queen Elizabeth I (and the Fall of Archbishop Grindal) Revisited', in *The Monarchical Republic*, ed. McDiarmid, 129–47; Parry, *The Arch-Conjuror*, 207–16, 219–20.

[142] Patrick Collinson, 'The Politics of Religion and the Religion of Politics in Elizabethan England', in *This England: Essays on the English Nation and Commonwealth in the Sixteenth Century* (Manchester, 2011), 40, 43; John Guy, 'Introduction – the 1590s: The Second Reign of Elizabeth I?', in *The Reign of Elizabeth I: Court and Culture in the Last Decade*, ed. J. Guy (Cambridge, 1995), 1–19.

The Earl of Essex and Elizabethan Parliaments

PAUL E.J. HAMMER

This article challenges the old notion championed by J.E. Neale that Robert Devereux, 2nd earl of Essex (1565–1601), displayed 'megalomania' in his parliamentary patronage during the latter years of Elizabeth I's reign. In addition to surveying Essex's influence on the membership of late Elizabethan parliaments, this article addresses the likelihood that the earl was angling for the summoning of a parliament in the spring of 1601. Instead, thanks to the Essex rising of 8 February 1601, Essex himself was executed and posthumously attainted for treason at a parliament summoned in October 1601. Finally, the article speculates about the possible impact of Essex's example and political research on the 12 peers who sought to force Charles I to summon a parliament in 1640.

Keywords: Robert Devereux, 2nd earl of Essex; parliamentary patronage; Essex rising; Twelve Peers; Charles I

1

Robert Devereux, 2nd earl of Essex, has been accorded a certain notoriety in the history of Elizabethan parliaments. Thanks to his fame as a royal favourite (albeit one who had the unique distinction of ultimately being executed by Queen Elizabeth) and the survival of some of his letters concerning parliamentary patronage, Essex has often been cited as an exemplar of aggressive aristocratic intervention in the choosing of members of parliament. In his much-reprinted speech against a motion for parliamentary reform in 1822, for example, George Canning singled out Essex to demonstrate the unavoidable operation of political influence on elections even in 'the reign of Queen Elizabeth, the era to which, habitually and almost instinctively, the mind of every Englishman recurs for everything that is glorious'. According to Canning, the earl 'dictated without scruple or reserve the returns to Parliament, not only for the County of Stafford, but for every borough in the County'.[1]

In modern writings on parliamentary history, the reputation of Essex has overwhelmingly been shaped by Sir John Neale. In his influential survey of *The Elizabethan House of Commons*, Neale singled out Essex as the most immoderate and overreaching patron of parliamentary elections in the late 16th century: 'this unique peer showed the same fatal lack of moderation in parliamentary elections as in the more dramatic incidents of

---

[1] The printed version of this speech added the text of three letters from Essex relating to elections for the 1593 parliament, which Canning had not had 'at hand' when delivering the speech: *The Pamphleteer: Dedicated to Both Houses of Parliament*, xxi (1822), 240–1. Canning's speeches were much reproduced after his death. E.g., *Select Speeches of the Right Honourable George Canning*, ed. Robert Walsh (Philadelphia, PA, 1835), where the mention of Essex and his letters are printed at 349–51.

his whirlwind career'; 'it was characteristic of Essex that he could not remain content with backing his step-father'; 'his megalomania met with the repulse it deserved'.[2] Using a phrase from the earl's speech before his execution in 1601, Neale even likened his influence to a 'leprosy'.[3] In his later narrative account of Elizabethan parliaments, Neale repeated the theme, describing Essex's approach to patronage as 'a mania'.[4] This characterisation of Essex's pursuit of parliamentary patronage as excessive, and ultimately self-destructive, reflected Neale's broader judgment that the earl's youthful rashness was responsible for shattering the general political balance of Elizabethan England in the 1590s.[5] In fact, the importance which Neale attached to Essex was such that, despite his consistently hostile and dismissive judgments of the earl, he planned to write a biography of him. However, Neale never embarked upon this project because the latter part of his career was 'hijacked' by his determination to oversee a large-scale prosopographical study of the Elizabethan house of commons. Rather cruelly (but not inaccurately), Patrick Collinson observed that the final fruits of Neale's emphasis on 'biographical' history, which were embodied in the three Elizabethan volumes of the History of Parliament in 1981, 'contained much rich biographical information, [but] the last thing to emerge was a history of parliament'.[6]

Since the 1970s, Neale's interpretation of Elizabethan parliamentary history, and of Elizabethan history more generally, has, of course, been dramatically eroded. G.R Elton and Michael Graves directly challenged Neale's whiggish narrative of Elizabethan parliaments and his famous (or perhaps notorious) 'puritan choir' in the Commons.[7] Neale's

---

[2] J.E. Neale, *The Elizabethan House of Commons* (rev. edn, 1963), 56–7.

[3] Neale, *Elizabethan House of Commons*, 223, 230.

[4] J.E. Neale, *Elizabeth I and her Parliaments, 1584–1601* (1957), 243.

[5] See esp. Neale's hugely influential published lecture: 'The Elizabethan Political Scene', *Proceedings of the British Academy*, xxxiv (1952 for 1948), 97–117. An early outline of Neale's view of Essex can be seen in his famous biography, *Queen Elizabeth I* (1934), which itself may have been partly inspired by antipathy towards Lytton Strachey's controversial pyscho-historical study, *Elizabeth and Essex: A Tragic History* (1928).

[6] Patrick Collinson, 'Neale, Sir John Ernest (1890–1975)', *ODNB*. Although edited down, Neale's influence remains strongly evident in *The History of Parliament: The House of Commons, 1558–1603*, ed. P.W. Hasler (3 vols, 1981) [hereafter cited as *HPC, 1558–1603*].

[7] See esp. G.R. Elton, 'Parliament in the Sixteenth Century: Functions and Fortunes', *Historical Journal*, xxii (1979), 255–78; G.R. Elton, 'Tudor Government, the Points of Contact, 1: Parliament', *Transactions of the Royal Historical Society*, 5th ser., xxiv (1974), 183–200; G.R. Elton, *The Parliament of England, 1559–1581* (Cambridge, 1986); Michael A.R. Graves, 'Thomas Norton the Parliament Man: An Elizabethan M.P., 1559–1581', *Historical Journal*, xxiii (1980), 17–35; Michael A.R. Graves, 'The Management of the Elizabethan House of Commons: The Council's Men-of-Business', *Parliamentary History*, ii (1983), 11–38; Michael A.R. Graves, *The Tudor Parliaments: Crown, Lords and Commons, 1485–1603* (1985); Michael A.R. Graves, 'Patrons and Clients: Their Role in Sixteenth Century Parliamentary Politicking and Legislation', *Turnbull Library Record*, xviii (1985), 69–85; Michael A.R. Graves, *Elizabethan Parliaments 1559–1601* (2nd edn, Harlow, 1996); Michael A.R. Graves, 'The Common Lawyers and the Privy Council's Parliamentary Men-of-Business, 1584–1601', *Parliamentary History*, viii (1989), 189–215; Michael A.R. Graves, 'Managing Elizabethan Parliaments', in *The Parliaments of Elizabethan England*, ed. David M. Dean and Norman L. Jones (Oxford, 1990), 37–63; Michael A.R. Graves, *Thomas Norton: The Parliament Man* (Oxford, 1994). A belated partial defence of Neale's view of parliamentary politics was offered by Patrick Collinson in his 1987 Neale Memorial Lecture, which was published as 'Puritans, Men of Business and Elizabethan Parliaments', *Parliamentary History*, vii (1988), 187–211. Cf. Michael A.R. Graves, 'Elizabethan Men of Business Reconsidered', *Parergon*, xiv (1996), 111–27.

heavy-handed emphasis on factionalism, with its excessive reliance upon evidence from the final years of Elizabeth's reign, has also been severely qualified by subsequent scholarship.[8] Even more dramatic has been the reinterpretation of the earl of Essex himself. No longer is Essex seen as a kind of playboy figure, whose ultimate failure was predetermined by his supposed rashness and lack of political competence. Instead, Essex has increasingly emerged as a serious, committed and notably popular aristocratic leader who was executed for treason after losing a prolonged political struggle about war policy and positioning for the looming crisis over the royal succession, which Elizabeth's adamant refusal to nominate an heir during her own lifetime seemed to make inevitable.[9]

The changes in historical scholarship on Elizabeth's reign over the past four decades leave our understanding of Essex's involvement in parliament in an awkward position. On the one hand, there is now a radically-altered appreciation of Essex and his significance in Elizabethan politics and political culture from that which still obtained even in the 1980s. On the other hand, almost the only published work on Essex and parliament remains that of Neale or publications strongly influenced by him.[10] This article seeks to revisit the connection between Essex and parliament, challenging the lingering image of him as a parliamentary patron driven by 'megalomania'. In place of the old Nealean narrative, it suggests a more complex and mixed picture of Essex's parliamentary patronage, with its peak coming in 1592–3, not 1597. In its second half, this article examines the hopes which Essex and his supporters placed in the projected calling of a parliament in early 1601. This event never took place, but the ideas which drove Essex and knowledge of his failure may have had previously-unsuspected resonances in the actions which culminated in the calling of the Long Parliament in 1640.

---

[8] See esp. the work of Simon Adams, such as *Leicester and the Court: Essays on Elizabethan Politics* (Manchester, 2002); Simon Adams, 'Eliza Enthroned? The Court and its Politics', in *The Reign of Elizabeth I*, ed. Christopher Haigh (Basingstoke, 1984), 55–77; Simon Adams, 'Faction, Clientage and Party: English Politics, 1550–1603', *History Today*, xxxii, No. 12 (Dec. 1982), 33–9. See also *The Reign of Elizabeth I: Court and Culture in the Last Decade*, ed. J. Guy (Cambridge, 1995), esp. the essays by Simon Adams, Paul E.J. Hammer and Natalie Mears.

[9] See, e.g., Paul E.J. Hammer, *The Polarisation of Elizabethan Politics: The Political Career of Robert Devereux, Second Earl of Essex 1585–1597* (Cambridge, 1999); Paul E.J. Hammer, 'The Smiling Crocodile: The Earl of Essex and Late-Elizabethan "Popularity" ', in *The Politics of the Public Sphere in Early Modern England*, ed. Peter Lake and Steven Pincus (Manchester, 2007), 95–115; Paul E.J. Hammer, 'The Uses of Scholarship: The Secretariat of Robert Devereux, Second Earl of Essex *c.*1585–1601', *English Historical Review*, cix (1994), 26–51; Alexandra Gajda, '*The state of Christendom*: History, Political Thought and the Essex Circle', *Historical Research*, lxxxi (2008), 423–46; Alexandra Gajda, *The Earl of Essex and Late Elizabethan Political Culture* (Oxford, 2012); Roy Strong, 'Faces of a Favourite: Robert Devereux, 2nd Earl of Essex, and the Uses of Portraiture', *British Art Journal*, v, 2 (2004), 80–90; R.C. McCoy, ' "A dangerous image": The Earl of Essex and Elizabethan Chivalry', *Journal of Medieval and Renaissance Studies*, xiii (1983), 313–29; L.W. Henry, 'The Earl of Essex as Strategist and Military Organizer (1596–7)', *English Historical Review*, lxviii (1953), 363–93.

[10] In addition to Neale's own writings and the 1981 History of Parliament volumes edited by Hasler, note also A.H. Dodd, 'North Wales in the Essex Revolt of 1601', *English Historical Review*, lix (1944), 348–70. The latter provides important context for the contested elections in Denbighshire of 1588 and 1601, which Neale had discussed in 'Three Elizabethan Elections', *English Historical Review*, xlvi (1931), 209–38. Neale's work was based upon original research by his student (and, later, his wife), Elfreda Skelton. Dodd himself not only wrote numerous entries on Welsh subjects for the Hasler volumes, but also contributed an essay to the festschrift for Neale: 'Mr. Myddelton, the Merchant of Tower Street', in *Elizabethan Government and Society: Essays Presented to Sir John Neale*, ed. S.T. Bindoff et al. (1961), 249–81.

2

According to P.W. Hasler: 'where so many statements [in Elizabethan parliamentary history] have to be qualified, where so much remains obscure, it may be stated unequivocally that Essex was the one man in this period, not excepting his great political rival, Sir Robert Cecil, with whom parliamentary patronage became an obsession'.[11] Hasler also notes (following Neale) that Essex's concern with parliamentary elections drew him to anticipate the practice of later centuries both by collecting the high stewardships of parliamentary boroughs and by exploiting his strong political position in Wales to ensure the election of his followers in Welsh constituencies.[12] The general thrust of Hasler's statements may be correct, but such emphatically 'unequivocal' judgments risk pushing the evidence rather too far. At the very least, this characterisation of Essex and Elizabethan parliaments requires qualification.

In some ways, the emphasis which Neale and Hasler place upon Essex's aggressive pursuit of parliamentary seats is itself based upon a false (or, at least, oversimplified) understanding of the nature of patronage in Elizabethan England. While great patrons like Essex might sometimes actively seek parliamentary seats for their own political reasons, the initiative for these requests often seems to have come from the gentlemen who were seeking to become MPs (for example, to avoid arrest for debt). While the accounts of Neale and Hasler imply that Essex sought to impose candidates of his own choosing on as many constituencies as possible, it seems more likely that Essex was usually responding to multiple requests from individual gentlemen for a parliamentary seat and was consequently forced to utilise any opportunities that might be open to him to gratify these requests. In most cases, borough officials were also very willing to please an influential nobleman like Essex, especially if it relieved them of the need to pay wages for one or both burgesses for the forthcoming parliamentary session.[13]

Because he focused specifically on parliamentary history, Neale observed that Essex collected the high stewardships of numerous parliamentary boroughs across the realm and drew the conclusion that the earl did so for the specific purpose of accumulating opportunities for parliamentary patronage. However, Essex also accepted other similar local offices which had no direct connection with parliament, such as the supervisorship of the mustering of all the tenants of the dean and chapter of Canterbury or the stewardship of the manors of Trinity College, Cambridge. The opportunity occasionally to nominate one or more burgesses for a parliament was only one of a range of benefits which accrued to Essex for accepting such local offices. As a military man, and frequent commander of overseas expeditions during the 1590s, Essex may well have been equally interested in the influence which these offices gave him in raising troops for his expeditions.[14] Moreover, these offices were offered to him by local notables who expected to advance their own political interests by creating a formal association with Essex. Essex's appointment as high steward at Hereford in 1597, for example, arose from

---

[11] *HPC, 1558–1603*, i, 63.

[12] *HPC, 1558–1603*, i, 64; Neale, *Elizabethan House of Commons*, 223ff.

[13] For an extended discussion of Essex's patronage (and especially the 'upward' pressure on him from current and would-be clients), see Hammer, *Polarisation*, esp. 269–315.

[14] Hammer, *Polarisation*, 277.

a local factional struggle and brought him no ability to nominate burgesses there, while a small local oligarchy at Newcastle-upon-Tyne instituted the payment of annuity to Essex with an eye to ensuring his support protecting their monopoly over the lucrative coalmining business.[15] Despite the clear and simple narrative offered by the Nealean view of Essex, the exercise of patronage was a much more complex (and often a more contingent) affair than this narrative suggests.

Essex first intervened to ensure the return of a member of parliament in 1584, when he requested the election of John Breton as a burgess for Tamworth.[16] At the time, Essex was only 18 years old and still under royal wardship. In 1586, newly freed from wardship by a knighthood on the battlefield, Essex apparently nominated two MPs.[17] When writs were sent out for the next parliament at the end of 1588, Essex's position had been transformed. Not only had he played a prominent role in the great military mobilisation against Spain's *Gran Armada* over the summer, but the recent death of his stepfather, Robert Dudley, earl of Leicester, Elizabeth's great favourite, placed a new burden of expectation upon him from former adherents of Leicester.[18] When the new parliament assembled in February 1589, the Commons included at least five burgesses directly nominated by Essex and two knights of the shire who were clearly elected by his influence.[19] Another two knights of the shire had probably had their own electoral prospects boosted by the earl's endorsement, while two more burgesses were servants of his who were returned for boroughs dominated by other patrons.[20] Presumably, Essex requested the return of these servants, or at least approved their approaches to the borough patrons concerned.[21]

Essex's efforts in 1588–9 were significant for a young nobleman who was not a member of the privy council. However, when the next parliament was called for February 1593, Essex was determined to secure the return of a far more impressive contingent of MPs. In part, he may have been concerned to ensure strong support for

[15] *HPC, 1558–1603*, i, 175, 221–2; *The History of Parliament: The House of Commons, 1604–1629*, ed. Andrew Thrush and John P. Ferris (6 vols, Cambridge, 2010), ii, 170–1, 302–3; W.J. Tighe, 'Courtiers and Politics in Elizabethan Herefordshire: Sir James Croft, his Friends and his Foes', *Historical Journal*, xxxii (1989), 257–79.

[16] *HPC, 1558–1603*, i, 244, 484. The reasons for Essex's backing for Breton remain mysterious, especially as it meant that Essex's own servant, Richard Broughton, who was recorder for the borough, was denied a seat (*HPC, 1558–1603*, i, 498).

[17] Richard Broughton at Lichfield (perhaps partially making amends for 1584) and Walter Bagot at Tamworth. Both were long-time gentlemen servants of Essex and his family (*HPC, 1558–1603*, i, 385–6, 498).

[18] Hammer, *Polarisation*, 76ff.

[19] Henry Bourchier (Stafford), Richard Broughton (Lichfield), Edward Devereux (Tamworth), Robert Wright (Tamworth), Gelly Meyrick (Carmarthen Boroughs), George Devereux (Pembrokeshire), and Herbert Croft (Carmarthenshire). Details of these men and those mentioned below can be found in the relevant constituency and personal articles of *HPC, 1558–1603*.

[20] The two knights of the shire were Thomas Gerard I and Sir Walter Harcourt, both of whom were elected for Staffordshire. Both men had sufficient property and status to represent the county on multiple occasions, but were known to be supporters of Essex in the earl's native county. The two burgesses were Thomas Crompton II (Steyning) and Thomas Smith (Cricklade). Crompton was a lawyer who served Essex in numerous property transactions, while Smith was his senior secretary.

[21] The patron at Cricklade was Giles Brydges, 3rd Baron Chandos, while that at Steyning was probably Essex's 'cousin' and fellow veteran of the Low Countries' war, Sir Thomas Sherley (spelled as Shirley in the Hasler volumes). Chandos was a friend of long standing to Leicester and Essex subsequently became close to Chandos's family in the 1590s.

a bill to restore in blood his brother-in-law, Sir Thomas Perrot.[22] More importantly, though, Essex expected to be elevated to the council.[23] By demonstrating the growing power of his patronage in the new parliament, he clearly hoped to confirm Elizabeth's decision by a conspicuous demonstration of his rising political significance in the realm. He was also fully supportive of the council's objective of securing a substantial boost in war funding from the new parliament. As a result, no fewer than 15 burgesses were returned through Essex's direct patronage in 1593, along with at least two (and possibly four) knights of the shire.[24] At least two more burgesses were elected by Essex's intercession with other patrons.[25]

In many ways, the 1593 parliament showed Essex at his most aggressive as an electoral patron. The letters cited by Canning in 1822 all relate to elections in 1593. A letter of 31 December 1592, directed by Essex to his three leading gentlemen followers in Staffordshire, lists the six men whom he has nominated at four boroughs in the county.[26] A second letter, dated two days later, expresses Essex's 'exceeding desire' that his stepfather, Sir Christopher Blount, should be elected as a knight of the shire for Staffordshire. The postscript to this letter has been much quoted to demonstrate what Neale extravagantly termed as Essex's 'megalomania': 'I perswade myself thatt my creditt is so good with my contrymen as the using of my name in so small a matter wilbe enough to effect yt, butt yett I pray yow use me so kindly in yt as I take no repulse.'[27]

---

[22] Sir John Perrot, Sir Thomas's father and a former lord deputy of Ireland, was condemned for treason in April 1592 and died as a prisoner in the Tower five months later. In the event, the Bill for the Restoration of Sir Thomas Perrot arrived in the parliament already bearing the sign manual and passed both Houses in only four days: David Dean, *Law-Making and Society in Late Elizabethan England: The Parliament of England, 1584–1601* (Cambridge, 1996), 218; *HPC, 1558–1603*, iii, 208.

[23] Essex took his oath as a privy councillor on the afternoon of 25 Feb. 1593, six days after the opening of the parliament: Hammer, *Polarisation*, 119.

[24] Sir Thomas Baskerville (Carmarthen Boroughs), Henry Bourchier (Stafford), Richard Broughton (Lichfield), Sir Conyers Clifford (Pembroke Boroughs), Sir Nicholas Clifford (Haverfordwest), Thomas Crompton II (New Radnor Boroughs), Sir Ferdinando Gorges (Cardigan Boroughs), Dr John James (Newcastle-under-Lyme), Sir Matthew Morgan (Brecon Boroughs), Henry Savile (Dunwich), Thomas Smith (Tamworth), Sir Francis Vere (Leominster), Charles Wednester (Reading), Sir John Wingfield (Lichfield), and Robert Wright (Shrewsbury). In addition, the return of John Ferrers at Tamworth (who had a family interest in the borough) was approved, if not necessarily supported, by Essex. Sir Christopher Blount (Staffordshire) and Sir Thomas Perrot (Pembrokeshire) relied heavily on Essex's support for their election. As in 1589, Sir Walter Harcourt's election for Staffordshire was at least significantly assisted by Essex's backing. Sir Thomas Coningsby's election as the senior knight of the shire for Herefordshire may also have been aided by Essex, under whom Coningsby had served during the Rouen campaign of 1591–2. Before his connection with Essex, Coningsby's ambitions in Herefordshire had been thwarted by the Croft family: Tighe, 'Courtiers and Politics in Elizabethan Herefordshire'.

[25] Anthony Bacon at Wallingford and Richard Theakston at Whitchurch. Wallingford was controlled by Essex's maternal grandfather, Sir Francis Knollys. Hasler's article on the constituency of Whitchurch, which was owned by the dean and chapter of Winchester, misses the crucial point that the dean of Winchester, Martin Heton, was a client of Essex: *HPC, 1558–1603*, i, 172–3; Brett Usher, 'Heton, Martin (1554–1609)', *ODNB*.

[26] The version of all three letters included with the printed version of Canning's speech (*Pamphleteer*, xxi, 240–1) describes them as being addressed only to Richard Bagot, Esq. This error is also repeated, e.g., in *Lives and Letters of the Devereux Earls of Essex*, ed. Walter Bourchier Devereux (2 vols, 1853), i, 280–2. Presumably, this reflects from a common source deriving from Blithefield, the home of the Bagots. In fact, the three letters were all addressed to Sir Edward Littleton (of Pillaton), Sir Edward Aston, and Bagot. They now survive as Folger Shakespeare Library, Washington, DC, Bagot Family Papers, MSS L.a.468–70.

[27] Folger Lib., MS L.a.469.

Essex's third letter, a week later, urged the recipients to work for the election of Sir Thomas Gerard as the county's other knight of the shire and repeated the injunction from the previous letter: 'I should thinke my credicte little in my owne cuntrie if I should not afford so smale a matter as this, esspeciallie the men beinge so fit.'[28] Unfortunately, this request conflicted with the desire for re-election in 1593 of Sir Walter Harcourt, Gerard's colleague in 1589 and another Essexian. In the end, Gerard's extensive estates in Lancashire enabled him to win election as a knight of the shire there, leaving the two places in Staffordshire to Blount and Harcourt.[29] This outcome demonstrated both that Essex really did have 'credicte . . . in my owne cuntrie' in early 1593 and that a number of partisans of the earl, like Gerard, were able to find seats for themselves in the parliament using their own local political resources.

Essex reinforced the impression by this demonstration of his ability to return men to parliament with his own purposeful behaviour in the Lords. In February 1593, the newest addition to the privy council showed that he could be a true parliament man: 'hys lordship is become a newe man, cleare forsakinge all hys former youthfull trickes, cariinge hymsealf with very honorable gravyty and singulerly lyked of boath in Parliament and at [the] Counsayle table, both for his speeches & judgment'; 'every forenone betwen vi & viii his lordship is in the higher Parliament house & in the afternones upon comittees for the better pennyng & amendment of matter in bills of importance'.[30] Essex also later stood up to the queen when she singled out some MPs for their complaining speeches in the debates in the Commons on the Subsidy Bill: 'I told her yf yow did err in any thing yow were no heretick, for yow did reforme yourself unto her will as soone as yow did understand yt. I told her yt was an ill example to other men thatt for one displeasure or misconceyte all the merite & service of a man's lyfe shold be overthrown.'[31] In a dramatic change from his attendance patterns at previous parliaments, Essex also made himself almost omnipresent in 1593, attending 91% of the sittings in that parliament.[32]

3

According to the interpretation of Essex's parliamentary patronage which has been shaped by Neale, the calling of the next parliament in 1597 saw a further escalation of the earl's 'megalomania'. Indeed, Neale argued that Essex's pursuit of nominations for parliamentary seats was so aggressive in 1597 that Sir Robert Cecil felt compelled to mount a co-ordinated response. Cecil, the principal secretary of state, was commonly perceived as the earl's chief rival for future dominance of the council and became the

[28] Folger Lib., MS L.a.470.

[29] *HPC, 1558–1603*, i, 186–7, 239.

[30] Folger Lib., MS L.a.45, 269.

[31] Hatfield House, Cecil Papers, CP 19/65 (cal. in HMC, *Salisbury MSS*, iv, 452–3). For Unton's part in the subsidy debate, see Neale, *Elizabeth I and her Parliaments, 1584–1601*, 303–4, 306–8, 312.

[32] Essex first took his seat in the Lords on 23 Feb. 1587. He subsequently attended 30% of the remaining sittings in that session. In 1589, he attended 63% of the sittings. All these figures are calculated against the total number of sittings for which the clerk recorded attendance. On some occasions, the clerk failed to enter attendance into the Lords journal: Hammer, *Polarisation*, 122.

central figure in the anti-Essex coalition which emerged at Elizabeth's court in the late 1590s. In addition to drawing upon the parliamentary patronage in his own hands as chancellor of the duchy of Lancaster, Cecil sent out numerous letters to other parliamentary patrons across the realm, asking them to transfer their nominations to him. This tactic by Cecil broke with previous Elizabethan political practice by 'organizing and canalizing nominations' – a policy which Neale condemned as 'the antithesis of high Elizabethan practice' and a 'noxious' foretaste of what he regarded as the 'vulgar corruption and 'foul elections' of the early Stuart period.[33] Essex's feverish pursuit of parliamentary patronage again in 1597, therefore, supposedly triggered a reaction from his political rivals (and especially from Sir Robert Cecil) which had a more lasting and powerful impact on English politics and political culture than Essex's own efforts.

Unfortunately, there are numerous problems with this analysis, even aside from Neale's notably censorious views of post-Elizabethan politics. For a start, the high-water mark of Essex's parliamentary patronage arguably came in 1592–3, not in 1597. When a new parliament was called in late 1597, Essex and most of his large military following were occupied in trying to resurrect an amphibious expedition aimed at attacking the Spanish fleet at Ferrol. Essex's force originally set sail in July, but was damaged and driven home again by a fierce storm. It took six weeks and the dismissal of most of the army before the fleet was ready to sail again on 17 August. This second sailing also hit storms, which cost it any chance of attacking Ferrol, and the expedition ended up as an unplanned voyage to the Azores in the hope of capturing a Spanish treasure fleet inbound from the New World. Essex did not return to Plymouth until late October.[34]

Essex certainly knew before he set sail for Spain that Elizabeth intended to call a parliament soon. In an undated letter, which may have been written in June or July 1597, Sir Robert Cecil assured Essex that 'I will do all in me to keepe the Parliament from beginning tyll you may be retorned, for before the xijth of October I have told the Queen wilbe to soone. It can not be worse for your freends and I am resolved in my sowle it shall not be for me, whom no devise nor humour shall make a changeling.'[35] In mid-August, Cecil informed Essex that the parliament would now start on 8 November.[36] Essex himself urged Cecil that it would be 'inconvenient' for the parliament to meet before the outcome of his impending expedition was known, especially as he foresaw difficulties if the queen sought 'extraordinary meanes to maintayne the warres' by seeking approval for a new large grant of multiple subsidies. A similar demand in the 1593 parliament had caused loud complaints in the Commons, a brief stand-off with the Lords and a heavy-handed intervention by the queen. Essex feared a repeat if

[33] Neale, *Elizabethan House of Commons*, 233–5.

[34] Paul E.J. Hammer, *Elizabeth's Wars: War, Government and Society in Tudor England, 1544–1604* (Basingstoke, 2003), 200–4.

[35] TNA, SP12/264/5, f. 7r. Cecil's letter (which is written entirely in his own hand) refers to newly-arrived intelligence from Brussels. Unfortunately, this (nearly illegible) intelligence report is itself undated: TNA, SP77/5, f. 225Br.

[36] TNA, SP12/264/67, f. 97r. This holograph letter by Cecil is misdated in *CSP Dom., 1595–7*, where it is assigned a date of 'July?' (p. 482). The correct mid-August dating is fixed by Cecil's mention of the letters carried by Sir Anthony Sherley, whom Essex had sent to court from Plymouth on Thursday, 11 August: Hatfield House, CP 54/39 (cal. in HMC, *Salisbury MSS*, vii, 350). Citations from the Cecil Papers are made with the gracious permission of the marquess of Salisbury.

the same approach was adopted in 1597: 'I feare yow will find yt was not well
forethowght of.'[37] Despite (or perhaps because of) such concerns, Essex had already
begun preparing for the new parliament.

On the previous day, 13 August, he wrote to the town authorities at Shrewsbury to
request the nomination of their two burgesses for the impending parliament. Essex
assured them that he would be returned from his expedition by the time nominations
were required. Since his departure was imminent, he asked the Shrewsbury bailiffs and
aldermen to signify their answer to his secretary, Edward Reynoldes, who would remain
at court to oversee his interests during his absence.[38] As it happened, the start of the
parliament was soon brought forward to 24 October, while Essex's frustrating expedition continued far longer than expected or planned.[39] Although the earl had undoubtedly left some instructions to cover this eventuality, it put Reynoldes in a difficult
position, especially as some of those gentlemen whom Essex would have wanted to see
chosen as MPs were still at sea with him when the returns were made. Reynoldes,
therefore, had to do the best he could. These efforts resulted in the return of some 11
MPs (including Reynoldes himself) for borough seats and two knights of the shire.[40] At
least two more men won county seats, by utilising their association with Essex to
reinforce their own local standing.[41] Another three men probably also owed their
borough seats to the earl's patronage, although each of these cases involves a degree of
uncertainty which may reflect organisational confusion deriving from Essex's absence.[42]
Finally, Essex's original secretary, Thomas Smith, no longer needed to find a seat,
because he was appointed clerk of the parliaments in 1597.[43]

[37] Hatfield House, CP 54/47 (cal. in HMC, *Salisbury MSS*, vii, 352). For the 1593 Subsidy Bill problems,
see Neale, *Elizabeth I and her Parliaments, 1584–1601*, 298–312.

[38] HMC, *5th Report*, Appendix, 342. The fleet began its embarkation on 14 August. For Edward
Reynoldes, see Paul E.J. Hammer, 'Reynoldes, Edward (d. 1623)', *ODNB*.

[39] The final date of 24 October, when the 1597 parliament did actually begin, was known no later than
21 August: Hatfield House, CP 54/75 (cal. in HMC, *Salibury MSS*, vii, 361).

[40] Arthur Atye (Dunwich), Anthony Bacon (Oxford), Francis Bacon (Ipswich), Henry Bourchier (Stafford),
William Fowkes (Lichfield), Henry Lindley (Newcastle-upon-Tyne), Joseph Oldsworth (Lichfield), James
Perrot (Haverfordwest), Thomas Rawlins (Cardigan Boroughs), Edward Reynoldes (Andover), William
Temple (Tamworth), Sir Christopher Blount (Staffordshire), and Sir Gelly Meyrick (Pembrokeshire).

[41] Sir Thomas Coningsby (Herefordshire) and John Lloyd (Denbighshire).

[42] Thomas Crompton II was returned both at Leominster and Beverley. Crompton was a trusted servant
of Essex and the earl was high steward at Leominster, while Crompton himself was steward at Beverley. It
is unclear which seat he took. Sir Oliver Lambert was a military comrade of Essex and was returned at
Southampton, where the earl had influence by virtue of his sweet wines monopoly. However, Lambert was
a native of Southampton and was able to take the seat only at the last minute because Essex's original choice,
Francis Bacon, chose to represent Ipswich (where he also seems to have been nominated by Essex). Nicholas
Trott was returned at Bramber, but seems to have had only rather tenuous ties to the earl himself (*HPC,
1558–1603*, i, 171, 248–9, 256–7, 262, 285, 680–1; ii, 433–4; iii, 531–2). For Trott, see also below, note 47.

[43] Smith had formally moved from Essex's service to royal service in 1595, when he became a clerk of the
privy council. This entailed a close working relationship with Sir Robert Cecil, who secured the clerkship of
the parliaments for him while Essex was still absent on the Azores expedition: Paul E.J. Hammer, 'Smith, Sir
Thomas (c.1556–1609)', *ODNB*; Hammer, 'Uses of Scholarship', esp. 28, 33. With Essex absent, Smith's
appointment as clerk of the parliaments in 1597 was facilitated by Cecil: Hatfield House, CP 53/30 (cal. in
HMC, *Salisbury MSS*, vii, 299). Neale's assertion that Smith won the post 'through his master's [i.e., Essex's]
unscrupulous pressure' is inaccurate: Neale, *Elizabeth I and her Parliaments, 1584–1601*, 332.

The circumstances of the 1597–8 parliament meant that the group of MPs associated with Essex in that parliament were notably different from those in the 1593 parliament. In 1593, the most striking feature was the number of highly-prominent military men returned by Essex's influence: Sir Thomas Baskerville, Sir Christopher Blount, Sir Conyers Clifford, Sir Nicholas Clifford, Sir Thomas Coningsby, Sir Ferdinando Gorges, Sir Walter Harcourt, Sir Matthew Morgan, Sir Francis Vere, and Sir John Wingfield – a veritable who's-who of the Elizabethan military establishment in the early 1590s.[44] Essex's brother-in-law, Sir Thomas Perrot, was perhaps another, slightly less militarily-eminent member of this group. Most of these battlefield knights served on committees in the Commons for the Subsidy Bill or for relief of maimed soldiers and sailors. In 1597, by contrast, this overwhelming military presence among the earl's nominees was absent. Several of the 1593 men were dead, while others were serving with Essex on the Azores voyage or elsewhere.[45] Other officers who might have replenished the ranks of Essex's parliamentary following in 1597 were similarly occupied in serving with Essex at sea. This meant that many of those nominated in Essex's name in 1597 were men chiefly notable for their friendship with Edward Reynoldes. They included eight servants of Essex,[46] Anthony and Francis Bacon (who were close friends both of Essex and Reynoldes), Arthur Atye, a former secretary to Leicester and friend to Reynoldes and Anthony Bacon, and Nicholas Trott, who was a friend of the Bacon brothers (especially Anthony) and whose return was probably arranged by Reynoldes at Anthony's request.[47]

The confusion surrounding Essex's involvement with the 1597–8 parliament continued after his return to England at the end of October. Although the session opened on 24 October, 'through the negligence of the messenger unto whom the same was delivered', Essex did not receive his writ of summons until 17 November.[48] By this time, however, he was claiming to be too ill to attend. Essex may have had some residual health problems after his exhausting military efforts, but the chief reason for his prolonged absence from attendance in the Lords was his anger at the recent creation of the lord admiral as earl of Nottingham, partly on the basis of a military victory at Cadiz in 1596, for which Essex himself had long claimed the prime credit. Like Sir Robert

---

[44] The chief omissions were officers associated with Sir John Norris, a lesser, but rival, military patron to Essex in these years.

[45] Sir Thomas Baskerville, Sir Nicholas Clifford, Sir John Wingfield, and Sir Thomas Perrot were dead by late 1597. Sir Conyers Clifford was in Ireland and Sir Matthew Morgan was in the Low Countries, while Sir Christopher Blount and Sir Francis Vere joined the Azores voyage.

[46] Thomas Crompton II, William Fowkes, Henry Lindley, Sir Gelly Meyrick (despite his absence on the Azores voyage), Joseph Oldsworth, Thomas Rawlins, William Temple, and Edward Reynoldes himself.

[47] The close friendship between Reynoldes and the Bacon brothers (especially Anthony), and their connection to Atye (or Atey) and Trott, is most readily seen in the Anthony Bacon Papers now at Lambeth Palace Library (MSS 647–62). Extensive excerpts from these papers were published in Thomas Birch, *Memoirs of the Reign of Queen Elizabeth from the Year 1581 till her Death* (2 vols, 1754). In the case of Trott, Reynoldes may have approached Lord Buckhurst for a seat at Bramber at the request of Anthony Bacon, albeit in Essex's name. In late 1597, Reynoldes was busy (along with Henry Lindley) in ensuring that Essex's crucial customs farm of sweet wines would be renewed: Hammer, 'Uses of Scholarship', 40; Hammer, *Polarisation*, 77, 227, 229, 322. This entailed considerable contact with Buckhurst, who was increasingly acting as Lord Burghley's understudy as lord treasurer. Like Sir Robert Cecil with Sir Thomas Smith's suit for the clerkship of the parliaments, Buckhurst was also eager to do small favours for Essex during the summer and autumn of 1597 to demonstrate his continued goodwill towards the absent earl.

[48] *LJ*, ii, 198.

Cecil's sudden appointment as chancellor of the duchy of Lancaster in early October, this important decision by Elizabeth during his absence infuriated Essex and his follow-ers. The queen's maladroit handling of the lord admiral's promotion embittered relations at court and on the council and prompted Essex effectively to boycott the parliament, which further exacerbated matters with the queen and his conciliar colleagues. In the end, Elizabeth agreed to restore Essex's superiority over the lord admiral by creating him earl marshal on 28 December. As a result, Essex finally threw himself into business in the Lords after the parliament reconvened on 11 January 1598 and became a zealous attender for the final 12 sittings of the session.[49]

The 1597–8 parliament was the last assembly called during Essex's lifetime. When a parliament next met, at the end of October 1601, it was eight months after Essex's execution for treason. This would prove to be the final parliament of Elizabeth's reign. Essex's record of parliamentary patronage was certainly impressive by Elizabethan stand-ards, but it was also brief – really only two parliaments (in 1593 and 1597), the second of which was elected in his absence and on which his influence was distinctly limited. It also seems hard to endorse P.W. Hasler's judgment that Essex was 'unequivocally . . . the one man in this period . . . with whom parliamentary patronage became an obsession'. Essex may have been the first high steward of Ipswich to nominate an outsider as an MP for the borough, but he failed to use comparable local offices to secure any nominations at Hereford, Maldon, or Great Yarmouth. Presumably because of his absence abroad at the time, Essex (or, perhaps, Edward Reynoldes acting in his name) also failed to repeat his previous successes at Newcastle-under-Lyme and Reading in 1597. Essex's request to Shrewsbury, before he set sail in 1597, also failed to repeat his previous success in securing the nomination of an MP for that town. Essex's mother, the dowager countess of Leicester, was also convinced that his absence had allowed her husband, Sir Christopher Blount, to be belittled by being elected as only the junior knight of the shire for Staffordshire.[50]

If the claims about Essex's parliamentary patronage are exaggerated, what about Neale's assertion that Sir Robert Cecil felt driven by Essex's example to muster an unprecedented number of nominations in 1597? Even before his appointment as chan-cellor of the duchy of Lancaster on 8 October (which brought its own very substantial patronage resources), Cecil seems to have sent out a large number of letters seeking the choice of nominations held by other patrons. Although he sent a request for one or both nominations at East Grinstead by the middle of September, his letter did not arrive until the burgesses there had already been elected. Similar requests by Cecil directed to Colchester and Stockbridge over the following weeks proved similarly untimely.[51] Requests to other patrons to give him their nominations also produced mixed results. Lord Cobham, Cecil's former brother-in-law and newly appointed as warden of the Cinque Ports, promised him the use of his single nomination at New Romney. A general request to the archbishop of York also secured a single nomination at Ripon.[52]

---

[49] Hammer, *Polarisation*, 122–3, 384–8.

[50] *HPC, 1558–1603*, i, 240–1; Warwickshire RO, MI 229, item no. 39: Lettice countess of Leicester to earl of Essex, [Nov. 1597].

[51] HMC, *Salisbury MSS*, vii, 385, 415, 432.

[52] HMC, *Salisbury MSS*, vii, 404, 429.

On the other hand, a similar letter to the bishop of Durham prompted the startled response that the county palatine had never had any representation in the parliaments of England.[53] Another awkward error occurred at Doncaster, where Cecil sought to use his office as high steward to nominate burgesses, only to be informed that 'their towne auncientlie had made burgesses', but none had sat in parliament in recent times.[54] Such missteps suggest the very broad net which Cecil was casting for seats in 1597. This effort certainly brought results. In the 1597 parliament, at least 30 MPs took their seats through Cecil's efforts, while a similar number did so in the 1601 parliament.[55]

Neale seems correct in suggesting that Sir Robert Cecil dramatically escalated his efforts to secure parliamentary patronage in 1597. However, Neale's claim that Cecil launched this effort as a direct counter to Essex's pursuit of parliamentary patronage seems much less compelling. While Cecil and some of his allies (most notably, Lord Cobham, who was a bitter personal enemy of Essex) may have been determined to ensure that their own adherents in the Commons would be a more conspicuous and impressive group than those associated with Essex, the earl's absence from the realm throughout the whole period when MPs were being chosen makes this speculative interpretation seem unconvincing as Cecil's primary motive.[56] A more plausible explanation would be the warning which Essex offered Cecil in his letter of 14 August: 'looke abowt yow to provide extraordinary meanes to maintayne the warres'. Cecil himself had introduced the Subsidy Bill at the 1593 parliament and would have remembered only too well the acrimony which it had provoked. Given the queen's need for substantial new war funding in 1597, the desire for greater support in the Commons seems a more likely explanation for Cecil's new electoral tactics in the autumn of 1597 than the factional animosity towards Essex, which only really exploded after Essex's return to England at the end of October.

4

The preceding discussion shows that Essex could mobilise significant influence on the composition of the house of commons, as he did in 1592–3. However, he was less successful in 1597, both in terms of the number of MPs chosen through his patronage and in the social standing and prestige of those MPs. With Essex and many of his chief military dependents absent from the realm, the motley group of Devereux servants and friends of Edward Reynoldes elected in 1597 were notably less distinguished than the

[53] Hatfield House, CP 55/82 (cal. in HMC, *Salisbury MSS*, vii, 405).

[54] Hatfield House, CP 56/45 (cal. in HMC, *Salisbury MSS*, vii, 442). The town had last been represented in a parliament in 1337. If Cecil's request actually encouraged an attempt to return two burgesses for Doncaster in 1597, it seems that the attempt was unsuccessful. The town tried to revive its ancient representation in 1621, when a motion was also advanced for the creation of parliamentary representation from Durham: E. De Villiers, 'Parliamentary Boroughs Restored by the House of Commons, 1621–1641', *English Historical Review*, lxvii (1952), 176–7.

[55] *HPC, 1558–1603*, i, 573–4, 575. These figures (and the names of the MPs concerned) are given in the biographical entry on Sir Robert Cecil. Remarkably, even though this entry was written by Hasler himself, the index to his Introduction for the publication fails even to list Sir Robert Cecil – an extraordinary omission.

[56] 'This, if true – and we are unfortunately reduced to speculation – would explain the counter-activities of Sir Robert Cecil': Neale, *Elizabethan House of Commons*, 231.

military officers returned with Essex's support in 1592–3. Clearly, circumstances worked against Essex's parliamentary representation in 1597. Nevertheless, the precedent of 1592–3 showed what Essex could achieve if he committed himself to making an impression on a new parliament.

Essex's track record with parliament became potentially very important in late 1600, when he was released from the prolonged period of detention which had followed his unexpected return to court from Ireland in September 1599. Essex emerged from this humiliation sequestered from the exercise of his chief offices (earl marshal, master of the ordnance, the fourth most senior member of the privy council) and banned from access to the queen at court. He was convinced that his political rivals had not only unjustly engineered his exclusion from power, but were also bent upon diverting the royal succession away from James VI of Scotland to ensure that they would control the realm after Elizabeth's death. As James's chief supporter in England, Essex calculated that his enemies were determined to prevent his return to power – and the likelihood of political payback against them which might follow – by secretly working to prevent James succeeding to the English throne. This logic was clearly apparent to Essex's most bitter opponents like Lord Cobham and Sir Walter Raleigh, as well as to Sir Robert Cecil, who played a more subtle game and sought to maintain as much flexibility as possible.[57]

In the late summer of 1600, Essex still hoped that Elizabeth would follow up on her encouraging responses to his efforts to accommodate himself to her royal wishes. However, with Coham and Raleigh still seeking to wreck his hopes, Essex looked for concrete evidence that the queen would ignore their slanders against him (as he saw it) and restore him to his former prominence at court and council. In Essex's eyes, one crucial test was Elizabeth's willingness to renew his lucrative grant of the customs farm on sweet wine imports, which lapsed at Michaelmas 1600.[58] A second test involved the rumoured calling of a new parliament, which was expected to meet about the same time. Essex not only hoped to be allowed to attend the parliament, but also to be restored to the exercise of his offices there.[59] The rumours of this new parliament were strong enough to encourage the unstable earl of Lincoln to attempt to hide himself from creditors until it met.[60] However, the parliament was not called and the queen refused to renew Essex's sweet wines grant. These blows convinced Essex that he would need to take active steps to remove his enemies from around the queen. At Christmas 1600, he wrote a letter calling upon James VI to intervene in English affairs by sending an ambassador who could finally force Elizabeth to hear Essex's detailed charges against his enemies.[61]

---

[57] For Cecil's recognition of the analysis embraced by Essex, see Leo Hicks, 'Sir Robert Cecil, Father Persons and the Succession, 1600–1601', *Archivum Historicum Societatis Jesu*, xxiv (1955), 124.

[58] Essex's efforts to reintegrate himself with royal favour in 1600 (and the bitter struggle which this triggered among his partisans) are detailed in a long account by Lord Henry Howard, which is discussed in Paul E.J. Hammer, ' "Like droppes of cold water caste into the flame": Lord Henry Howard's Notes on the Fall of the Earl of Essex', in *'In the prayse of writing': Early Modern Manuscript Studies*, ed. S.P. Cerasano and Steven W. May (2012), 70–92.

[59] Hatfield House, CP 83/108; printed in *Correspondence of King James VI of Scotland with Sir Robert Cecil and others in England during the reign of Queen Elizabeth, with an appendix containing papers illustrative of transactions between King James and Robert, Earl of Essex*, ed. J. Bruce (Camden Society, old ser., lxxviii, 1861), 107.

[60] HMC, *Salisbury MSS*, x, 312.

[61] H.G. Stafford, *James VI of Scotland the Throne of England* (New York, 1940), 214–16, 219–24.

While Essex waited for the arrival of James's ambassador, the earl of Mar, new reports circulated in January 1601 that the queen was about to summon a parliament.[62] This news raised fresh expectations with Essex and his friends that they might be able to use this opportunity, perhaps even to raise openly the same charges which were being readied for Mar's future audience with the queen. In Scotland, the reports of the impending new parliament at Westminster provided diplomatic cover to explain why James was rushing to send Mar and Edward Bruce into England.[63] If the writs had been issued, Essex and his friends would undoubtedly have sought to return even more MPs for this parliament than in 1592–3 or 1597. More importantly, Essex's urgent political need would presumably have driven him to demand of these MPs what had not been asked in the past – that they act as a distinct and active bloc in the Commons to support his political objectives. Given the number of MPs returned by means of Cecil and his allies, the confrontation in the parliament which might have ensued between the rival groups would have been truly explosive. However, before the Essexians could begin preparing for the new parliament, Elizabeth, again, changed her mind. By late January, the council finally accepted that it could not convince her to proceed with the idea.[64] With the prospect of a parliament dashed and Mar's departure from Scotland running well behind the schedule which had been set out in Essex's letter, the discussions among Essex and his inner circle of friends and followers turned to more direct action.[65]

During the early days of February 1601, Essex, his cousin the earl of Southampton, and a handful of other trusted men, began to prepare a plan for a sudden irruption into the queen's court at Whitehall. Prominent enemies of Essex would be detained at their homes, the royal guards would be disarmed to avoid any violence, and then Essex and a delegation of like-minded lords would 'humbly' petition the queen for the arrest of Cecil, Cobham and Raleigh and the restoration of Essex.[66] One subsequent account claimed that Essex sought 'to kneele before the Queen half a score noble men at the least'.[67] Another report claimed that these aristocratic petitioners would be 'I & 12 others of the greateste of the nobilitye of Englande, with many other of our noble ffreindes & kinsemen, lordes, knightes & gentlemen'.[68] This action was planned for about 15 or 16 February, but it never took place. On the preceding weekend, Essex and his co-conspirators were tricked by his enemies and spooked into a hastily improvised scheme to seek safety with the lord mayor and aldermen of London on Sunday 8 February. This plan – which has subsequently become known as the Essex rising or

---

[62] Expectations of a new parliament were current in East Anglia by 3 Jan. 1601: Bodl., MS Eng.lett.c.130, f. 145r.

[63] TNA, SP52/67, ff. 16r, 18r; David Calderwood, *The History of the Kirk of Scotland*, ed. Thomas Thomson (8 vols, Edinburgh, 1842–9), vi, 102.

[64] Northamptonshire RO, MS Winwood 1 (unfoliated): Sir Henry Neville to Ralph Winwood, 29 Jan. 1600/1: printed in *Memorials of affairs of state in the reigns of Q. Elizabeth and K. James I, collected (chiefly) from the original papers of . . . Sir Ralph Winwood*, ed. Edmund Sawyer (3 vols, 1725), i, 292.

[65] In his letter to James VI of 25 Dec. 1600, Essex had requested Mar's arrival in London by 1 February.

[66] For an overview of what follows here, see Paul E.J. Hammer, 'Shakespeare's *Richard II*, the Play of 7 February 1601, and the Essex Rising', *Shakespeare Quarterly*, lix (2008), 1–35.

[67] BL, Add. MS 64871, f. 69r.

[68] BL, Sloane MS 756, f. 8v.

Essex revolt – went disastrously wrong and resulted in Essex and some of his followers being condemned and executed for rebellion and treason.[69]

Although the crown's lawyers misconstrued and mingled together Essex's plans to claim that he intended a *coup* that was never actually planned, the interrogation of his supporters soon revealed that parliament would have played a central role in his plans. Even though Essex himself tried to deny it, his co-conspirators clearly expected that the presentation of the lords' petition to the queen and the arrest of Essex's enemies would be followed by the calling of a parliament at which the latter would be called to account.[70] As Cecil reported to the lord deputy of Ireland, this parliament would have 'condemned all those that should have been scandallized to have misgoverned the State'.[71] The attorney general, Edward Coke, even claimed that one of Essex's secretaries, Henry Cuffe, would have been chosen Speaker of the Commons for this parliament.[72] The latter suggestion may have been somewhat fanciful, but, if such a parliament had been called in these circumstances in the spring of 1601, it would undoubtedly have been very much an Essexian assembly. The impressive body of MPs whom Essex had helped to return in the 1592–3 parliament would have paled by comparison with the contingent of members he would have recruited to ensure that his political victory in successfully petitioning the queen was confirmed by parliament. This task would have been made easier by the imprisonment of Cecil and other rivals and by the eagerness of gentlemen across the realm to benefit from the consequent redistribution of royal offices and grants. Essex and his numerous aristocratic friends would also have been able to dominate the Lords. Coke and Cecil seem to have had little doubt about the likely fatal outcome of this parliament for Essex's rivals. However, neither Coke nor Cecil was willing to speculate openly about what would surely have been the most important initiative in Essex's putative parliament in the spring of 1601: a move to recognize formally the claim of James VI as Elizabeth's future successor. This was an issue which was so sensitive in 1601 that it remained unspoken. Nevertheless, the logic of Essex's appeal to James at Christmas 1600 made it inevitable that the earl would have tried to use a parliament to resolve England's long-running succession crisis by installing the Scottish king as Elizabeth's heir apparent.

All these speculations assume that Elizabeth would have accepted Essex's petition and his charges against his enemies. Given our knowledge of Elizabeth, it is by no means certain she would have done so, even after seeing the extent of Essex's support. Her refusal would have created a terrible political problem. However, as Alexandra Gajda has recently noted, Essex would surely have recognized the relevance to his needs in 1601 of a treatise which argued that a prince could legitimately be 'corrected' by drawing upon the combined authority of nobility and parliament.[73] Running to almost 300 pages in its later printed form, *The state of Christendom* was produced within what might

---

[69] *Complete Collection of State Trials*, ed T.B. Howell (33 vols, 1811–26), i, cols 1333–60, 1409–52.

[70] E.g., BL, Cotton MS Vitellius C. XVII, f. 342v; Hatfield House, CP 83/87 (cal. in HMC, *Salisbury MSS*, xi, 70).

[71] TNA, SP12/278/125, f. 247r: 'Scandallized' here means those (like Cecil himself) who would be unjustly accused.

[72] *State Trials*, ed. Howell, i, col. 1445. Cuffe had never been an MP and this suggestion seems to be an invention of Coke himself.

[73] Gajda, '*The state of Christendom*', esp. 445–6; see also Hammer, 'Shakespeare's *Richard II*', 12–13.

loosely be called Essex's extended secretariat in late 1594 or early 1595 to justify opposition to the king of Spain. It was conceived as a companion piece to Antonio Perez's autobiographical *Relaciones*, which was printed in London in 1594 for illicit dissemination in Spanish territories. An English translation of Perez's book and *The state of Christendom* were both prepared for publication in 1595, but the planned print campaign was ultimately abandoned.[74] *The state of Christendom* itself remained unpublished until 1657, when it was erroneously attributed to Sir Henry Wotton, one of Essex's secretaries in the 1590s.[75]

According to *The state of Christendom*,[76] the key to solving the problems of royal misgovernment in any state lies in its 'high court of parliament, unto which princes either can be contented, or be constrained, to submit themselves, and wherein subjects may speak unto their King freely, so they speak reverently, any thing that may benefit their country'. However, if a prince chooses not to summon a parliament (as Elizabeth did in January 1601) and if 'the outrages grow once to be so extream that they are no longer to be endured' (as Essex and his friends emphatically believed in early 1601), the nobility should 'enforce him to call a parliament'. If the nobility as a whole failed to act in this way, some bold 'confederates' must band together as 'humble petitioners unto the princes to reform such abuses as are notoriously known to be abuses'. This was precisely what Essex and his friends were planning to do in February 1601: 'wee wowld have cum to her Majestie's feet armed with papers, and not with weapons, to satisfie her Majesty and her nobilitie'.[77] The clear logic of *The state of Christendom* was that this 'humble petitioning' of Elizabeth should be followed by the calling of a parliament to confirm the removal of Essex's enemies and their 'abuses' once and for all. The ambitious plans for taking over various parts of the palace at Whitehall, which Essex's co-conspirators considered at a secret meeting at Drury House, also reflected the tract's emphasis on the crucial importance of maintaining decorum in confronting a sovereign, 'lest they [i.e., the confederates] mar a good cause with evil handling thereof'. As shown by the conduct of 'Richard Earl Marshal of England unto King Henry the Third', extreme care was required even of an earl marshal – an office which Essex still retained in February 1601.

Despite taking all possible care, those who confronted an unwilling prince with unpalatable information were inevitably committing a 'kind of violence'. As such, they might face a rebuff, 'when neither their humble suits may prevail, nor their gentle connivance or toleration mitigate the wrath, or moderate the affections, of their sovereign'. In this case, the 'confederates' must look for their protection and support to

[74] G. Ungerer, *A Spaniard in Elizabethan England: The Correspondence of Antonio Perez's Exile* (2 vols, 1974–6), ii, 249ff. The Spanish edition of the *Relaciones* was secretly printed by Richard Field in London in 1594 for dissemination in territories controlled by the king of Spain, such as Aragon and Flanders. The English translation of this work was prepared by Arthur Atye, whose return at Dunwich was arranged by Reynoldes in 1597.

[75] The treatise was printed in 1657 as *The state of Christendom: or, a most exact and curious discovery of many secret passages, and hidden mysteries of the times* (1657). A 'Supplement' discussing Perez's book was appended to the end of the main text (beginning a new pagination at sig. Aaa). *The state of Christendom* was reprinted several times in the 1660s and 1670s. In her 2008 article, Dr Gajda argued that Essex's special 'friend', Anthony Bacon, was a more probable author than Sir Henry Wotton. More recently, Dr Gajda has characterised authorship of the tract as 'a group production by members of the earl's circle, coordinated by Anthony Bacon': Gajda, *Essex and Late Elizabethan Political Culture*, 88. This seems eminently plausible.

[76] *The state of Christendom*, 201–7.

[77] BL, Add. MS 64871, f. 75v.

those noblemen 'better disposed then others', whom God will 'raise up . . . to judge of wrongs, to redress injuries, and to repress evil-disposed princes'. In the final resort, therefore, a sovereign who wilfully ignores the urgings of 'the peers of the realm' and proved to be 'evil-disposed' could be resisted with force and might even risk their crown, even in England.[78] Indeed, 'it cannot justly or truly be said that that is against the law or without law which is done by an high court of parliament'.

This ultimate sanction was very far from Essex's intention in February 1601. He and his friends believed implicitly that Elizabeth was being deluded by the 'corrupte orators'[79] who were his enemies and that she would recognize how far her regime had been harmed by their malign influence – and act decisively to change things – as soon as Essex told her what he believed to be the truth of their actions. Nevertheless, the specific medieval precedents cited in *The state of Christendom* suggest that the extraordinary size of Essex's planned aristocratic delegation to Elizabeth may have had a political significance beyond the simple desire to impress upon the queen the seriousness of the charges against his rivals. In a passage describing historical precedents for the 'chastening' of princes who permitted injustice to take hold in their realm, *The state of Christendom* notes that:

> although our Kings [i.e., of England] . . . are the greatest and most absolute Kings of the world, next unto the Kings of France, yet the barons, after the battel of Lewis, in the time of Henry the Third, ordained that two earls and a bishop elected by the commonalty should chose to them nine other persons, whereof three should always remain about the King, and by *the whole twelve* both the Court and the realm should be governed. So in the fourth year of the reign of Edward the Second, the prelates, earls and barons made Ordinances for the state and government of the realm, which because the King would neither confirm, nor allow, were confirmed by sentence of excommunication against all them that should go to break the same. So the Scotch-men in the time of John their King, being moved thereunto by his negligence, *chose twelve peers*, and four bishops, four earls, and four barons, by whose advice and counsel the King should govern the realm.[80]

If Essex and his co-conspirators took this passage seriously, the fact that he hoped to be accompanied into the queen's presence by 'tenne or twelve honorable persons whoe had just occasion of discontent, though not equall with myne'[81] may suggest that some thought was given to the possibility of issuing orders 'for the state and government of the realm' in the event that Elizabeth proved unreceptive to the lords' petition. In light of the medieval precedents cited in *The state of Christendom*, Essex and his band of aristocratic confederates might have felt that, in the final resort, they possessed the authority jointly to issue ordinances and even summon a parliament, regardless of the queen's wishes.

---

[78] Although the tract is couched as having European-wide relevance, Gajda notes that a section discussing the Aragonese revolt of 1591–2 explicitly opens the way for the notion of legitimate resistance by the nobility against a tyrannical prince to be applied to England itself: Gajda, *Essex and Late Elizabethan Political Culture*, 96–7.

[79] BL, Sloane MS 756, f. 7v.

[80] *The state of Christendom*, 206 (emphasis added).

[81] BL, Add. MS 64871, f. 69r; Stowe MS 399, f. 18r.

Ultimately, these suggestions can only be speculative, because Essex's aristocratic irruption into Elizabeth's court never took place and because the crown's investigation which followed the events of 8 February 1601 conflated the secret preparations for the former with a misconstrued understanding of the latter. There was no inquisition into which lords would have accompanied Essex to Whitehall, no interrogation of Anthony Bacon and no mention of *The state of Christendom*. By the late 1590s, the sort of claims which it advanced about the potential 'correctability' of a sovereign by their nobility, however delicately hedged around with conditions and injunctions to respectfulness, constituted a kind of political heresy. As Essex had learned to his cost over the past few years, political actions which had been acceptable earlier in the reign were now increasingly deemed to be utterly unacceptable, as the Elizabethan regime became ever more absolutist in manner and tone. Essex himself was, therefore, deliberately evasive when questioned about his plans for calling a parliament after his arrest on 8 February 1601: he knew that his own fate was already sealed, but he may have realized that giving an explicit answer would only give his enemies more ammunition against him and alert his interrogators to the ideas contained in *The state of Christendom* and the men who wrote it. Nevertheless, Essex's surviving close associates knew what he had intended and why, even if they could not say so openly. The 'true' story of Essex's thwarted plans and defeat in 1601 was relegated to libels and the deniable format of literary allusions and partisan manuscript accounts of Essex's trial.[82]

5

As noted above, Essex did not live to see Elizabeth's next (and final) parliament, which met in October 1601. He was executed on 25 February and attainted in the parliament. However, Essex's abortive plans for a parliament in the spring of 1601 may, perhaps, have had an unlikely, and hitherto unappreciated, after-life of their own. In a despatch of September 1640, the Venetian ambassador in England reported that 'several earls, barons and other leading men of the Puritan party came to this city and after secret conferences they have united to send letters to the King', urging him:

> that this kingdom has been brought to a state of most serious calamity by the sole fault of his Majesty's evil ministers and there is no remedy except the summoning of a parliament. They beg him to consent to this, otherwise they protest that they will summon it themselves, in order to escape greater trouble for their country.[83]

The 'letters' were actually a petition which was signed by 12 deeply disaffected lords at the end of August and presented to the king at York in early September.[84] The petition of the so-called 'Twelve Peers' urged that, 'for remedie ... & prevention of the daungers that my ensue to your Royall Person & to the whole state', the king should:

[82] Edited texts of the surviving libels can be found online at *Early Stuart Libels* (especially sections A, B, D, I and K): available at *http://www.earlystuartlibels.net/htdocs/index.html* (accessed 13 Dec. 2014).

[83] *CSP Ven., 1640–2*, no. 109, pp. 76–7.

[84] Charles I responded to the petition by calling a great council of peers at York, before summoning a new parliament himself which finally met at the beginning of Nov. 1640.

summon a parliament within some shorte & convenient tyme, whereby the causes of
theise & other great greivances which your people lye under may be taken away;
And the authors & counsellors of them may be brought to such legall tryall &
condigne punishment as the nature of theire severall offences shall require.[85]

Although the lords in 1640 did not share Essex's need to force his way into the court,
this otherwise seems strikingly reminiscent of the sort of 'humble petition' which Essex
and his friends had planned to present to Queen Elizabeth in February 1601.

The petition of the 'Twelve Peers' of 1640 itself offers no explicit support for the
Venetian ambassador's assertion that the lords threatened to summon a parliament
themselves if the king failed to do so. Nevertheless, Conrad Russell and John Adamson
have both argued that this claim is entirely credible, because of antiquarian research into
England's medieval past. Russell suggests that the threat reflected the peers' willingness
to revive medieval precedents and assert themselves 'as a sort of caretaker government'.
Adamson makes a more specific claim, arguing that the petitioning of the king by the
'Twelve Peers' demonstrated 'a power vested in twelve noblemen to summon a
parliament in their own right where the King failed to do so'. Adamson notes that:
'within less than a year of this discovery' of 'thirteenth century baronial powers', the
right of 12 or more lords of parliament to summon a parliament regardless of the
sovereign was given statutory force in the Triennial Act of early 1641.[86]

Russell and Adamson each support their claims by citing the same manuscript source:
part of a single page in a series of antiquarian notes by Oliver St John, a noted lawyer
and the reputed draftsman of the petition of the 'Twelve Peers'.[87] Below half a page of
notes in French about the clergy in parliament taken from a history of Richard II,
St John simply noted: 'The parliament in H3 time att Oxford that erected the 12 peares
auctoritie is called parliamentum insanum, that of H4 after lawyers excluded
parliamentum indoctum.'[88] This brief note mentions 'the 12 peares auctoritie', but does
not explain what it was. Moreover, the description of the parliament of 1258 ('the
parliament in H3 time att Oxford') is hardly a ringing endorsement of that 'auctoritie':
it is the Mad Parliament ('parliamentum insanum'). This mention of the parliament of
1258 was also far from novel. Essex's old enemy, Sir Walter Raleigh, twice mentioned
it (and at some length) in his *The prerogative of parliaments*, which was printed after his
death in multiple editions on the Continent in 1628 and which was reprinted in London
and dedicated to the parliament in 1640. Raleigh's tract also makes it clear that the
Oxford parliament would hardly be an appealing precedent for the 12 peers: 'the madde

[85] TNA, SP 16/465/16, f. 33r. The signatories were: William Cecil, 2nd earl of Exeter; Francis Russell,
4th earl of Bedford; William Seymour, 2nd earl of Hertford; Robert Devereux, 3rd earl of Essex; George
Manners, 7th earl of Rutland; Robert Rich, 2nd earl of Warwick; Oliver St John, 1st earl of Bolingbroke;
Edmund Sheffield, 1st earl of Mulgrave; William Fiennes, 1st Viscount Saye and Sele; Edward Montagu, styled
Viscount Mandeville; Edward Howard, 1st Baron Howard of Escrick; and Robert Greville, 2nd Baron
Brooke.
[86] C. Russell, *The Fall of the British Monarchies, 1637–1642* (Oxford, 1991), 150–1; J. Adamson, *The Noble
Revolt: The Overthrow of Charles I* (2007), 47–8. Russell suggests that the original research underlying this claim
may date from the 1630s (151 n. 21), but seems to agree with Adamson that the realization of the apparent
implications of this work was new in the early autumn of 1640.
[87] For St John, see sub 'St John, Oliver (c.1598–1673)', *ODNB*; Adamson, *Noble Revolt*, 152ff.
[88] BL, Add. MS 25266, f. 113v.

Parlament, which was no other then an assembly of rebels ... a constrained consent is the consent of a captive & not of a K., & therefore was nothing done there either legally or royally'.[89] In this light, the heavy evidential weight which Russell and Adamson place upon St John's note seems to strain it almost to breaking point.

However, an alternative, and more convincing, explanation for the petition of the 12 lords in 1640 and their apparent claim to be able to summon a parliament on their own authority, may lie in the Elizabethan example of Essex and his plans for a parliament in 1601. The noblemen who petitioned Charles I in 1640 included: Essex's son, the 3rd earl of Essex; Essex's nephew, the 2nd earl of Warwick; Essex's son-in-law, the 2nd earl of Hertford, who was married to Essex's daughter, Frances, who had been born in 1599; the 7th earl of Rutland, who had been knighted by Essex as a young man; the 2nd Lord Brooke, who was the cousin and adoptive son of Essex's very close friend, Fulke Greville; the 1st earl of Mulgrave, who was Essex's exact contemporary and had known him personally; and the 1st earl of Bolingbroke, whose father had served on the jury of peers which condemned Essex in 1601.[90] More than half the 'Twelve Peers', therefore, had a direct connection to Essex and would have been intimately familiar with Essex's posthumous reputation as 'the great earl'.[91] Some of these lords (not least his son, nephew and son-in-law) must surely have have sought detailed explanations for his shocking fall in 1601 from those who had known him (as Rutland and Mulgrave did). The earl of Rutland – then merely Sir George Manners – had even participated in the 'rising' of 1601 himself and had been forced to buy his pardon with a substantial fine.[92]

---

[89] [Sir Walter Raleigh], *The prerogative of parlaments in England: proved in a dialogue (pro & contra) betweene a councellour of state and a justice of peace* (Hamburg, 1628), 15.

[90] In addition, the 2nd earl of Exeter's father had been the nobleman who proclaimed Essex a traitor in the streets of London on 8 Feb. 1601. The 4th earl of Bedford's late cousin, the 3rd earl, had also been caught up in the rising that day and arrested and fined for his involvement in it.

[91] E.g., K. Lindberg, ' "Your father's perfection shall be your blemish": the 3rd earl of Essex and the development of a legend', *Medievalia et Humanistica*, xxxii (2006), 117–31. In addition to the very extensive circulation and copying of manuscripts relating to the 2nd earl of Essex, there were, apparently, much oral traditions about him, some of which were later reflected in Francis Osborne's *A miscellany of sundry essayes, paradoxes and problematicall discourses, letters and characters together with politicall deductions from the history of the earl of Essex, executed under Queen Elizabeth* (1659). Numerous printed works also lionised him, including: Robert Pricket, *Honors fame in triumph riding: Or, The life and death of the late honorable earle of Essex* (1604); Thomas Scott, *Robert earle of Essex his ghost* ('Paradise' [i.e., London], 1624); Gervase Markham, *Honour in his perfection, or A treatise in commendations of the vertues and renowned vertuous vndertakings of the illustrious and heroycall princes Henry earle of Oxenford, Henry earle of Southampton, Robert aarle of Essex, and the euer praise-worthy and much honoured Lord, Robert Bartue, Lord Willoughby, of Eresby: with a briefe cronology of theirs, and their auncestours actions* (1624); *Profitable instructions describing what speciall obseruations are to be taken by trauellers in all nations, states and countries; pleasant and profitable. By the three much admired, Robert, late earle of Essex. Sir Philip Sidney. And, Secretary Davison* (1633); Henry Wotton, *A parallel betweene Robert late earle of Essex, and George late duke of Buckingham written by Sir Henry Wotton* (1641); *Certaine choise and remarkable observations selected out of a discourse written long since by the late and ever famous earle of Essex, very usefull for these times; whereunto is annexed the advice of that worthy commander, Sir Edward Harwood, Collonell, written by King Charles his command upon occasion of the French kings preparations and presented in his life-time by his owne hand unto His Sacred Majesty ; all tending to the securing and fortifying of the kingdome both by sea and land . . .* (1642); *The earle of Essex his letter to the earle of Southampton in the time of his troubles containing many pious expressions and very comfortable for such are in any troubles, Septemb. 29, 1642* (1642).

[92] Sir George's older brothers, Sir Roger Manners, 5th earl of Rutland (1576–1612), who married Essex's step-daughter, Elizabeth Sidney, and Francis Manners, later 6th earl of Rutland (1578–1632), were also arrested and fined for their involvement in the rising. Sir George and Sir Roger were both knighted by Essex in Ireland in 1599 (Sir Roger on 30 May and Sir George on 12 July): W.A. Shaw, *The Knights of England* (2 vols, 1906), ii, 95, 96.

As they sought to challenge Charles I in 1640, at least some of the 12 lords were, therefore, likely to have been deeply conscious of the last time a substantial body of noblemen sought to overturn royal policy and personnel – Essex's pre-empted attempt to petition Elizabeth in February 1601.[93] They would also have been painfully aware of the fatal consequences of Essex's failure to present his petition and determined to ensure they would not share a similar fate.[94]

Given this context, it would seem highly probable that the events and plans of Essex in 1601 had an important (but hitherto unnoticed) formative influence on the petitioning of the 12 peers. For lords seeking to force an unwilling sovereign into calling a parliament and sanctioning the arrest and trial of leading ministers, Essex's plans in 1601 would seem an obvious place to seek legal and ideological justification for their actions. Several of the group surely had privileged access to papers from Essex and his friends and servants which survived the 'rising' of 1601. Since the earl of Warwick and his friends had secretly been considering this plan for more than three years, by August 1640, they would also have had plenty of time to search through any old papers relating to Essex and his intentions in 1601.[95]

Instead of Oliver St John's antiquarian notes, therefore, a more convincing source of evidence to support the claim about the baronial authority of the 12 peers in 1640 would be knowledge of Essex's plans in 1601 and access to a manuscript copy of *The state of Christendom*.[96] This treatise spells out 'the twelve peers' authority' more explicitly and powerfully than St John's brief note. Moreover, it connects it to De Montfort's parliament of 1265, rather than the problematic Mad Parliament of 1258: 'the barons, after the battel of Lewis, in the time of Henry the Third, ordained that two earls and a bishop elected by the commonalty should chose to them nine other persons, whereof three should alwayes remain about the King, and by the whole twelve both the Court and the realm should be governed'. If this speculation is correct, Essex's dashed hopes of seeing his enemies condemned and James VI confirmed as Elizabeth's heir in 1601 may well have helped a later generation of aristocrats to undermine James's son and set the scene for the summoning of what would become the Long Parliament of 1640–60.

[93] Adamson's erroneous dismissal of Essex's 1601 actions as 'little more than an instance of chivalric grandstanding' (*Noble Revolt*, 32) reflects the unsatisfactory historical understanding of the Essex rising which was still current in 2007.

[94] As Russell and Adamson note, at least some of the 12 peers of 1640 were treasonously conspiring with the enemy of their king (the Scots) during a time of active war: Russell, *Fall of the British Monarchies*, 151; Adamson, *Noble Revolt*, 46ff.

[95] In mid-Jan. 1637, an earlier Venetian ambassador to England had reported that 'many of the leading men of the realm are determined to make a final effort to bring the forms of government back to their former state. They hold secret meetings for the purpose . . . It is said that they have decided to draw up a paper which many will sign, to be handed to his Majesty in the name of all, with an open request for the convocation of parliament': *CSP Ven., 1636–9*, no. 139, p. 125.

[96] The survival of at least six manuscript copies of the treatise suggests it may have had some limited circulation in scribal form, at least among a few of Essex's trusted friends or servants: Gajda, '*The state of Christendom*', 424 n. 5.

The Development of Parliamentary Privilege, 1604–29*

PAUL M. HUNNEYBALL

The early Stuart parliaments witnessed a dramatic expansion in the exercise and scope of parliamentary privilege. What had once been essentially a mechanism for avoiding disruption to parliamentary business came, instead, to be seen as a personal benefit for members, or even a political weapon for use against the crown. While such developments occurred in both Houses, it was the Lords which normally led the way, continually pushing the boundaries of privilege as part of a general reassertion of its rights and status. While the Commons also proved capable of innovation in this field, it is the Lords which emerges from this survey as the more assertive of the two Houses, better organised and much more effective in exploiting the advantages that parliamentary privilege now provided.

Keywords: privilege; house of lords; house of commons; convocation; committee for privileges; freedom from arrest; freedom from legal process; precedent(s); letters of protection; prorogation days

When, in 1977, Michael Graves published his seminal article on peers' freedom from arrest, he was venturing into relatively uncharted territory. Parliamentary privilege has not proved a popular topic with early modern historians in recent decades.[1] While a handful of 17th-century cases are recognized as important precedents which helped to lay the foundations of the modern British constitution, much of the surviving data is both mundane and repetitive, not perhaps an obviously fruitful field of study.[2] However, the object of this article is not to tease out long-term legal implications, but rather to consider the evidence as a whole, and to explore how privilege was understood and exercised by those who attended the first seven Stuart parliaments, in both institutional and political terms. While it cannot be disputed that some of this period's strongest statements on privilege, such as the famous 1621 protestation of the Commons, were made with one eye on posterity, it is equally true that most debates were generated by issues of immediate, and often personal, concern. Privilege was seen as a valuable tool for solving problems. It was also a vital means of self-definition for parliament as a whole, and for the two Houses individually. But privilege was not set in stone. Between

* I am grateful to Linda Clark, Ben Coates, Hannes Kleineke, Chris Kyle, and Andrew Thrush, for their comments and contributions towards this article.

[1] Michael A.R. Graves, 'Freedom of Peers from Arrest: The Case of Henry Second Lord Cromwell, 1571–72', *American Journal of Legal History*, xxi (1977), 1–14. For the house of lords there is a useful discussion in Elizabeth Read Foster, *The House of Lords 1603–1649: Structure, Procedure, and the Nature of its Business* (Chapel Hill, NC, 1983), 137–48. There is currently no equivalent overview of the house of commons.

[2] Peter Leyland, *The Constitution of the United Kingdom: A Contextual Analysis* (Oxford, 2007), 91.

1604 and 1629, it evolved in some quite surprising ways, and analysis of that process reveals a great deal about the development of parliament itself.

Parliamentary privilege in its narrowest sense indicates certain specific legal immunities enjoyed by members of the Lords and Commons. However, before these are examined in detail, it must first be observed that, in the early 17th century, the term was used quite freely in a variety of different contexts which embraced most aspects of parliamentary life. In the 1621 protestation, for example, the house of commons attempted to spell out the full extent of its rights. Accordingly, the text asserted 'that the liberties, franchises, privileges, and jurisdictions of Parliament are the ancient and undoubted birthright and inheritance of the subjects of England'.[3] Fine words indeed, appropriate for a perceived constitutional crisis. However, privilege was also routinely invoked in relation to the personal dignity of individual members, and the decorum with which parliamentary proceedings were, in theory at least, conducted. In February 1621, when the earl of Berkshire jostled Lord Scrope while entering the Lords chamber, apparently in the belief that his path was being deliberately blocked, he was made to kneel at the bar, sternly reminded that he 'should be tender to the privileges of the House', and consigned to the Fleet prison for three days to ponder his offence.[4]

Again, the jurisdictional boundary between the Lords and Commons was routinely defined in terms of privilege. For all their talk of desiring 'good correspondency', both Houses were, in practice, highly sensitive to any perceived infringements of their respective rights.[5] In these intermittent border squabbles, the language of privilege was used both for attack and defence, as is well illustrated by one particular example from James I's reign. In May 1621, the house of commons seriously overreached itself when, in what can best be described as a fit of corporate hysteria, it decided to inflict an exemplary punishment on a catholic lawyer, Edward Floyd, who had slandered the king's daughter and son-in-law. In their zeal and excitement, members overlooked one vital consideration, namely that the Commons lacked the power to sentence offenders unless they had infringed the House's own privileges. They could make complaints about other individuals, but judgment lay with the Lords and the crown. This awkward fact was pointed out to them the next day, in a message from the king himself, whereupon members embarked on the painful process of extricating themselves from an untenable position. On 3 May, they assured James 'that it was not ther meaneing to proceed in judgment further then theay hav president by Parliament to winn unto them selves any larger power and priveledg'.[6] The king, in fact, took a relatively tolerant, albeit unyielding, view of this fiasco, but it was a different story in the Lords. Two days later, the peers took formal notice of the Floyd affair, observing that it 'doth trench deep into the privilege of this House', and resolving 'not to suffer any thing to pass which might prejudice their right in this point of judicature'. Their lordships were almost certainly well aware that most members of the Commons were, by now, mortified at their own behaviour, and keen to put the whole affair behind them. Nevertheless,

---

[3] *Constitutional Documents of the Reign of James I*, ed. J.R. Tanner (Cambridge, 1952), 288–9.

[4] *LJ*, iii, 19–20, 22–3.

[5] *LJ*, iii, 110; *CJ*, i, 548.

[6] *CJ*, i, 600–3; *Commons Debates, 1621*, ed. Wallace Notestein, Frances Helen Relf and Hartley Simpson (7 vols, New Haven, CT, 1935) [hereafter cited as *CD, 1621*], iii, 151.

a challenge had been made, and the Lords must, for form's sake, respond to it. Accordingly, they arranged a conference with the Commons, with the object of 'accommodating that business, in such sort as may be without any prejudice to the privilege of either House'. At this meeting, the Commons was allowed to present what precedents it could to justify its behaviour. A second conference was then held, to confirm that the lower House had failed to produce any evidence that it could exercise judicature beyond the traditional limits. Finally, a subcommittee was set up, at which representatives of the two Houses hammered out a joint statement: 'that the proceedings lately passed . . . against Edward Floud be not, at any time hereafter, drawn or used as a precedent, to the enlarging or diminishing of the lawful rights or privileges of either House; but that the rights and privileges of both Houses shall remain in the self-same state and plight as before'. Having thus restored the normal balance of power, the Lords proceeded to investigate Floyd itself, and eventually imposed much the same sentence as the Commons had originally devised nearly a month earlier.[7]

This episode not only demonstrates that the term 'privilege' was used in a variety of contexts, to describe the rights enjoyed by the two Houses, but also underlines the importance attached to the upholding of those rights. According to the prevalent constitutional doctrine of this era, the power balances within the current English political system had existed almost since time immemorial, and could not be altered without undermining the entire edifice. In theory at least, no novelties could be introduced without the sanction of the past, hence the endless search for precedents.[8] Although parliamentary judicature had only just been revived, it was modelled on medieval patterns, whereby the Commons assembled charges, and the Lords dispensed justice.[9] Judicature was a very valuable parliamentary weapon, and the Lords' highly charged reaction to Floyd's case was doubtless, in part, born of fears that the Commons' behaviour might undermine the legitimacy of this new procedure. Nevertheless, the priority for both Houses, as the dispute developed, was to restore the normal balance, so that neither side emerged with its rightful privileges diminished. In general, during this period, the demarcation line between the Lords and Commons was more honoured than breached, and this mutual sensitivity to privilege was a vital means by which disputes were kept to a minimum. And yet here we have one of the fundamental contradictions of early Stuart politics, the disparity between the rhetoric of time-honoured continuity and the reality of steady change. Both houses of parliament routinely claimed to be merely defending their constitutional birthright, but in practice, both repeatedly devised new powers for themselves. Parliamentary privilege in its narrower sense offers a good tool for examining that process of change. During the early 17th century, the Lords and Commons both extended the scope of their privilege, but in subtly-contrasting ways which reveal differences of outlook and ambition between the two Houses. That will be the subject of the remainder of this article but, before embarking on this discussion, it is first necessary to consider briefly what legal immunities the Lords and Commons enjoyed by 1604.

[7] *LJ*, iii, 110–11, 113, 116, 119, 132–3.

[8] Glenn Burgess, *The Politics of the Ancient Constitution* (University Park, PA, 1992), 5–7.

[9] Colin Gerald Calder Tite, *Impeachment and Parliamentary Judicature in Early Stuart England* (1974), 5, 7.

The basic concept of freedom from arrest for those attending parliament can be traced back to regulations for the Anglo-Saxon 'witanagemot', but there was a fundamental difference between this early model and its Stuart manifestation. As late as the 14th century, privilege was understood as belonging to the crown, rather than to parliament. In other words, it was a means by which the king could ensure that the men summoned to advise him at these assemblies were not prevented from attending. Over time, this situation was reversed, so that by the 17th century, privilege was held to be vested personally in the members of both Houses. Meanwhile, the actual scope of privilege also expanded. By the late medieval period, it was increasingly defined as offering protection in essentially civil matters, such as trespass, debt, and contractual disputes; the more serious charges of treason, felony and breach of the peace were not covered, nor, understandably, was condemnation by parliament itself. Within those limits, members of the Lords and Commons, and also their servants, were, in principle, free from the threat of prosecution, arrest and imprisonment.[10] Until 1542, all writs of privilege were issued by chancery, but from then on, the house of commons was allowed to order the release of its own members. This was, of course, less of an issue in the upper House, where the lord chancellor or lord keeper was the presiding officer, though the *status quo* was clarified in 1601, when the Lords' collective authority failed to secure the release of a peer's servant held under execution in Newgate gaol, and Lord Keeper Egerton had to issue a writ himself. As late as 1585, the Commons was denied the right to freedom from subpoenas, but this privilege, too, was secured by the end of Elizabeth I's reign.[11] Meanwhile, in 1572, Lord Cromwell's case brought all peers substantial protection against arrest, and in 1601 it was finally determined that the crown's servants were also covered by privilege, a logical step, given that the monarch formed part of the parliamentary trinity.[12]

The other great innovation of the Elizabethan period was the establishment in the Commons of a committee for privileges. Beginning with the 1584–5 parliament, select committees for this purpose were set up, and from 1593 oversight of electoral matters was added to their remit.[13] The Buckinghamshire election case of 1604 saw the Commons finally wrest control of electoral scrutiny from chancery, and from then on the standing committee for privileges and returns was, unquestionably, the most prestigious body within the House, though the bulk of its business related to the examination of disputed elections.[14] During the early 17th century, the committee grew substantially, in part probably because of the personal cachet that membership bestowed. In 1604, it consisted of the two privy councillors then sitting in the Commons, and 25 other senior members. By 1628, the total number had swollen to

[10] *Parliamentarians at Law: Select Legal Proceedings of the Long Fifteenth Century Relating to Parliament*, ed. Hannes Kleineke (Parliamentary History: Texts & Studies, 2, 2008), 4–7.

[11] Michael A.R. Graves, *Elizabethan Parliaments 1559–1601* (2nd edn, Harlow, 1996), 44, 46; *LJ*, ii, 238, 240.

[12] Graves, 'Freedom of Peers from Arrest', 10–13; *LJ*, ii, 230–4.

[13] Graves, *Elizabethan Parliaments*, 52.

[14] *The History of Parliament: The House of Commons, 1604–1629*, ed. Andrew Thrush and John P. Ferris (6 vols, Cambridge, 2010) [hereafter cited as *HPC, 1604–29*], i, 50, 69, 150.

an unmanageable 88, though the number of active participants was undoubtedly rather smaller.[15]

The Lords initially dealt with privilege cases either in the House, or by specially appointed committees. Not until 1621 did it set up a designated standing committee 'to take consideration of the customs and orders of this House, and of the privileges of the peers of this kingdom, and lords of Parliament'.[16] As should be clear from that remit, the new body was tasked with far more than just scrutiny of privilege claims. The timing of this innovation has never been fully explained, but it was evidently linked to current concerns that the position of the English aristocracy was under threat. The committee was established barely a fortnight before 33 members of the Lords signed a petition to James I protesting at the recent elevation of English commoners to Irish or Scottish peerages. Tellingly, when an irate king sought to face down the petitioners, they responded by asserting their collective status as lords of parliament, and attempted to get the petition formally adopted as parliamentary business.[17] Similarly, from the outset, the committee approached parliamentary privilege as just one aspect of the wider privileges of the peerage, and used the house of lords as a powerful platform for addressing grievances which had nothing to do with parliament. In 1621, for example, the committee led opposition to the notion that peers should be made to give evidence in court under oath, rather than swearing on their honour, and also commissioned the lawyer and historian, John Selden, to compile a comprehensive survey of the rights of the peerage. Alongside these broader issues, it also became effectively the Lords' executive committee, providing leadership across most aspects of the business of the House.[18] As established in 1621, it had a membership of 32, with a smaller subcommittee, and the numbers remained fairly stable until 1629, when 45 lords were appointed.[19]

Even without the Lords' standing committee, the 1604 parliament began with an impressive foundation of privileges, and it was one on which both Houses were happy to build. However, delineating the developments of the next 25 years is not an entirely straightforward process. While the journals of the house of lords provide a detailed and polished record of deliberations in the upper House, with fairly consistent accounts of privilege cases, the Commons journal for this period is a compilation of draft texts only, and entries are frequently much less informative or, indeed, clear. Many of the missing details can be culled from related documents, but the narrative for the lower House remains comparatively uneven. Allowing for that caveat, it appears that 132 privilege

---

[15] *CJ*, i, 149–50; *Commons Debates, 1628*, ed. Robert C. Johnson, Mary Frear Keeler, Maija Jansson Cole and William B. Bidwell (4 vols, New Haven, CT, 1977–8) [hereafter cited as *CD, 1628*], ii, 28–9.

[16] *LJ*, ii, 497–8, 597–8; iii, 10.

[17] Charles R. Mayes, 'The Early Stuarts and the Irish Peerage', *English Historical Review*, lxxiii (1958), 248; Arthur Wilson, *The History of Great Britain* (1653), 186–7; *The Court and Times of James the First*, ed. Thomas Birch (2 vols, 1848), ii, 230–2; *Notes of the Debates in the House of Lords, 1621, 1625, 1628*, ed. Frances Helen Relf (Camden Soc., 3rd ser., xlii, 1929), 10–11.

[18] *LJ*, iii, 21, 41–2, 176.

[19] *LJ*, iii, 10; iv, 6; *Proceedings in Parliament 1625*, ed. Maija Jansson and William B. Bidwell (New Haven, CT, 1987) [hereafter cited as *Procs 1625*], 45; *Proceedings in Parliament 1626*, ed. William B. Bidwell and Maija Jansson (4 vols, New Haven, CT, 1991–6) [hereafter cited as *Procs 1626*], i, 48; *Lords Proceedings 1628*, ed. Mary Frear Keeler, Maija Jansson Cole and William B. Bidwell (New Haven, CT, 1983) [hereafter cited as *Lords Procs 1628*], 72–3.

cases were considered by the Lords and 183 by the Commons between 1604 and 1629.[20] Of these, two examples in the Lords and seven in the Commons were actually requests to waive privilege in relation to lawsuits.[21] In the upper House, a further three cases were dropped, while 29 were ostensibly never resolved. However, only 20 requests for privilege were definitely rejected, which means that at least 60% of all applications made to the Lords were successful. In the lower House, one case went to arbitration, 19 had no known outcome, and four were rejected, which indicates a massive 86% approval rate. At first glance, these figures imply that the Commons took much greater advantage of privilege during this era. Nevertheless, it is important to note that the Commons generated only 35% more claims than the Lords over the same period, despite having roughly four times as many members.[22] Contrary to its popular reputation as the more assertive of the two Houses, the Commons was actually, in *per capita* terms, a great deal less active on this particular front.

Beyond these basic quantitative considerations, there were also marked variations in the type and distribution of cases, which, in part, reflected the membership of the Lords and Commons. In the upper House, as mentioned earlier, the lords enjoyed wide-ranging personal protection from arrest, and all but 22 of the cases debated there were claims made on behalf of their servants. Indeed, until 1621, complaints were exclusively about the arrest of servants, and this remained the biggest single category throughout the 1620s. By comparison, the dominant issue in the Commons was privilege against lawsuits and other legal processes. This accounted for 70% of all cases, of which nine out of ten related to members personally. In short, here is another fundamental difference between the two Houses. If privilege was intended to prevent interference to the vital work of parliament, then peers were mainly distracted by the troubles of their servants, while members of the Commons were far more concerned about being sued.

Having said that, the detailed picture within each House was, of course, more complicated. It is somewhat easier to detect trends within the Lords, due to the relatively complete record of cases there, and the overall picture suggests a fairly steady increase in the number and variety of privilege claims during this period. During the five sessions of the 1604–10 parliament, there were 21 cases in total, whereas that was the average figure for each of the five parliaments of the 1620s. Clearly, the latter decade saw a lot more business of this kind. It also became much more diversified. In one sense, this was to be expected, given that the Lords dealt with privilege claims not just from

---

[20] The statistics presented here are derived from the following sources: *LJ*, ii–iv; *CJ*, i; *The Parliamentary Diary of Robert Bowyer 1606–1607*, ed. David Harris Willson (New York, 1971) [hereafter cited as *Bowyer Diary*]; *Proceedings in Parliament 1610*, ed. Elizabeth Read Foster (2 vols, New Haven, CT, 1966); Hampshire RO, 44M69/F2/15/1: diary of proceedings in the house of commons of Sir Richard Paulet, 1610; *Proceedings in Parliament 1614 (House of Commons)*, ed. Maija Jansson (Philadelphia, PA, 1988); *CD, 1621*; Edward Nicholas, *Proceedings and Debates of the House of Commons, 1621* (2 vols, Oxford, 1766) [hereafter cited as Nicholas, *Commons, 1621*]; TNA, SP14/166: Edward Nicholas's diary for 1624; *Procs 1625*; *Procs 1626*; *CD, 1628*; *Lords Procs 1628*; *Commons Debates for 1629*, ed. Wallace Notestein and Frances Helen Relf (Minneapolis, MN, 1921) [hereafter cited as *CD, 1629*]. They cover only cases where the personal rights of members of either House were at stake. Examples of members invoking privilege without a formal request being made to either House have been excluded from these figures, as have grants of privilege to non-members, such as witnesses summoned before committees.

[21] Both requests to waive privilege in the Lords were approved; three in the Commons were rejected.

[22] In 1604, the Lords had 93 members, the Commons 462; by 1629, these figures stood at 144 and 493, respectively.

peers and bishops, but also from the crown, the legal assistants attending the House, and, very occasionally, members of convocation, who possessed their own privilege, but were obliged to channel their complaints through the Lords.[23] Even so, it is striking that, compared with the first Jacobean parliament's unwavering litany of reports about the arrest of servants, the 1628 session's quota also included lawsuits directed against peers, one peer's wife and several servants, as well as the seizure of goods of both a lord and a retainer. It is difficult to escape the conclusion that, by the late 1620s, the upper House was finding many more uses for privilege than it had done two decades earlier.

The Lords was, of course, very proud of its status as a court of law, and the evidence suggests that it took a more rigorous approach to the assessment of privilege cases than did the Commons. While privilege was almost automatically granted to members of the lower House in receipt of subpoenas, the Lords generally reserved judgment on its privilege cases until the full facts were established, and was statistically more likely to reject claims which failed to meet the correct requirements.[24] In 1604, for example, a bid to free the earl of Cumberland's servant, William Allome, from Newgate gaol, failed when, upon closer inspection, it emerged that Allome was not one of the earl's 'menial or ordinary' servants, 'nor . . . employed in any necessary place of attendance about his lordship', the traditional qualifications.[25] It displayed a similar scrupulosity in 1614, when two servants employed by Lord Morley and Lord Eure were detained in Newgate. A preliminary inquiry established that they had both been arrested for breach of the peace, and that their cases had already been heard by a local justice of the peace, whereupon the matter was referred back to the same magistrate to establish definitively whether or not the servants came within the current scope of privilege.[26] Again, in 1626, the Lords threw out a petition from the earl of Nottingham's solicitor, who was being sued at the Sussex assizes, on the grounds that the correct procedure was for him to request a stay of trial before the assize judges began to hear the case, not when it was already underway.[27]

However, it should be noted that the employee in that last case would most likely not have passed the 'menial servant' test a couple of decades earlier. By the 1620s, more or less any servant was considered worthy of privilege, provided that the relevant peer was prepared to vouch for them. This was a significant relaxation of the original rules, and a symptom of the changes being made by the Lords to the privilege system. For example, in May 1628, the House agreed to award privilege to the earl of Danby's chaplain, John Randall. Although a claim had been made on behalf of another chaplain, four years earlier, that case was, apparently, never resolved, so Randall's grant was a novelty. Accordingly, the committee for privileges was instructed to consider whether it set a precedent for all peers' chaplains. Just four days later, before the committee had reached a conclusion, the Lords was presented with a second case involving a subpoena

[23] *Procs 1625*, p. 139; *Procs 1626*, i, 496; *Lords Procs 1628*, pp. 445, 684.
[24] *Bowyer Diary*, 175.
[25] *LJ*, ii, 285, 290–1.
[26] *LJ*, ii, 714–15.
[27] *Procs 1626*, i, 239.

granted against the earl of Essex's chaplain, and the culprit was promptly hauled in and punished for breach of privilege. This apparently settled the issue, and the committee never reported back.[28]

Similarly, by the 1620s, it was widely accepted in the Lords that servants were personally protected, and that peers could claim for their own goods, but there was no precedent for servants' possessions also being covered. Then, in December 1621, Thomas Cole, a servant of the earl of Oxford, petitioned for the restoration of property seized over a debt. This was recognized as a new departure, and the issue was duly debated when the offender appeared before the House. According to the *Journal*, 'there fell a doubt amongst the lords, whether the privileges of Parliament do extend to the immunity of the lands and goods, as well as of the person, of a nobleman's servant', and the question was referred to the committee for privileges. The session ended just two days later, pre-empting a report, and the matter was allowed to rest until 1625.[29] The next case demanded more urgent attention, as it related to a yeoman of the king's chamber, whose property had been confiscated while he was on royal service. When summoned before the Lords, the men responsible not unreasonably explained that they were unaware that privilege extended to servants' goods. Under the circumstances, they were discharged with a verbal warning, but they were also ordered to restore the yeoman's possessions.[30] This then became a precedent which was cited in 1628 when a servant of the earl of Cleveland claimed privilege for his belongings, though the final outcome of that case is unclear.[31]

Meanwhile, more fundamental issues of privilege were also under debate. Until 1614, it was assumed, as a precondition for grants, that the lord to whom a claim related must be personally present at parliament. Then, in May that year, George Kember, a servant to Lord Clifton, complained that he had been arrested. This would have been a routine matter, but for the fact that Clifton was not actually attending the House, and had merely sent a proxy. It took five days for Kember and his adversary to appear before the Lords and, in the meantime, some careful thought had clearly been given to this problem. Kember's petition was, again, read in the House, whereupon 'it was proposed by the Lord Chancellor, and by all the lords without opposition agreed, that any lord, a member of this House, being absent with licence, and having made a proxy, may enjoy the privilege of this House for his servants, as if such lord were personally present'.[32] This was a considerable conceptual leap. In effect, the personal bond between peers and privilege was deemed to be so strong that actual physical participation in a parliament was no longer essential, so long as any absences were officially sanctioned. The new *status quo* was effectively confirmed in 1626, when Lord Vaux claimed privilege over a Star Chamber suit. This was another pivotal case, because Vaux was a catholic who routinely stayed away from parliament in order to avoid taking the oath of allegiance. Not surprisingly, the Lords took a less benevolent view of his request than it had of Kember's, but it was still prepared to give him a second chance. The deciding

[28] *LJ*, iii, 342; *Lords Procs 1628*, pp. 500, 535, 572.

[29] *LJ*, iii, 183–4, 198.

[30] *Procs 1625*, pp. 52, 55, 84.

[31] *Lords Procs 1628*, pp. 353, 359, 376–7.

[32] *LJ*, ii, 700, 702.

issue was spelt out by Viscount Saye and Sele: 'our privileges are that we be free to attend the service of this House. He that makes himself uncapable thereof, [is] not capable of the privileges.' Accordingly, Vaux was presented with an ultimatum. If he wanted to be granted privilege, he must first conform over the oath of allegiance, and start attending the Lords again. Having indicated that he would do so, he was promptly allowed a stay of the Star Chamber proceedings. As an extra precaution, it was further agreed that, in future, all peers should take the oath once in every parliament. Even so, there was clearly some residual embarrassment about this episode, for it was resolved that when Vaux's grant of privilege was entered in the journal, the events surrounding it should not be recorded.[33]

Having dispensed with the need for personal attendance, the Lords also extended the time span within which privilege might be claimed. It was already accepted that some allowance should be made, either side of an actual sitting, for the time spent travelling to and from Westminster. However, the issue suddenly became much more important in 1621 when, in a major break with tradition, parliament was merely adjourned over the summer, and the same session resumed in November, rather than there being a prorogation and two separate sessions. According to convention, privilege was suspended once parliament was prorogued, but continued to apply during a normal, short adjournment. It was unclear which option should apply in this novel situation of a long adjournment. The Lords consulted the judges, who failed to find a suitable precedent. Accordingly, the House generated one of its own, ruling on 4 June 'that the lords do know, that the privileges of themselves, their servants and followers, do continue, notwithstanding the adjournment of the Parliament'.[34] During the second sitting, the topic was revisited, and the committee for privileges produced a draft order that, specifically in relation to peers' servants, privilege should 'continue twenty days before and after every session; in which time the lords may conveniently go home to their houses in the most remote parts of this kingdom'. This order was presented to the House, but no decision was reached on it.[35] Then, in 1624, a further complication emerged, which forced a review of this proposal. In March that year, the Lords heard a petition from Sir Edward Osbaldeston, servant to the earl of Derby, who had been arrested two months earlier. Osbaldeston had declared his status at the time, but there was a problem over the date. Although parliament had been summoned on 30 December 1623, it had not actually assembled until mid-February, and Osbaldeston had been detained on 13 January, a whole month beforehand. According to precedent, that should have meant that he did not qualify for privilege. However, the Lords was disinclined to be so pernickety. Having decided that Derby's absence from parliament should not affect its verdict, it proceeded to address the one remaining obstacle in Osbaldeston's path, and agreed on 16 March that 'the privileges of Parliament do begin with the date of the writ of summons'. In a move that smacked of deliberate obfuscation, this innovation was justified by the wider concern that delays in the delivery of the writs might penalise people who failed to realize in time that they were entitled to

[33] *Procs 1626*, i, 39–40, 49, 61.

[34] *LJ*, iii, 151, 153, 155, 157.

[35] *LJ*, iii, 194–5.

privilege. Following further debate in the subcommittee of the committee for privileges, the House rubber-stamped this resolution in May 1624.[36]

These were dramatic changes. In the course of just three parliaments, the Lords had decided that servants could request privilege regardless of whether their masters were attending the House, and that the critical period for claims now extended from the moment parliament was summoned until 20 days after a session, or, in the case of an adjournment, indefinitely. However, there was still scope for further expansion. In 1626, yet another question arose when a petition was received from Sir Francis Browne, a servant of James I until the king's death in the previous year. The case was, in fact, an old one, as Browne had been arrested in February 1625, and confined ever since. Parliament was not actually in full session when he was first detained, but it had been appointed to meet then, before the government opted to prorogue it for a further month, James's demise latterly forcing a dissolution. As the basis for a privilege claim, a superseded prorogation date was distinctly dubious. Nevertheless, it was normal practice for a handful of members to assemble at Westminster to witness the formal statement of postponement. That being the case, and given that Browne was arrested on the very day of the prorogation, was he entitled to privilege? A number of lords thought that he was, and the only person recorded as arguing against this view was the man who had Browne detained in the first place. In the event, parliament was dissolved before a final ruling could be made, but the viability of a mere prorogation date as a time of privilege had now been tacitly accepted.[37] This, in turn, paved the way for a further claim which would have been inconceivable three decades earlier.

In January 1629, the Lords was petitioned by a prominent lawyer, John Glanville, currently a member of the Commons, who accused Roger Clay of breaching the privileges of the upper House. The facts of this case were as follows: since February 1628, Glanville and Clay had been in competition for the right to appoint the next vicar of Lamerton, Devon. Glanville had won a suit of *jure patronatus*, and secured the bishop of Exeter's approval for his nominee, John Cooper. However, Clay and his candidate, John Segar, had then appealed to a higher authority, the archbishop of Canterbury's court of audience. The bishop had been summoned before this court to answer Clay's complaint, but failed to attend. Consequently, the hearing went against him, and the court agreed to Segar's institution as vicar. This dispute might not seem to have any obvious bearing on the smooth running of parliament, but there was one more vital detail in Glanville's petition to the Lords. The bishop's summons was served on him on 4 October 1628, just 16 days before a date to which parliament had been prorogued. As with the Browne case, the government had changed its plans, and postponed the next session until the following January. Nevertheless, if an isolated prorogation day counted as a meeting of parliament, then privilege should logically extend 20 days either side, as Glanville had realized. On that basis, the Lords could properly rule on whether the court summons was a breach of privilege. It is not recorded whether the House sought the bishop's opinion, but he was clearly co-operating with Glanville, and did nothing to obstruct what was, in effect, a requisitioning of his personal privilege for another man's private benefit. The committee for privileges considered the case in detail, and on 5

[36] *LJ*, iii, 205–7, 261, 264, 417–18.
[37] *Procs 1626*, i, 388–9, 536–7, 610.

February reported the facts to the Lords, which promptly ruled that Segar was in breach of privilege. Glanville's victory, for it was, after all, as much his as the bishop's, was comprehensive. Segar was instructed to have his own appointment as vicar cancelled in every particular, prior to a further legal hearing to decide whether he or Cooper was the rightful incumbent. Having achieved their objective, Glanville and the bishop graciously waived their parliamentary privilege so that the law could run its course without further delay. A few days later, Cooper was himself instituted as vicar.[38] By any measure, this is a remarkable case. In the upper House at least, privilege had now become so clearly defined as an abstract legal concept that a clever lawyer like Glanville could construct an argument which rested entirely on the bishop of Exeter's personal entitlement, without the non-parliamentary reality of the circumstances obtruding on the Lords' deliberations. The way had undoubtedly been prepared, by the increasingly outlandish appeals made on behalf of peers' servants, but Glanville's tactics remain breathtaking in their audacity. Whether the bishop had previously retained his services as a lawyer is not known, but Glanville did not claim any such connection, and, moreover, he did not need to. His dispute with Clay gave him no scope for a claim in the Commons using his own privilege, but he had found a way to twist the Lords' regulations to his own advantage.

While the upper House presents a picture of steady development in the use and range of privilege, the sequence of events in the Commons is more confused. Problems with the source material have been mentioned already but, in addition, the number of privilege claims per session fluctuated quite wildly during this period. The first Jacobean parliament considered eight cases in its first session and 12 in the second, then the figures for the next two sessions jumped dramatically to 27 and 36, respectively. The fifth session is known to have generated only three claims, though the Commons journal does not survive for this phase of the parliament, and there may have been others which went unrecorded. There again, the short-lived 1614 parliament saw just two claims. Although 13 cases were heard in both 1621 and 1624, the plague-interrupted 1625 parliament produced only eight. However, numbers then soared again, with 28 claims in 1626, and 33 in 1628–9.[39] Such wide variations are difficult to explain. In part, they doubtless reflect the greater turnover of membership in the lower House, compared with the relatively stable personnel of the Lords. In other words, with a larger pool of people, whose presence was not guaranteed from one parliament to the next, there was more scope for individual personalities to skew the figures. For example, in the first session of 1610, which produced the biggest Commons' total of these years, three members each made two privilege claims. Of these three, Nicholas Steward and Sir William Waad never sat again after that parliament, and Sir Nicholas Saunders was not re-elected until 1626.[40] Even so, this lack of consistent progress towards greater exploitation of privilege remains a defining characteristic of the lower House, during this period.

---

[38] *LJ*, iv, 12, 17, 21–2; *HPC, 1604–29*, iv, 376; Parliamentary Archives, HL/PO/JO/10/1/37: 26 Jan., 5 Feb. 1629; Clergy of the Church of England Database, available at *http://theclergydatabase.org.uk/* (accessed 29 September 2014), (*sub* Lamerton, Exeter).

[39] For the sources of these statistics, see note 20.

[40] *HPC, 1604–29*, vi, 212–14, 434–6, 639–40.

Having said that, it is clear that some of the developments already seen in the Lords also occurred in the Commons. As in the upper House, the definition of personal servants was relaxed over time. Initially, members were fairly scrupulous about this issue. In February 1607, Sir Michael Sondes sparked controversy by claiming privilege for a former servant who was now an attorney in the court of common pleas. The House reluctantly agreed to this, after Sondes affirmed that the man had continued to live in his house and take his wages, but it then took steps to restrict future claims to the traditional category of personal, menial attendants.[41] By June 1621, however, Sir Francis Popham felt able to request privilege for some of his tenants in relation to a lawsuit. The final outcome of this case is unclear, as an initial stay of trial was challenged, but Sir Francis Foljambe in 1626 and Sir John Hotham in 1628, both successfully made claims on behalf of tenants.[42]

Significantly, the Commons also went through the same process of defining the temporal limits of privilege. Although there was already a precedent from 1587 which advocated 20 days' grace either side of a session, a narrower option was actually adopted in 1606. The issue was raised when Christopher Brooke was arrested a few days after the 1605 emergency adjournment of parliament triggered by the discovery of the Gunpowder Plot. In the ensuing inquiry, the 1587 case was cited, but it was generally felt that 16 days was 'a reasonable tyme of priviledge and freedome before and after every cession'.[43] That decision was revisited in October 1610. Sir Vincent Skinner had been arrested for debt exactly 16 days after the end of the previous session, but released upon claiming privilege. His narrow escape gave members pause, and a few even argued that the time limit should vary according to the distance that they had to travel to and from parliament. However, the 16-day rule was eventually upheld, and thereafter became set in stone.[44]

The next stage was the utilisation of prorogation days, and this was addressed in Sir Robert Howard's case of 1626. Howard, a younger son of the 1st earl of Suffolk, had served in the 1624 parliament, which was scheduled to begin a second session on 15 March 1625 until, as noted earlier, events forced a change of plan. Five days before this prorogation date, Howard was excommunicated by the court of high commission for adultery with the wife of Viscount Purbeck. Although he asserted his privileged status as a member of the Commons, the court dismissed his claim and went ahead with its sentence. Howard was, again, elected to parliament in the following month, but did not initially pursue the privilege question, which was thus left unresolved until 1626. His case was raised on 17 February that year, when the House was reassured that there were solid precedents for a breach of privilege in one parliament being pursued in a later session. Even so, the circumstances behind Howard's case were unusually complex, and it was not until 21 March that privilege was finally granted, and a precedent created in the Commons for claims built around prorogation days. Intriguingly, this was just over a month before Sir Francis Browne's equivalent case was brought before the Lords and,

[41] *Bowyer Diary*, 209–10.

[42] *CJ*, i, 634; Nicholas, *Commons, 1621*, ii, 200–1; *Procs 1626*, ii, 194, 197; *CD, 1628*, iv, 293.

[43] *Bowyer Diary*, 35–6.

[44] *Proceedings in Parliament 1610*, ed. Foster, ii, 306–8, 387–8.

although the records of the upper House make no mention of the Howard inquiry, it must be suspected that word filtered through, and that for once the Commons set the pace in this area.[45]

It should be clear, by now, that the history of parliamentary privilege during the early 17th century is not simply one of enhanced scope, but also of changing function. By 1629, the original concept of preventing disruption to parliament, while not completely forgotten, had become secondary to the personal needs of members. Both Houses were aware that this could lead to abuse of the protection that privilege afforded, and, indeed, that proved to be the case. In 1621, for example, the Lords considered a request from Edward Shereborne, who had been arrested for debt. Initially, he presented himself as a servant to Lord Mordaunt, but it finally emerged that he was actually basing his claim on his appointment by Lord Chancellor St Alban as a collector of the Lords' subsidy tax. That most certainly did not qualify him for privilege and, in any case, St Alban had only recently been disgraced and barred from membership of the Lords, which would have invalidated any genuine ties between him and Shereborne.[46] Accordingly, the claim was rejected. Shereborne's case was sufficiently far-fetched to be almost amusing, but there was nothing funny about the behaviour of Lord Deincourt, who claimed privilege in both 1626 and 1629 in a bid to avoid financial obligations to his own family, to whom he owed more than £2,000. This was a blatant abuse of privilege and the Lords, while upholding the Elizabethan precedent of Lord Cromwell that peers should not be arrested, otherwise supported the battle waged in chancery by Deincourt's relatives as they tried to recover their money.[47]

In contrast, the Commons generally took a more relaxed attitude to debt problems. Although the crown warned against the lower House acting as a shelter for bankrupts, there is no question that it did so. In 1614, as many as 11 men may have sought election to the Commons to gain temporary respite from their creditors, and such cases can be detected in most parliaments of this period.[48] The attitude of the lower House, where the bulk of the members were probably in debt to some degree, was almost invariably to focus on the legal niceties, while turning a blind eye to the underlying problem. In 1625, for example, Arthur Bassett won a seat at Fowey, Cornwall, while imprisoned for debt, and then claimed privilege in order to secure his release. The only issue of concern to his fellow members was the precise grounds on which he had been interned, and once it was established that he was still bailable, there was no argument about privilege being awarded.[49] In the following year, no doubt emboldened by this episode, one of Bassett's kinsmen, the even more heavily indebted Sir Thomas Monck, tried the same tactic, and arranged for his own election at another Cornish borough, Camelford. However, in this instance the strategy failed, as Monck was not simply in gaol awaiting trial, like Bassett, but had already received judgment in court over his debts. Privilege did not apply in these circumstances, and the Commons, instead, ruled that Monck's election was invalid.[50]

[45] *HPC, 1604–29*, iv, 814; *Procs 1626*, ii, 60–1, 64–5, 327–9.

[46] *LJ*, iii, 120.

[47] *Procs 1626*, i, 445; *LJ*, iv, 16, 27–9.

[48] *HPC, 1604–29*, i, 67–9, 90–1.

[49] *Procs 1625*, pp. 257, 353–4.

[50] *HPC, 1604–29*, vi, 929–30; *Procs 1626*, ii, 339, 356.

Such cases probably attracted little attention outside Westminster, but one area of abuse briefly brought privilege into serious and widespread disrepute. By 1621, a new practice had grown up whereby members of both Houses issued letters of protection to those dependants whom they wished to benefit from their own privilege. The recipients could then produce these documents, if they found themselves in trouble, as proof of their connection to the member concerned. In theory, this was supposed to dispel uncertainty and reduce the number of cases being brought before parliament, but it took little imagination to realize that this valuable ability to offer protection from the law might have a lucrative side. That became all too obvious when the momentous decision was taken by both Houses, in June 1621, that privilege would remain in force through-out the forthcoming adjournment.[51] Parliament did not resume for nearly six months and, when it did so, it was faced with a crisis of its own making. As the newsletter writer, John Chamberlain, reported, on 24 November, in the Commons 'their first work was to call in and disannull protections, which were growne to great excesse, so that marchants, tradesmen, and all maner unthrifts and debtors walked securely under sombodies name during the Parlement, which was generally misliked, and thought a grosse error that they who take upon them to set all straight shold geve way to such an abuse'. As for the Lords, 'yt be saide they are more faultie in this kind, insomuch that the report goes the Lord Stafford hath geven above three hundred to some very base and meane companions for five shillings apeece more or lesse'.[52] The house of commons moved swiftly to distance itself from such abuses, bringing in tough new regulations governing the future issuing of protections. Arguably, there was an element of cover-up, as the matter was then treated as closed.[53] In the Lords, the problem was raked over at much greater length, for Lord Stafford himself complained, on 26 November, that forged protections had been issued in his name by seven individuals, thereby initiating an inquiry which ran on until the end of the session. Lord North came forward at the same time with a similar tale while, four days later, the House heard that Viscount Rochford had also fallen victim to a forger, the appropriately named Con Conner. One man eventually admitted to manufacturing fake protections in Lord Stafford's name, and it is clear that a number of these letters changed hands for money, though the precise quantity is not known, and the going rate was apparently only three shillings.[54] There is no proof that Stafford himself profited from this trade, though he certainly seems to have handed out genuine protection letters more freely than did most peers. In November and December 1621, the Lords considered five different privilege claims by his servants, almost half of all the cases heard during that sitting.[55]

It would, of course, be incorrect to suggest that abuse of privilege was anything new in the 17th century, and examples can be found back into medieval times.[56] Neverthe-less, the organised corruption of the 1621 protections' scandal was unprecedented, even if it cannot be proved that parliamentarians benefited from it financially. The crucial

---

[51] *LJ*, iii, 157; *CD, 1621*, vi, 477.

[52] *The Letters of John Chamberlain*, ed. N.E. McClure (2 vols, Philadelphia, PA, 1939), ii, 409.

[53] *CJ*, i, 641; *CD, 1621*, iii, 430–1.

[54] *LJ*, iii, 170, 172, 176, 180, 199.

[55] *LJ*, iii, 169, 176, 183–4, 186.

[56] *Parliamentarians at Law*, ed. Kleineke, 7.

point is that privilege was increasingly a resource which could be taken for granted. Once the rules were more clearly defined, and their application more predictable, it became possible for them to be manipulated for personal advantage, as John Glanville demonstrated in his 1629 case. Privilege became not just a form of defence, but also a means of attack, and by the later 1620s it was demonstrably being exploited for purely political ends, though a successful outcome was by no means guaranteed.

There are, for example, good reasons for believing that Sir Robert Howard's case in 1626 was politically motivated. This was the parliament which saw the most concerted attack on the royal favourite, the duke of Buckingham. Howard's lover, Lady Purbeck, was the duke's sister-in-law, the wife of his elder brother, John. This was particularly significant, because Buckingham had obtained a patent in 1617 whereby, if he died without male heirs, John and his offspring would inherit his titles. Viscount Purbeck's marriage broke down four years later but, because he did not obtain a divorce, any children born to his wife were legally his own. Thus, when Lady Purbeck had her first illegitimate son by Howard in 1624, there was nothing to prevent the child from succeeding to a string of honours, as Buckingham still only had a daughter himself. Not surprisingly, the duke suddenly became very keen to have his brother's marriage annulled, and was the driving force behind the High Commission action against Howard and Lady Purbeck. The guilty couple both tried to claim privilege, but without success. Howard was excommunicated, but Lady Purbeck continued to protest her innocence, and the hearings dragged on.[57] By the time the 1626 parliament met, Howard's penalty had already been lifted, so his claim for privilege was, in effect, superfluous, and most likely intended to remind his fellow members of the scandal as a way of embarrassing Buckingham. Tellingly, the case was managed in the Commons by John Selden, a client of the earl of Hertford, one of the duke's opponents in the Lords. Selden actively misled the Commons, denying that Howard's excommunication had been cancelled, and alleging that the other members risked incurring the same penalty by association. Even after Howard was granted privilege on 21 March, Selden kept the issue alive by pushing for the High Commission formally to revoke Howard's sentence.[58] Meanwhile, in the Lords, where Selden's patron, Hertford, was chairing its committee for privileges, Lady Purbeck herself had two claims approved, after she and one of her servants were arrested. Even though these latter two cases were apparently coincidental, it can hardly have escaped their lordships' notice that she was claiming in the right of her estranged husband, so this was still a calculated snub to Buckingham.[59]

However, if the Howard case was primarily about causing embarrassment to the government, there were other issues where privilege was deployed for more serious reasons. One of the most pressing concerns in the Lords in 1626 was the exclusion of members by the king. The bishop of Lincoln and earl of Bristol were denied their writs of summons before the parliament met and then, on 5 March, the earl of Arundel was unexpectedly committed to the Tower of London. This was ostensibly over a private

[57] G.E. Cokayne, *The Complete Peerage of England, Scotland, Ireland, Great Britain and the United Kingdom*, ed. Vicary Gibbs *et al.* (14 vols in 15, 1910–98), ii, 392–3; x, 684–5; Roger Lockyer, *Buckingham* (1981), 285–6, 408; *Letters of John Chamberlain*, ed. McClure, ii, 605, 607–8.

[58] *HPC, 1604–29*, vi, 267; *Procs 1626*, ii, 61, 64–5, 330–3; iii, 150.

[59] *Procs 1626*, i, 70, 75–7, 96–7, 256, 603, 615.

matter, the earl's son having just secretly married one of Charles I's cousins without permission.[60] Indeed, as soon as the matter was raised in the Lords on 14 March, a message was delivered from the king reassuring the House that Arundel's detention had nothing to do with parliamentary matters. Nevertheless, it was generally believed that the earl had been imprisoned for opposing Buckingham, and the incident was, in any case, yet another example of arbitrary interference with the Lords' membership. Other critics of the duke, such as Viscount Saye and Sele, were soon stirring up fears that a precedent would be set if Arundel's confinement was not challenged.[61] The ensuing stand-off between the Lords and the king lasted for nearly three months, with Charles refusing to explain the reasons for his action, and Arundel's allies maintaining that it was a breach of privilege for a lord to be committed during a parliamentary session without a trial or the judgment of his fellow peers. The more the king tried to fob them off, the more the Lords insisted on Arundel's return to the House.[62] At length, taking its cue from a similar incident involving a member of the Commons, Sir Dudley Digges, the Lords went on strike. After a fortnight of suspended business, Charles capitulated and released Arundel, unwilling to surrender the point that the Lords had no automatic right to be informed of matters of state, but equally unable to find a convincing argument that his continuing silence was not a breach of its privilege.[63]

This was an impressive victory for the Lords, but it depended on three factors: its collective determination to stand up to Charles; the solid body of precedents that it was able to bring to bear on Arundel's case; and the king's realization that he could not afford to alienate his peers entirely at a time when he was already in dispute with the Commons. When the lower House attempted to use privilege for political ends in 1629, the outcome was very different. John Rolle's case was ostensibly a simple claim for recovery of property, but the manner in which it was pursued constituted a serious challenge to the crown's powers of taxation. Rolle was a merchant who had had some of his goods confiscated for non-payment of tunnage and poundage. These traditional levies on merchandise were normally awarded for life to each monarch at the start of their reign but, due to continual disputes in parliament, Charles I had failed to secure this vital grant, and was, therefore, obliged to collect tunnage and poundage without parliamentary approval. This, in turn, came to be seen as a major grievance, and the 1628 session ended with a declaration by the Commons effectively inciting merchants to withhold payment. That was the context in which Rolle made his own stand.[64] It was generally recognized by both crown and parliament that this situation needed to be resolved, and parliament reconvened in 1629 with the principal purpose of finally passing a Tunnage and Poundage Bill. However, the Commons was deeply divided between members who saw such legislation as the only constructive solution to the crisis, and others who believed that Englishmen's liberties had been trampled on by the government, rendering some measure of redress a vital precondition for any fresh start.

[60] *Procs 1626*, i, 108, 192; TNA, SP16/20/43.

[61] *Procs 1626*, i, 151, 157–9; Conrad Russell, *Parliaments and English Politics, 1621–1629* (Oxford, 1979), 287.

[62] *Procs 1626*, i, 256–7, 286–7, 290, 349, 351, 394–5, 398, 407.

[63] *Procs 1626*, i, 495, 533, 543, 553–4, 556, 558–9, 561, 564.

[64] *HPC, 1604–29*, vi, 87–8.

When Rolle brought his complaints to the House, on 22 January, his bid to recover his goods rapidly became a test case on whether the Commons could force concessions from the government. From the outset, it should have been obvious that this was a flawed strategy. Even if Rolle won, the precedent created would be of no benefit to other merchants who were not members of the House. Moreover, his privilege claim rested on the fact that his merchandise had been confiscated ten days after an isolated prorogation day in October 1628. Despite the Howard case in 1626, the basing of claims on the prorogation day argument was still a novelty, and many members remained doubtful about it, despite the assurances offered by John Selden and others.[65] However, the real nub of the question was far more problematic. Privilege was understood to be effective for recovery of goods seized by private individuals, but not for property taken by the crown. Rolle's goods had been confiscated by the customs' farmers who were contracted to collect tax revenues on behalf of the king, so his claim was viable only if it could be proved that these officials had detained his merchandise for their own benefit, rather than that of the crown. The Commons spent many anxious days questioning the customs' farmers and examining their contract, in search of a definitive answer, and at length a majority of members were persuaded that the farmers had acted on their own behalf. Rolle was awarded privilege on 23 February. By this time, though, Charles had given up all hope of securing a formal grant of tunnage and poundage, and he was in no mood for compromise. Having informed the Commons that he took full responsibility for the customs' farmers' actions, thereby effectively invalidating Rolle's grant of privilege, he proceeded first to adjourn and then dissolve parliament. Rolle's claim had proved to be nothing more than a distraction from the real business that the Commons did not want to address.[66]

Rolle's case illustrates both the limitations and potential of parliamentary privilege by 1629. The lower House had clearly overreached itself by challenging the crown with a relatively weak claim, but the very fact that members could be persuaded to pursue this strategy at all is a measure of just how much privilege had evolved since 1604. What had once been merely a means of protecting the Lords and Commons from external distractions was now increasingly viewed as a political weapon. In a sense, the trans-formation of privilege was one manifestation of parliament's growing assertiveness during this period. On the one hand, its members awarded themselves additional rights, in keeping with their own burgeoning sense of constitutional self-importance. On the other hand, privilege came to impinge more heavily on the world outside parliament, both in the range of possible breaches and in the scope for abuse. As John Chamberlain observed of the 1621 protections' scandal, there was an inherent risk that if members' rights took precedence over their responsibilities, the image of parliament as a vehicle of reform could become tarnished, though in the event that episode did nothing to slow the rate of change.

This expansion of privilege was an issue affecting parliament as a whole. The Lords and Commons had slightly different requirements, and the pace of development varied accordingly between the two Houses, but there was broad agreement that the rights of members could, and should, be extended, provided that the existing demarcation lines

---

[65] CD, 1629, pp. 7–8, 228–34.
[66] CD, 1629, pp. 83–95; CJ, i, 932.

within parliament were respected. Where Lords and Commons diverged was in their perceptions of the purpose of privilege. For the lower House, parliaments provided intermittent opportunities to address the nation's grievances, and privileges afforded them a measure of protection while they engaged in that task. As Sir Edward Coke put it, in August 1625: 'the privilege of the House of Commons was the heartstring of the commonwealth'.[67] Regardless of how those rights were actually deployed, they were seen as existing primarily for the benefit of the wider population. In contrast, for the peers, parliamentary privilege was merely a supplement to the many rights they already enjoyed in normal life, as was spelt out in the remit given to the Lords' committee for privileges in 1621. Consequently, the most significant benefit for the peers was not their individual immunities but, rather, the political muscle available to them when they invoked their collective rights as members of the upper House. This distinction became more apparent, as tensions grew between parliament and the crown in the later 1620s. Rolle's case demonstrated that, if the Commons abandoned serious negotiations over taxation, its traditional means of leverage, then privilege was not an effective means of influencing government policy. However, when the peers challenged Charles I over the detention of the earl of Arundel, it was their unyielding defence of their privileges which forced him to capitulate. At a private level, privilege benefited both Houses fairly evenly, but in political terms it was the Lords which emerged the stronger, reasserting its status as the one body that the crown could not afford to alienate.

---

[67] *Procs 1625*, pp. 382–3.

'Wrangling Lawyers': Proclamations and the Management of the English Parliament of 1621

CHRIS R. KYLE

This article examines the fall of lord chancellor, Sir Francis Bacon, Viscount St Alban, during the parliament of 1621. It reviews Bacon's drafting of two controversial proclamations relating to the calling of the parliament and James I's intense displeasure at the actions of his lord chancellor. While Bacon sought to inform the political nation of English policy towards the Spanish match and the Thirty Years' War, James closed down all such talk and railed against the legal profession in general and 'wrangling lawyers' in particular. When allegations of corruption against Bacon surfaced during the 1621 parliament, James did not defend him, in part because of his long-standing antipathy towards lawyers.

Keywords: Sir Francis Bacon; parliament; impeachment; proclamations; James I; lawyers; parliamentary elections; Spanish match; George Villiers, duke of Buckingham; Sir Edward Coke; Francis Brakin; freedom of speech; censorship

1

The calling of a parliament was always a fraught occasion for any early modern monarch. Accustomed to ruling the country from on high and in conjunction only with their personal appointees on the privy council, the assembling of a parliament opened up a forum in which the governing class had the opportunity to critique (gently or robustly) government policy, attempt to force new directions in that policy, both foreign and domestic, and, by and large, make a nuisance of themselves. No early modern monarch looked forward to these meetings and one thing was certain – there were always going to be a few members, the perennial firebrands, who would overstep the mark and require censuring by the parliament and monarch. They were, as one might expect, usually lawyers.

The third Jacobean parliament of 1621 was set to open at a particularly awkward time and would require extensive management from the crown, especially given the chequered history of Jacobean parliaments. The 1604–10 sessions had been marred by bitter disputes over the union with Scotland and the failure of the Great Contract and the 1614 parliament was named a convention not a parliament as, after failing to pass any legislation, it was 'addled', following allegations of royal packing and interference in elections.[1]

---

[1] See Wallace Notestein, *The House of Commons, 1604–1610* (New Haven, CT, 1971); David L. Smith, *The Stuart Parliaments, 1603–1689* (1998), 101–9; *The History of Parliament: The House of Commons, 1604–1629*, ed. Andrew Thrush and John P. Ferris (6 vols, Cambridge, 2010) [hereafter cited as *HPC, 1604–29*], i, pp. xxxv–xliii; Thomas L. Moir, *The Addled Parliament of 1614* (Oxford, 1958); Conrad Russell, *The Addled Parliament of 1614: The Limits of Revision* (The Stenton Lectures, Reading, 1992); *The Crisis of 1614 and The Addled Parliament*, ed. Stephen Clucas and Rosalind Davies (Aldershot, 2003).

Adding to this potentially fiery situation in 1621, the Thirty Years' War and the loss of the landed possessions of James's daughter and son-in-law in that war, meant that English foreign policy was to the fore of 'public' debate. The omens for a successful parliament, or at least a peaceful one, were not great.

But parliaments were always about management and, after all, Henry VIII had survived his by removing the opposition beforehand; Elizabeth had struggled through hers by sheer force of will and some useful tacticians in the house of commons; and James had managed to secure a substantial sum of money in 1604–10 despite his other problems. However, the Great Contract negotiations of 1610 had left a rather bitter scar on James – he had come to regard the 'negotiations' that had taken place as not the right way for a king to engage with his subjects.[2] The point was how to get parliament on board with the royal agenda – keep the peace but help his children abroad; conclude a successful marriage treaty with Spain; and convince the parliament to vote for substantial subsidies. Into this effort, the lord chancellor, Sir Francis Bacon, Viscount St Alban, was drafted.

In terms of domestic grievances, the 1621 parliament was most concerned with the issue of egregious monopoly patents.[3] Problems with crown grants of monopolies had a long and complex legal history, dating back to Elizabeth's reign and involving the law courts in a number of landmark cases, most importantly *Darcy* v. *Allen* (1602) and the *Cloth-workers of Ipswich* v. *Sheninge* (1614). Despite these cases, and Jacobean proclamations and the king's declaration in the 1610 Book of Bounty, monopoly patents continued to be granted and executed. As in 1601, one of the first actions in the house of commons was to debate legislation on this very issue.[4]

In the parliament of 1621, grievances ran through two processes – one was the traditional model of legislation and the other was through complaint and petition. As soon as the house of commons started investigating, the scale of the problem became clear. Tales of exploitation and woe poured into parliament and soon the blame for this started to be shared around. Obviously, as Sir Edward Sackville noted, the king was too busy to examine personally all the grants: 'inquiry might be made towching his Majesties referments of the Peticions uppon which such graunts ensued, and soe the faults might be taken from his Majestie and lye uppon the Refferrees who misled his Majestie and are worthie to beare the shame of their owne worke'.[5]

---

[2] On the Great Contract, see Neil Cuddy, 'The Real Attempted "Tudor Revolution in Government": Salisbury's Great Contract', in *Authority and Consent in Tudor Government*, ed. George W. Bernard and Steven J. Gunn (Aldershot, 2002), 249–70; Eric N. Lindquist, 'The Failure of the Great Contract', *Journal of Modern History*, lvii (1985), 617–51; A.G.R. Smith, 'Crown, Parliament and Finance: The Great Contract of 1610', in *The English Commonwealth, 1547–1640*, ed. Peter Clark, A.G.R. Smith and Nicholas Tyacke (Leicester, 1979), 111–27, 237–9.

[3] Robert Zaller, *The Parliament of 1621: A Study in Constitutional Conflict* (Berkeley, CA, 1971); Conrad Russell, *Parliaments and English Politics, 1621–1629* (Oxford, 1979), ch. 2; Chris R. Kyle, ' "But a New Button to an Old Coat": The Enactment of the Statute of Monopolies, 21 James I cap.3', *Journal of Legal History*, xix (1998), 203–23; Elizabeth Read Foster, 'The Procedure of the House of Commons against Patents and Monopolies, 1621–1624', in *Conflict in Stuart England*, ed. W.A. Aiken and B.D. Henning (1960), 57–85.

[4] For the history of these cases, see Kyle, 'Enactment'.

[5] *Commons Debates, 1621*, ed. Wallace Notestein, Frances Helen Relf and Hartley Simpson (7 vols, New Haven, CT, 1935) [hereafter cited as *CD, 1621*], iv, 19–20.

In the following days and weeks, the rhetoric heated up – the Inns patent held by an MP, Sir Giles Mompesson, was so hideous, Sir Edward Coke thought, 'that no King in Christendom would have granted it'.[6] The furore just would not abate and it quickly became clear that the Commons could do little to one of its members except send him to the Tower. Ironically, the quest to punish Mompesson would lead through the Tower where the ancient records were kept. William Noy and William Hakewill searched the records and Coke presented the solution. In medieval times, the house of lords had acted as a court of law – if its judicial function could be revived, then Mompesson could be prosecuted for a 'general grievance' against the state. All the while, the grievances that flooded into the Commons flowed closer and closer to Bacon. One which looked particularly odious was the gold and silver thread patent. Information on this came from Sir Henry Yelverton, the ex-solicitor general, over whose trial for corruption Bacon had recently presided.[7] Yelverton confessed that he thought the patent dubious, but Bacon had approved it. In the days of early March, MPs fell over themselves in condemning these grants: Sir Dudley Digges was quite modest with his proposal that patents and referees (certifiers) be 'damned to posterity'.[8] Sir Edward Giles liked the phrase 'bloodsuckers'; Sir Hamon L'Estrange, 'Jesabells' and 'Achitophells';[9] and Sir John Walter bizarrely suggested sending them all before the convocation of Canterbury so they could be cursed.[10] If this was not sufficiently dangerous to Bacon, it then came to light that he had accepted money in conjunction with suits in chancery over which he had presided as lord chancellor.

Events moved swiftly. Charges were prepared in the Commons and indictments laid before the Lords. Bacon denied only a few of the charges, confessing 'that I am guilty of corruption', and he was impeached. Although fined £40,000 and imprisoned at the king's pleasure, he, in fact, was in the Tower for only three days and the fine was not enforced. However, he was barred from holding any office of state or coming within the verge of the court.[11] This, then, is the traditional, centuries-old picture of the fall of Bacon, sacrificed by a king whose concern was to protect his favourite, the duke of Buckingham, who was the real target of the monopolies investigation. A scapegoat was needed – Bacon was it – and, as Linda Levy Peck has recently argued, James could not tolerate corruption in his own royal judges – they represented him and their corruption could easily be seen as his corruption.[12] Peck's judgment on this is undoubtedly correct and Bacon himself described royal judges as 'Lions under the throne'.[13]

[6] *CD, 1621*, ii, 108.

[7] *The Letters and Life of Francis Bacon*, ed. James Spedding (7 vols, 1861–74), vii, 133–40.

[8] *CD, 1621*, ii, 167.

[9] *CD, 1621*, v, 272.

[10] *CD, 1621*, v, 25–6; *CJ*, i, 539.

[11] Colin Gerald Calder Tite, *Impeachment and Parliamentary Judicature in Early Stuart England* (1974), chs 4–5; *Bacon*, ed. Spedding, vii, 182–227; Simon Healy, unpublished draft biography of Francis Bacon, History of Parliament Trust, House of Lords 1604–1660; Lisa Jardine and Alan Stewart, *Hostage to Fortune: The Troubled Life of Francis Bacon, 1561–1629* (New York, 1998), 444–69.

[12] Linda Levy Peck, *Court Patronage and Corruption in Early Stuart England* (1990), 186–9.

[13] *Francis Bacon: The Major Works*, ed. Brian Vickers (Oxford, 2002), *Essays or Counsels, Civil or Moral: Of Judicature*, 449.

However, there were other issues that may well have influenced Bacon's fall and the king's willingness to let him go – in particular, the lord chancellor's advocacy of parliaments in the constitution and politics of England. This, combined with James's increasing distaste of lawyers, ultimately weakened Bacon's standing with the king and helped ensure his removal from office.

2

In late 1620, the lord chancellor, Sir Francis Bacon, drafted two proclamations in anticipation of the forthcoming parliament. The first called for the election of the 'worthiest' citizens to serve as MPs while the second forbade the discussion of matters of state in public.[14] Coming shortly after the publication and suppression of Thomas Scott's controversial anti-Spanish tract, *Vox Populi*,[15] and in the wake of the failed parliament of 1614, James I was desperate to ensure that a tractable parliament assembled and one in which discussion of English foreign policy in relation to the Thirty Years' War did not become the talk of the town. However, in an extraordinary moment of royal control, James dismissed Bacon's work on the election proclamation and drafted his own version, dripping with venom at the 'wrangling lawyers' who dominated the house of commons, and deleting all references to foreign policy.

James, having dismissed the intellectual capacity of his subjects to understand European affairs, embarked on an extraordinary course of royal authorship and management. Thus, summarily dismissed was the advice of his privy council committee on parliament and his senior government officer, while James bent himself to the task of writing a proclamation. Out, of course, went any reference to why parliament was being called and James even altered the wording on who was fit to be an MP. Lawyers took the brunt of James's ire. Bacon's original draft had recommended that voters 'not disvalue or disparage the House' with 'lawyers of mean account and estimation'. James, over the fervent protestation of both Bacon and the earl of Pembroke, changed the wording.[16] Between 1,000 and 1,500 copies were printed and read out in town halls, yelled out in market squares and perused in the drawing rooms of stately homes, including James's own words: 'no wrangling lawyers'.[17] James singularly failed to follow his own advice, so clearly laid out in *Basilikon Doron*: 'Flatter not your selfe in your laboures, but before they be set foorth, let them firste bee priuelye censured by some of the best skilled men in that craft.'[18]

---

[14] *Stuart Royal Proclamations: James I*, ed. James F. Larkin and Paul Hughes (Oxford, 1973), 493–6.

[15] Thomas Scott, *Vox Populi. Or, Newes from Spayne* (1620). See Simon Adams, 'Captain Thomas Gainsford, the "Vox Spiritus" and the *Vox Populi*', *Bulletin of the Institute of Historical Research*, xlix (1976) 141–4; Peter Lake, 'Constitutional Consensus and Puritan Opposition in the 1620s: Thomas Scott and the Spanish Match', *Historical Journal*, xxv (1982), 805–25.

[16] *Bacon*, ed. Spedding, vii, 152–6.

[17] On the numbers of proclamations printed in Jacobean England, see BL, Add. MS 5756, f. 140.

[18] James VI and I, *Basilikon Doron: Or His Majesties Instructions to his Dearest Sonne Henrie the Prince* (Edinburgh, 1603), 118.

That Bacon as lord keeper was actually drafting the proclamations was in itself unusual. The attorney general normally wrote proclamations, but the office was in abeyance at this time. Sir Henry Yelverton, the previous incumbent, had recently been dismissed for alleged charges of corruption or, more accurately, for being an implacable enemy of the duke of Buckingham and refusing to bribe him.[19] Thus the task fell to the experienced Bacon who, as lord chancellor, had just presided over Yelverton's trial. Having served before as attorney general, he had already penned some 30 proclamations for the Jacobean government.[20] The first proclamation concerned parliamentary elections and the other was 'against excess of lavish and licentious speech of matters of state'.[21] Both turned out to be rather problematical, although in somewhat different ways. Bacon was concerned, and rightly so as it turned out, that the recent events on the Continent, as well as the rapprochement with Spain, would prove to be contentious issues in parliament, mirroring the already worrying open discussion of these matters in general. He thus recommended to the king, via the duke of Buckingham, that a proclamation be drafted and issued to restrain speech about these matters of state, which he found were being discussed by the 'vulgar' sort. Subsequently drafted by Bacon, James was delighted with his lord chancellor, as Buckingham informed him: 'his Majesty liketh in every point so well, both in matter and form, that he findeth no cause to alter a word in it, and would have your lordship acquaint the council with it (though he assureth himself no man can find anything in it to be changed) and to take order for the speedy setting foorth of it'.[22] Or as the Venetian ambassador noted: 'A vigorous proclamation has been published here against those who speak or write too freely of the government and of matters of state, but when everyone is silent air and earth ultimately cry out.'[23]

However, Bacon's other proclamation concerning parliament met with severe royal disapproval. In simple terms, what Bacon proposed, drafted and submitted to James was a robust declaration of the government's thinking *vis-à-vis* the Palatinate. In the proclamation, he wrote a full explanation of the royal policy towards the Palatinate. The aim of being so forthright was to enlist the assistance of parliament in regaining Bohemia for Frederick and Elizabeth. Bacon, though, acknowledged the king's power: 'for although the making of war and peace be a secret of empire, and a thing properly belonging to our high prerogative, royal and imperiall power: yet nevertheless, in causes of that nature which we think fit not to reserve but to communicate, we shall ever think ourselves much assisted and strengthened by the faithful advice and general assent of our loving subjects'.[24] Communication with his subjects in such a clear form was not, however, how James felt a king ought to rule. Bacon received the king's response in a letter from Buckingham:

I have showed your letter and the proclamation to his Majesty, who expecting only ... directions therein for the well-ordering of the elections of burgesses, findeth a

[19] See 'Yelverton, Sir Henry', *ODNB*.

[20] Calculated from *Stuart Royal Proclamations*, ed. Larkin and Hughes.

[21] *Bacon*, ed. Spedding, vii, 156–7; *Stuart Royal Proclamations*, ed. Larkin and Hughes, 493–6.

[22] *Bacon*, ed. Spedding, vii, 154–5.

[23] *CSP Ven., 1619–21*, no. 679: 8 Jan. 1621; *CSP Dom., 1619–23*, p. 202.

[24] *Bacon*, ed. Spedding, vii, 126.

great deal more, containing matter of state and the reasons for calling the Parliament, whereof neither the people are capable, nor is it fit for his Majesty to open now unto them ... His Majesty hath therefore extracted somewhat of the latter part of the draught you have sent, purposing to take a few days space to set down himself what he thinketh fit.[25]

These proclamations were issued at the same time as the first newspapers arrived in England and, just as the king failed to grasp the enormous propaganda value of starting an official news service, so, too, did James miss the opportunity to inform the governing class of his views before its representatives arrived at Westminster.

3

Except in a rather clinical fashion of compilation, proclamations have received little scholarly attention, and what they have received was either forged in the crucible of early revisionist politics or limited to proclamations on individual matters – for example, weights and measures.[26] What is missing from this picture is how proclamations became public and what that means? Proclamations had steadily become a more important and visible part of governing England in the 17th century by a variety of metrics – the number issued every year increased from Elizabeth's reign; more special messengers were employed to deliver them – four was the common number under Elizabeth, while five to six swept through the countryside with these printed bundles under James. The numbers printed increased as well; 400 seems to have been the normal Elizabethan print run, increasing to 1,000–1,500 in the early 17th century (400 would, by then, only service important local areas such as London).[27]

Away from simple metrics, proclamations are a staple of many gentry collections, as magistrates and local officials collected and enforced them, and scribbled notes in the margins. City and town councils entered them in their records as did London companies. In one way, there is nothing particularly problematic here – Bacon's election proclamation reached the core constituency of parliamentary voters. But the difficulty lies in display and their public performance. Proclamations were not only written reminders or edicts but also highly-visible signs of government policy. In Stratford-upon-Avon, a proclamation box in the church foyer held the latest issue for everyone to read (or be read to) as they went to church.[28] In Thetford, the bell corner post served

---

[25] *Bacon*, ed. Spedding, vii, 128.

[26] E.g., R.W. Heinze, *The Proclamations of the Tudor Kings* (Cambridge, 1976); Frederic A. Youngs jr, *The Proclamations of the Tudor Queens* (Cambridge, 1976). Some research has been done on parliament's attitude to proclamations and Henry VIII's controversial act in 1539, but the whole field remains ripe for reinterpretation. Michael Bush, 'The Act of Proclamations: A Reinterpretation', *American Journal of Legal History*, xxvii (1983), 33–53; G.R. Elton, 'Henry VIII's Act of Proclamations', *English Historical Review*, lxxv (1960), 208–22; Esther S. Cope, 'Sir Edward Coke and Proclamations, 1610', *American Journal of Legal History*, xv (1971), 215–21; R.W. Heinze, 'Proclamations and Parliamentary Protest, 1539–1610', in *Tudor Rule and Revolution*, ed. DeLloyd Guth and J.W. McKenna (Cambridge, 1982), 237–59.

[27] BL, Add. MS 5756, ff. 134–40.

[28] *Minutes and Accounts of the Corporation of Stratford-upon-Avon*, ed. Richard Savage (Dugdale Society, 4 vols, 1921–9), iv, 56.

as a convenient hanging place, littered with numerous proclamations, while anyone popping into the Sadler's shop in Watton could read proclamations.[29]

Nor was it necessary to be literate to discover what was in a proclamation – as their name implies, these documents were proclaimed, often with great fanfare. Throughout the country, proclamations were withheld until market days, where a greater proportion of the population could be reached. In many town and cities, the ritual was elaborate and very visible – trumpeters processed with local officials dressed in their regalia through the town, reading the proclamation at multiple sites and tacking up copies in markets, squares and other venues.[30] Crowds gathered, watched, listened, and occasionally reacted. In one particularly unfortunate instance in 1621, an Englishman stood on the toe of a Spaniard while the proclamation was being read that base persons should not abuse persons of quality – for his foot stomp, the Spaniard punched him and, when querying why, he punched him again. The rumour circulated that the proclamation had made the Englishman fearful of responding to this assault.[31] Proclamations were also visible in their enforcement. Elizabeth's 1581 proclamation on the carrying of weapons was enforced in London by sending men to all the gates in town to check the length of weapons. This action resulted in the arrest of a servant of the marquess of Northampton who scoffed at the London officials and the proclamation.[32]

James, at least until near the end of his reign, greatly valued printed proclamations, claiming, in 1621, that he had dictated every one of significance since becoming king. That same year, in response to the monopolies crisis, he claimed that 'Proclamations are for particular occasions and purposes . . . most of them myself doth dictate every word. Never any proclamation of state and weight which I did not direct; others I leave to ordinary means. And those which accompany patents and projects I meddle not with.'[33]

Despite the exaggeration of this claim, James recognized how proclamations reached a larger audience of his subjects than any other form of printed word (the Bible aside) and closely monitored their content. James was also authoring political poems at this time and he acknowledged that proclamations could not stop libels. As Curtis Perry noted, these poems show James's concern 'with writing, of his insistence upon arcana imperii and of the centrality of discursive imposition to his idea of authority'.[34] James was skeptical over the value of proclamations, despite his regarding them as law: his mocking poem of 1622 ordering the nobles to depart London, expressed his hope that a manuscript verse could do more than 'scarce a [printed] proclamation can expel'.[35] But it is clear that Bacon's proclamation would have done exactly what both he and James

---

[29] BL, Add. MS 22959, ff. 9, 29v, 32v–33.

[30] See, e.g., London: BL, Stowe 1047, ff. 268v–9; BL, Add. MS 4712, ff. 49v–50; Dover: BL, Add. MS 29623, f. 250v; Bristol: Bristol RO, 13748 (unfoliated): *Adam's Chronicle of Bristol*; Great Yarmouth: Hastings Museum and Art Gallery, A/H(a)1, f. 6v; Oxford: *Records of Early English Drama: Oxford*, ed. John R, Elliott (Toronto, 2004), i, 272.

[31] BL, Harleian MS 389, ff. 49–50: Joseph Meade to Martin Stuteville, 7 Apr. 1621.

[32] BL, Lansdowne MS 32, no. 6, f. 12.

[33] *CD, 1621*, iv, 71.

[34] Curtis Perry, ' "If Proclamations will not Serve": The Late Manuscript Poetry of James I and the Culture of Libel', in *Royal Subjects: Essays on the Writings of James VI and I*, ed. Daniel Fischlin and Mark Fortier (Detroit, MI, 2002), 224.

[35] Kevin Sharpe, 'Foreword', in *Royal Subjects*, ed. Fischlin and Fortier, 20.

did not want – and that is make visible to a large cross-section of the population, royal policy on the Palatinate and the fact it was up for debate.

But Bacon was possibly the ideal draftsman, so what went wrong? Bacon had substantial parliamentary experience. He had sat in every parliament since 1581 when he was 20 years old (he later boasted he was 17 years old when first elected), had served as attorney general during the 1614 parliament, in the rather unique position of sitting both in the Commons and serving in the Lords as well, and had drafted numerous parliamentary documents, including advice to the king on how to manage the 1614 session.[36] And, of course, Bacon now served on the privy council and as the lord chancellor, in which role he would preside as Speaker of the house of lords. But Bacon was also a dangerous choice for the king. He was one of the foremost supporters of the doctrine that at no time did the monarch stand so high as when he was 'King-in-Parliament' and was a fervent advocate of the necessity of consultations between the crown and parliament. Bacon had been heavily involved in the build-up to the 1614 parliament, advising on how to pack the Commons without looking like the elections were being manipulated and drawing up an agenda to appease the turbulent spirits in the Commons. In 1615, he had strenuously called for another parliament and put forward the suggestion that a proclamation on elections and the business of parliament should be issued.[37] After the commission for parliament was established in 1620, Chamberlain commented:

> yet in this short moment he resolved on a parlement to begin the 16 of January, and hath taken order for a commission and a proclamation as yt were two gentlemen-ushers to go before yt: the commission to survay all monopolies and patents that are grievous to the commonwealth: the proclamation to geve encouragement for a free election of knights and burgesses, and to forbid all recommendation by letters, and in case any be sent, to return them to him or his counsaile.[38]

These 'gentlemen ushers' of advance warnings of the business of parliament and electioneering were a recent innovation. In fact, it had only been tried once before at the start of James's reign. And this had spectacularly backfired, resulting in the *Goodwin* v. *Fortescue* case, the most controversial election dispute in the period and a standoff eventually won by the Commons over who had the right to determine election returns.[39]

For Bacon, parliaments were, and should be, the 'ancient and royal way of aid and provision for the King with treasure', as he noted in 1615.[40] Parliaments were of 'ancient

---

[36] On Bacon's parliamentary career, see *The History of Parliament: The House of Commons, 1558–1603*, ed. P.W. Hasler (3 vols, 1981); *HPC, 1604–29*; Healy, unpublished draft biography of Francis Bacon.

[37] *Bacon*, ed. Spedding, v, 176–91.

[38] *The Letters of John Chamberlain*, ed. N.E. McClure (2 vols, Philadelphia, PA, 1939), ii, 325: Chamberlain to Sir Dudley Carleton, 4 Nov. 1620.

[39] Linda Levy Peck, 'Goodwin v. Fortescue: The Local Context of Parliamentary Controversy', *Parliamentary History*, iii (1984), 33–56; see also Andrew Thrush, 'Commons v. Chancery: The 1604 Buckinghamshire Election Dispute Revisited', *Parliamentary History*, xxvi (2007), 301–9.

[40] *Bacon*, ed. Spedding, v, 176; see also Markku Peltonen, 'Bacon's Political Philosophy', in *The Cambridge Companion to Bacon*, ed. Markku Peltonen (Cambridge, 1996), 284–90.

dignity and splendour', but James had not benefited from this most royal way of governing because of poor advice. Parliament should not be negotiated with – it was an exchange.[41] Queen Elizabeth, he noted, had successfully managed her parliaments by standing aloof from them – in other words, James should not stake his personal reputation on the line by becoming too closely involved. There was tacit criticism of the king as well. James had eschewed the customary practice that the lord chancellor delivered the opening speech to the house of commons – the speech in which the government pressed its need for money and offered unpopular guidance. James, though, had undertaken this task himself in both 1604 and 1614. Despite the king's reluctance, after the 1614 failure, to ever call a parliament as long as he could help it, Bacon continued to push him forward. He must stop the muttered opinions 'that his Majesty will call no more Parliaments'.[42] James, however, ignored his advice. The 1615 series of memoranda that Bacon had written to the king on the necessity of a parliament went unheeded, as James entered what Andrew Thrush has called his period of 'personal rule'.[43]

James's attitude towards parliament was, as we have seen, reflected in his dismissal of Bacon's advice (again) in late 1620. In a small concession to Bacon, James did restore the traditional opening oration of the lord chancellor, which Bacon delivered on 3 February 1621. True to form, Bacon got to deliver the 'bad news' – the parliament was, of course, free to bring forward complaints but not to hunt down grievances nor bring scandal upon the state.[44] But James could not leave well enough alone and, while Bacon was preparing his own speech, James was hard at work on his own. It was a triumphal *tour de force* of everything Bacon had feared: the reason for calling the parliament, James told it, was 'to sustain *me* in my urgent necessities'. He continued: 'I have had less supply from my people than ever any King or Queen had, I know not for how many hundred years.'[45] It was just the display of weakness, negotiation, and personal intervention that Bacon had warned against.

By this point, James's antipathy to the legal profession extended not only to those 'wrangling lawyers' he thought dominated the house of commons, but to Bacon and the legal profession more generally. In fact, for the king, lawyers were essentially the root of all evil and his dislike can be traced both through parliament and outside of it. Of course, he did not actually write 'let's kill all the lawyers' and there is no evidence that James saw William Shakespeare's *Henry VI part 2* or that it was performed during his reign. Nevertheless, there certainly is evidence that it was a sentiment, taken literally, with which he may well have agreed, especially as his reign wore on. One such incident revolves around Cambridge's recorder and graduate of Gray's Inn, Francis Brakin.[46] Brakin served as Cambridge's deputy recorder from 1593 to 1608, and then as its recorder from 1608 until his retirement in 1624. As such, he was the chief negotiator

[41] *Bacon*, ed. Spedding, v, 1–3.

[42] *Bacon*, ed. Spedding, v, 85.

[43] Andrew Thrush, 'The Personal Rule of James I, 1611–1620', in *Politics, Religion and Popularity in Early Stuart Britain*, ed. Thomas Cogswell, Richard Cust and Peter Lake (Cambridge, 2002), 84–102.

[44] For Bacon's draft speeches and those delivered, see *Bacon*, ed. Spedding, vii, 171–9.

[45] Emphasis added. *CD, 1621*, ii, 7.

[46] The following is based on my biography of Brakin in *HPC, 1604–29*, iii, 293–4.

in the often stormy town/gown relationship and later, in 1617, was influential in Bacon's appointment as the chancellor of the university. The tense, and often conflicting, relationship between the corporation and the university frequently played out on college stages and Brakin was frequently lampooned on stage in student plays. Barkin was ridiculed in the Parnassus plays[47] and satirised as 'Ignoramus' in the eponymous drama designed to show the foolishness of lawyers.[48] The play was inspired by recent disputes between the university and town over who had precedence, the mayor or the vice chancellor. At the quarter sessions in 1612, the vice chancellor, Barnaby Gooch, a vitriolic opponent of the corporation, had attempted to evict the mayor from his seat. Brakin mediated, and the rather messy compromise of leaving the central chair vacant was enacted. Dinner that night was also served around a chair in which none dared sit. Gooch would not let the matter rest though and, at the next sessions, he had the mayor evicted and took the chair.[49] Gooch succeeded in winning the day after the privy council intervened in the university's favour. But the whole matter was marked by Brakin's 'pettifogging shifts' to promote the mayor's authority.[50] Ignoramus, staged in Latin in March 1615, was enormously enjoyed by the king despite its six-hour length.

Not everyone found the play so funny and various poetic interludes and verses critiquing Cambridge's reception and entertainment of James refer to Ignoramus. The courtier's censure of the entertainment at both universities included the lines:

> Oxford comicke Actours had; Cambridge a lawyer fool.
> Who Ignoramus chrisetn'd was by men of her owne schoole.
> And is this not strange, is not this strange?
> That both exceeded, neither needed fooles for fooles to change.
> Oxford acts in toto were well pleasing to some;
> But Ignoramus best pleased the King when done.[51]

The play certainly amused the king, but not the legal fraternity. The lord chief justice, Sir Edward Coke, had been noted in the court of king's bench and 'other places, hath galled and glanced at scholars with much bitterness'.[52] Wits, too, in the Inns of Court responded with ditties aimed unfavourably at university men.[53] But for James, it was ideal. So much so, that he resolved to return to Cambridge and, a month later, despite his desire that actors should come to him and not *vice versa*, made a special trip to Cambridge to see the play again. It was a performance that ended at 1 am with 'His Majesty much delighted and laughed exceedingly; and oftentimes, with his hands, and by words, applauded it'.[54]

[47] *The Three Parnassus Plays*, ed. J.B. Leishman (Oxford, 1942).

[48] G. Ruggle, *Ignoramus*, trans. R. Codington (1662).

[49] *Annals of Cambridge*, ed. C.H. Cooper and J.W. Cooper (5 vols, Cambridge, 1842–1908), iii, 46–7, 53.

[50] George Dyer, *The Privileges of Cambridge University* (2 vols, 1824), i, 138, 140–1.

[51] John Nichols, *The Progresses and Public Processions of Queen Elizabeth; among which are interspersed other solemnities, public expenditures, and remarkable events during the reign of that . . . Princess: . . . with historical notes. (To which are subjoined some of the early Progresses of King James, etc.)* (4 vols, 1828), iii, 74.

[52] *Letters of John Chamberlain*, ed. McClure, i, 597–8.

[53] *Letters of John Chamberlain*, ed. McClure, i, 597–8.

[54] *Annals of Cambridge*, ed. Cooper and Cooper, iii, 84–8.

That James, too, thought that the law, lawyers and judges should bend to his will, is evident in the treason case against Edmund Peacham, a matter that also involved Bacon as attorney general.[55] Peacham came to the attention of the authorities due to his puritanical beliefs and attacks on the bishop of Bath and Wells who presided over his parish in Somerset. In 1614, in a mood of open defiance, he also refused to pay the benevolence. A search of his papers revealed a draft sermon in which James's death was foretold as divine judgment for his support for the episcopate. It was a matter, Peacham concluded, which involved rebellion. Peacham was brought to London and, with the guidance of Bacon, and the king's law serjeant, Sir Henry Montague – the brother of the libelled bishop of Bath and Wells – was tortured. Peacham, however, remained silent and this then sparked off a legal controversy. Was Peacham, indeed, guilty of treason? James, at least, was convinced that Peacham had violated the 1571 Treason Act that distinctly included both writing and preaching as potentially treasonable. As Rebecca Lemon has noted: 'subjects and monarchs report on and narrate the crime not as it materialized but as it might have been'.[56]

The judge's hesitancy annoyed the king who could see no reason why it was not treason or why *his* judges sought to debate the matter. Peacham was to be tried before the assizes in Taunton. However, the judge on the western circuit was Sir Henry Hobart, chief justice of the common pleas, and one of those who had qualms about Peacham's legal guilt. So, summarily, James exiled him to the vastly more difficult home circuit as a punishment. His replacement was none other than Sir Henry Montague. This was royal manipulation of justice on a grand scale, coming from a man who distrusted the legal opinions of his highest counsel.

James's ire with the legal profession and his justices grew during his second decade of rule. In 1616 *the case of commendams* (*Colt* v. *Glover*) involved a clash between the common law and episcopal privilege. James had allowed the bishop of Coventry and Lichfield, John Overall, to take the profits from a rectory granted by him, *in commendam*. Sir Edward Coke objected, but Bacon supported James through a writ, *non procedendo rege inconsulto*. Bacon argued that the king had the right to protect royal interests but 'the judges countered unanimously, in a reply drafted probably by Coke, that the king's letter was "contrary to law" and that "our oath in express words is that in case any letter comes to use contrary to law that we do nothing by such letters, but certify your Majesty thereof, and go forth to do the law" '.[57] After James had called the judges before him, all relented except for Coke. Further disputes between Coke and the king arose over 'exhorbitant and exaggerated opinions' in his law reports that ultimately led to Coke's removal from the bench.

These instances, and many more, illustrate James's antipathy and disdain for lawyers and the legal process. Furthermore, James believed that his problems with parliament stemmed from the legal profession. It was lawyers who had raised the objections to the union between England and Scotland in 1606–7; lawyers who had derailed the Great

---

[55] On Peacham, see Roger N. McDermott, 'Edmund Peacham', *ODNB* (where he is quaintly described as 'Church of England clergyman and traitor'); *Bacon*, ed. Spedding, v, 90–128.

[56] Rebecca Lemon, *Treason by Words: Literature, Law and Rebellion in Shakespeare's England* (Ithaca, NY, 2006), 2.

[57] HMC, *9th Report*, pt 2, 372; 'Coke, Sir Edward', *ODNB*.

Contract in 1610; and lawyers who had wrecked the 1614 parliament. But his authorship of the election proclamation was an amazing incident for a number of reasons: not
the least because it revealed the king's great antipathy to the legal profession. But it also
highlighted James's extraordinary control and authorial intervention in the ordinary
business of state – a king so anxious that he did not even trust his own advisors. As
Kevin Sharpe has noted, if Elizabeth was a monarch of the image, then James was a
monarch of the word.[58] Both James's reputation as an author and as a king who created
a politico-cultural printed world in the early 17th century have recently been the subject
of increasing scholarship. Attention has been paid to the literary canon of James, be it
through his treatises on kingship, Petrarchan sonnets of the 1590s and political verses of
the 1620s. However, James's interventions in the daily workings of administration have
been ignored and deserve greater study before we can understand him as both a king
and author.

Of course, as the parliament of 1621 played out, James was proved right, although
perhaps not in the way he anticipated. The 'wrangling lawyers' were, indeed, elected to
parliament and took over. Led by Bacon's arch nemesis, Sir Edward Coke, the
Commons revived the ancient process of impeachment and brought down the lord
chancellor. For James, the choice was simple – he could let lawyer Bacon go or face the
prospect of a sustained attack on his favourite, Buckingham. Whether or not Bacon was
guilty was irrelevant – it certainly appeared that corruption in the legal system extended
right to the top. As Linda Levy Peck has noted, these were royal judges; their corruption
reflected on the king himself.[59] Whatever the cause of Bacon's fall, the king's opinion
on certain matters was very clear. Despite the disquiet of the peerage, which was
concerned at the elevation to the lord chancellorship of a lowly cleric, James appointed
the dean of Westminster, John Williams, to the vacant office. As John Chamberlain
wrote to his friend, Dudley Carleton, the king was 'resolved to have no more lawiers
(as men so bred and nousled in corruption that they could not leave yt)'.[60] He could
well have said: 'Our wrangling lawyers are so litigious and busy here on earth, that I
think they will plead their clients' causes hereafter, some of them in hell' – but that was
left to that earnest (some might say sycophantic) searcher for patronage, Robert Burton,
in the *Anatomy of Melancholy*, first published in 1621.[61]

4

The dismissal of Bacon in 1621 reflected not only the obvious corruption of the lord
chancellor – a situation that the king could not tolerate – and the instrumental role of
Bacon's arch-enemy, Coke, in the proceedings, but also a clash of views on how
England should be governed. For Bacon, the king stood highest and at his most effective
as a ruler when parliaments were summoned frequently and managed well. To do so,

---

[58] Kevin Sharpe, *Image Wars: Promoting Kings and Commonwealths in England, 1603–1660* (New Haven, CT, 2010), 17.

[59] Levy Peck, *Court Patronage and Corruption*, 162–72, 185–8.

[60] *Letters of John Chamberlain*, ed. McClure, ii, 383.

[61] Robert Burton, *The Anatomy of Melancholy* (1621); the lines are those of Democritus jr to the reader.

Bacon thought, required a mixture of compromise and reward. Supply would be forthcoming if legislation was introduced that benefited the commonweal and satisfied the local magistrates who formed the majority of the Commons, while a fulsome act of pardon would also appease the, often restless, spirits of MPs. Parliaments, too, would be more tractable if 'packed' full of those sympathetic to the wishes of the crown. Bacon recognized that the assembling of a parliament could be problematical, or perhaps more accurately *was* problematical, but it also represented the 'ancient' way that monarchs ruled the country in conjunction with the governing class. Furthermore, in his advice to James on calling a parliament, from the mid 1610s to the proclamations of 1620, Bacon emphasized repeatedly that a willingness to be open about royal policy would lead to a more manageable and effective parliament. It was advice that James ignored.

Preaching and English Parliaments in the 1620s

LORI ANNE FERRELL

This article evaluates the impact of a small cache of sermons, dating from the second half of the 1620s, which served as the prelude to the famous sermons preached to the Long Parliament. Few in number, concentrated in time, and disparate in location, these works have attracted little sustained attention from scholars of the parliamentary sermon. However, they represent a crucial turn in the discursive politics of that particular set of influential pulpits: before the 1640s, not one, but three, high-profile – and very distinct – sermon venues served as sites for the dissemination of opinions directly and intimately associated with the work of a sitting parliament. Considered together, these form one singular and note-worthy platform of political debate, allowing us to posit religious origins to civil war.

Keywords: sermons; parliament; William Laud; Commons; Lords; court

'Parliamentary sermons' brings to mind the great run – some 240 in all, regular and occasional – first delivered to the Long Parliament and then, into historical memory, by way of the bookseller and collector George Thomason.[1] This article is not about those sermons. Instead, it evaluates the impact of the sermons that served as their prelude, a much smaller cache dating from the second half of the 1620s. Few in number, concentrated in time, disparate in location, these works have attracted little sustained attention from scholars of the parliamentary sermon. This is unfortunate, for they represent a crucial turn in the discursive politics of that particular pulpit. Or, better said, *pulpits*: for, before the 1640s, not one, but three, high-profile – and very distinct – sermon venues served as sites for the dissemination of opinions directly and intimately associated with the work of a sitting parliament. Considered together, these form one singular and noteworthy platform of political debate.

While references to parliament abound in the printed sermons of early modern England, the deliberate printing of parliamentary sermons, as targeted and authorised political statements, was a Caroline innovation. In this article, I will identify only *printed* sermons with title pages that announced their parliamentary *bona fides*, as 'parliamentary sermons'. Many sermons were deliberately 'tuned', of course, to a sitting parliament's work, of which the Lenten sermons preached at Elizabeth I's behest and during her opening parliament are, perhaps, the most interesting example.[2] However, neither these,

---

[1] Hugh Trevor-Roper, 'The Fast Sermons of the Long Parliament', in Hugh Trevor-Roper, *Religion, the Reformation and Social Change: And Other Essays by Hugh Trevor-Roper* (1967), 294–5; British Museum, *Catalogue of Pamphlets, Books, Newspapers, and Manuscripts Relating to the Civil War, the Commonwealth, and Restoration, Collected by George Thomason, 1640–1661* (2 vols, 1908).

[2] Peter McCullough, *Sermons at Court: Politics and Religion in Elizabethan and Jacobean Preaching* (Cambridge, 1998), 59–60. For a description of Elizabeth's well-tuned Lenten parliament of 1559 and the rota of preachers for that series, see McCullough, *Sermons at Court*, 60 n., 210–12.

nor any other parliamentary sermon, were printed in her reign. Exactly two parliamentary sermons were printed in the waning years of James I's reign. In contrast, sermons directly related to parliament's work were a characteristic feature of Charles's early reign. Before 1625, no sermons preached at court to mark the opening of any early modern English parliament went into print. But those preached at the openings of the parliaments of 1625, 1626, and 1628–9, all did, immediately, and all three were preached by William Laud.

In this article, it will be argued that this brief, intense and immediate run of parliamentary sermons by Bishop Laud, *agent provocateur* to England's fracturing politics in the opening years of Charles I's reign, was an early warning system signalling the revolution that would turn the world of Charles I's England upside down in 1640–2, if we use, as I will, 'revolution' in the manner advocated by David Cressy: the radical shift in cultural opinion that preceded civil war and interregnum.[3] If, by the parliament of 1628–9, members of both houses were frantically broadcasting what Conrad Russell described as a 'constant state of alarm about the possibility that the king would put an end to all parliamentary institutions', then this assessment is first borne out in Laud's pulpit commentary on early Caroline parliaments.[4]

Nor are Laud's our sole sermonic witnesses: in 1628, the bishop's pronouncements found outraged answer in sermons commissioned by both houses of parliament and swiftly sent to the press (those commissioned by the Lords were ordered into print; those by the Commons were printed but not authorised).[5] What had once been an internal homiletic debate went viral in 1626, raging on the issue that proved most incendiary, as well as most amenable, to the medium of sermonic discourse: not the current course of plague, but the future course of religion in England.

Until the second half of the 1620s, the only reliable issue about which to demand occasional, if extraordinary, national religious observance was the outbreak of disease (the ordinary issue was the opening of a parliament). The detection of plague in England traditionally set off a chain of discursive events that had always prompted (and thus tacitly allowed) a sitting house of commons to take the initiative: remedial actions that began, invariably, with a call for local, regional, or national prayer and fasting. The outbreak of plague in 1625 was so severe as to delay, disrupt, and finally relocate Charles I's first parliament, but it also set an unusual precedent swiftly exploited by the lower House.

In doing so, the House was treading a path deeply marked for it by both venerable and recent practice. Each request for a general fast followed strict protocol: the Commons first took its case to the Lords, which then took the case to the king as a joint request. This punctilious attention to procedure undoubtedly reflects a hard lesson learned in 1580, when the Commons took up a similar matter, apparently without prior consultation:

> Upon a Motion made for a public Fast, with Prayer and Preaching to be exercised by this House . . . it was thereupon, after many Arguments and Speeches first had,

---

[3] David Cressy, *England on Edge: Crisis and Revolution, 1640–1642* (Oxford, 2006), 17–24.

[4] Conrad Russell, *The Crisis of Parliaments* (Oxford, 1971), 307.

[5] Cyndia Clegg, *Press Censorship in Caroline England* (Cambridge, 2008), 84.

both with, and also against the Motion, and whether the same Fast, Prayer, and Preaching, to be exercised by this House in some One Day of this Session, should be publick for the whole Society of this House, to be done by them all in One Place together, or else private, for every Man in his own Conscience: It was, upon the Division of the House, (after the Doubtfulness of the Voices) upon the Question, resolved, with the Difference of the Number of Fifteen Voices, that the said Fast, Prayer, and Preaching, should be public; *viz. with the public.* One Hundred and Fifteen; and with the private, but One Hundred: And it was then further agreed that the Privy Council being of this House, should nominate the Preachers, to the end they might be such as would keep convenient Proportion of Time, and meddle with no Matter of Innovation or Unquietness. The Day to be To-morrow Sevennight, at Eight of the Clock in the Morning; the Place to be in the Temple Church; and such of this House to be there as will, and conveniently may.[6]

Elizabeth I reprimanded the Commons for its untoward and disorderly behaviour in 1580, but in 1625, 1626, and 1628, Charles I acquiesced to similar importuning. Indeed, it may have been impossible for him to refuse, despite the critique encoded in the request. It also seems that the Commons became ever more anxious to exploit this new development in governmental style, becoming ever more prone to calling general fasts; in essence, declaring a state of national contrition in circumstances not medically, but spiritually, urgent.

Once agreed in principle, English government showed itself essentially *divisa in partes tres*: the king, the Lords, and the Commons each observed the national fast in different venues, commissioning and hearing very different sermons. The sermons preached before the king on these days went into print but, for the first time in 1628–9, so did others responding to the same call. In publishing *their* fast sermons, the Lords and the Commons also aired publicly their disagreements with the king. In the end, half a dozen sermons preached from the 1628–9 parliament's dedicated pulpits came out in print within the year, all touting their unique status as parliamentary sermons on their title pages. This cache of sermons thus presaged the revolutionary parliamentary homiletic of the 1640s and 1650s, in every way but one: they issued from *three* separate venues. The sermons of the Long Parliament were unicameral.

Still, they were a hard act to precede. The work of Hugh Trevor-Roper and John F. Wilson established the sermons of the Long Parliament as a distinct subgenre: regular fast sermons constructed from a heady mix of providential rhetoric, penitential doctrine, and a marked preference for Old Testament over New Testament exegesis.[7] The overheated style matched that of the scriptural texts themselves, and the scriptural texts spoke to incendiary and apocalyptic times – so well that the Long Parliament sermons have supported a historiographical argument for puritan revolution that has generally managed to dodge the cavils of political revisionism. This has mostly been a case of quiet

[6] *CJ*, i, 118: 21 Jan. 1581.

[7] Trevor-Roper, 'Fast Sermons', 294–344; John F. Wilson, *Pulpit in Parliament: Puritanism during the English Civil Wars, 1640–1648* (Princeton, NJ, 1969); see also Tom Webster, 'Preaching and Parliament, 1640–1659', in *The Oxford Handbook of the Early Modern Sermon*, ed. P. McCullough, H. Adlington and E. Rhatigan (Oxford, 2010), 404–20. Webster's essay is a tidy encapsulation of how the Long Parliament got its sermons, calling the fasts it commissioned, 'a monthly spiritual fix', 405.

disambiguation: scholars of post-Reformation English religion have been seeking revisable subjects elsewhere – in studies of English conformism, English catholicism, big-tent English christianity. In the 1980s and 1990s, the 1640s and 1650s were flyover country for most historians of religion, until it became clear that the puritanism we could not revise out of the record might account for the radicalism the revisionists could not quite revise – at least not plausibly – out of their monographs.[8]

This prompts a thoughtful glance back: if not at 'origins', then at least to telltale, if not exactly prophetic, signs. At first glance, nothing would seem less puritanical than the ceremonial practice of public fasting. The abnegatory prelude to feasts, fasts punctuated the ecclesiastical calendar of the pre-Reformation Church of England, demanding devotional expressions of a theological world-view that advocated the strenuous doing of good works in pursuit of eternal life. The retention of certain saints' days was one of the overcautious decisions that made the Elizabethan religious settlement so deeply unsettled in the 1570s and 1580s. '[D]ays are ascribed unto saints [and] . . . kept holy with fasts on the evens', fumed the virulently anti-catholic writers of the *Admonition* directed to the 1572 parliament, 'contrary to the commandment of God'.[9] But godly protestantism was also profoundly attuned to Old Testament syntax and style. Scorning the ostentatious hypocrisy of jewish ceremonial orthodoxy, the Jesus of the gospels can sound like one of the hotheaded writers of the *Admonition to the Parliament*. This is because the Hebrew Bible, unlike the 'New' Testament later grafted onto it, abounds with references to fasting as a personal or collective confession of sin, or as the necessary adjunct to prayers for the restoration of divine favour.[10]

This mixed exegetical legacy inspired an equally mixed message in a national Church increasingly wary of protestant sola scripturalism by the end of the 16th century. The politically timid progress of reformation in the Church of England made for ambiguous policy on fasting, and so the practice remained commendable, if not unto salvation. '[T]hose rites and customs of the old law bind us not', observed the Elizabethan homily on the subject, which notwithstanding then went on to describe the practice carefully as 'a withholding of meat, drink, and all natural food from the body for the determined time'. Fasting was a 'thing merely indifferent: but . . . made better or worse by the end that it serveth unto', a means that might or might not justify the ends. This extensive attention – the *Homily on Fasting* is, perhaps, the only sermon in this series to dwell so extensively and approvingly on a non-sacramental devotional practice – simply underscores fasting's cultural importance. It was becoming a metaphor of remarkable acquisitive power in a Janus-faced age.

Stripped of sacerdotal, but not social, meaning (much like the calendrical saints themselves), fasts swiftly became scripts ripe for revision, and the hotter sort of the

[8] There are important exceptions, of course, most if not all following up on Christopher Hill's pioneering and problematic (if exhilarating) work in one way or another: these include David Norbrook's *Writing the English Republic: Poetry, Rhetoric and Politics, 1629–1660* (Cambridge, 1999), and Nigel Smith's *Literature and Revolution in England, 1640–1660* (New Haven, CT, 1994), as well as Cressy's *England on Edge*.

[9] *An Admonition to the Parliament* (1572), reprinted in David Cressy and Lori Anne Ferrell, *Religion and Society in Early Modern England* (2nd edn, 2005), 98.

[10] *The Book of Common Prayer: The Texts of 1549, 1559, and 1662*, ed. Brian Cummings (Oxford, 2011), 805. Cummings observes that the term 'fast' referred both to an actual act of abstention and the 'day or season' appointed for that particular form of 'religious observance'.

queen's protestants soon began to reclaim the practice for godlier purposes.[11] The laboratory for their experiment was not the Church but a parliament. Distressed by the persistently under-reformed state of religion in England, the later Elizabethan house of commons first proposed the institution of regular fast days in 1580. What it had not counted on, perhaps, was how well the queen could detect the critique encoded in its request and how swiftly she would interpret this religious impulse as a declaration of independence on the part of the lower House.

To call for a general fast was apparently to suggest that only God could reform England and, by 1580, Elizabeth I was through with unsolicited offers of assistance. After controversies over prophesyings, injudicious archiepiscopal remarks, and the tracts of Martin Marprelate, the queen's heart had irrevocably hardened against anything that smacked of headstrong religious enthusiasm: she refused the request with strident fury. Commanded to beg pardon for its 'rash, unadvised, and inconsiderate Error', the Commons apologised within the week. Its calls for fasting to address what was, in essence, a political issue, were forever after associated with the kind of religious activism that reliably angered monarchs.[12]

It would take another 40 years, the accession of James Stuart and, even still, sufficient time to take *that* monarch's measure, to embolden the lower House once again to take up the work of commissioning religious observations, and the special prayers and sermons that went along with these, and in the absence of an uncontroversial threat – such as bubonic plague or foreign invasion – the house of commons began cautiously if unilaterally. In 1614, the Commons voted to institute a 'test' communion (the expression is Wilson's) requiring all members to demonstrate their fidelity to canon 20 of the Church of England, worshipping, for the first time, separate from the house of lords.[13] The sermon on that occasion was not printed, nor do we know who preached it. This seems to have raised no hackles on a king who appreciated ceremonial demonstrations of his authority and subjects' conformity; the House's request to hold that service, and all subsequent, in the more puritan-friendly St Margaret's, Westminster, rather than the Abbey, also seems to have caused no particular stir.[14] Six years later, James Ussher preached at the second such communion service; the House requested his sermon go into print that same year.

So the age of the parliamentary sermon as a new kind of printed public occasion began with Ussher's *The Substance of That Which Was Delivered in a Sermon before the Commons House of Parliament, in St. Margaret's Church at Westminster, the 18. of February, 1620*. The second such textual event was less successful. The sermon preached to the lower House by Isaac Bargrave on 3 February 1623, angered the king with its fulminations against 'evil councilors'; its subsequent printings in 1624 may simply have

---

[11] Richard Greaves, *Religion and Society in Elizabethan England* (Minneapolis, MN, 1981).

[12] Wilson, *Pulpit in Parliament*, 22–3.

[13] One important consequence of this decision was the Commons' vote also to change sacramental venues: from Westminster Abbey – where the use of wafers offended godlier members of the House, to St Margaret's, Westminster, where communion was administered with 'common bread'. The sermons preached on this first occasion by persons unnoted were not printed: Wilson, *Pulpit in Parliament*, 23–4.

[14] Wilson, *Pulpit in Parliament*, 22–3.

represented an attempt, on either Bargraves's part or the part of the Commons, to set the record straight.[15]

In *Pulpit in Parliament*, Wilson traced what he termed a 'genesis of the commons preaching program' precisely to Ussher's sermon, leaving subsequent scholars with a seemingly indelible impression: that the parliamentary pulpit thereafter belonged to the house of commons – not the Lords, and certainly not king-in-parliament.[16] Having made this point, he then shifted immediately to the Long Parliament – and never looked back. Wilson's identification of preaching with puritanism, puritanism with the house of commons, and the house of commons with a purpose-built homiletic broadcast system thus had the odd – and, presumably, unintended – effect of shifting the subfield's primary emphasis: away from preaching as general parliamentary strategy and onto the importance of the voice of the lower House. But by the 1970s, this supposition – that the house of commons once pursued an initiative in political affairs in the early 17th century that led directly to its management of government in the 1640s – was losing its allure in other fields of English history.

Notestein and company have long been vanquished by the forces of revisionism, but important work in religious historiography since the publication of Wilson's book suggests we should take another, perhaps more pointed, look at the symbiotic, as well as symbolic, relationship of religious language and political action in the earlier 17th century. For one thing, we are now far better acquainted with the politics of the early modern pulpit, and we assess it as the influential, if typically and necessarily circumscribed, agent of broadcast opinion that it was. As Peter McCullough has shown, court sermons were unusually packed at parliament time – and as Arnold Hunt has shown, English monarchs and their churchmen were adept at tuning the pulpit to the pitch of policy.[17]

McCullough's list of Elizabethan and Jacobean court sermons printed by command, reveals none with the expression *preached at* (or *to*) *parliament* in their titles until 1621. Given the limitations of analysis by searching the English Short Title Catalogue, this observation may seem less than revelatory until we go on to study the titles of sermons, both preached and printed, in the second half of the 1620s. Here we find a significant rise in title pages proudly bearing their parliamentary *bona fides* (and significant prepositional use): *A sermon preached before the kings maiesty at the opening of the last parliament; A Sermon preached to the . . . Commons house of Parliament; One of the Sermons Preacht at Westminster . . . to the Lords of the high court of PARLIAMENT.* So, looking forward from

---

[15] Isaac Bargraves's *A Sermon Preached before the Honorable Assembly of Knights, Citizens, and Burgesses of the Lower House of Parliament February the Last 1623*: Wilson, *Pulpit in Parliament*, 27–8; the 'royal displeasure' was first recorded by the preacher in BL, Lansdowne MS 985, f. 9; Sidney Lee, revised by Stephen Bann 'Bargrave, Isaac (*bap.* 1586, *d.* 1643)', *ODNB*. A sermon on Christian liberty, *adiaphora*, and the signs of the true church, preached by the conformist Christopher Hampton to the house of lords in the second session of the parliament of 1622, was also printed within a year of the preaching: *An Inquisition of the True Church, and those that revolt from it: being a sermon pronounced at the second session of Parliament. By Christopher Lo. Archbishop of Armagh, and Primate of All Ireland* (Dublin, 1622).

[16] Wilson, *Pulpit in Parliament*, 24–7.

[17] McCullough, *Sermons at Court*, 59–100; Arnold Hunt, 'Tuning the Pulpits', in *The English Sermon Revised: Religion, Literature and History 1600–1750*, ed. Lori Anne Ferrell and Peter McCullough (Manchester, 2000), 86–114; Arnold Hunt, *The Art of Hearing: English Preachers and their Audiences, 1590–1640* (Cambridge, 2010), 292–342.

1621 rather than back from 1640, the other decision made by the Commons – to have Ussher's parliament sermon printed and to declare intent by the medium of the title page – may actually manifest truly significant change, a transformation spurring on a governmental trifecta. For if, in the matter of instituting test communions (thereby proving their loyalty to the canons of the Church of England) and printing the sermons associated with these (thereby informing the public that they were, in fact, loyal, conforming puritans), the house of commons won any initiative in the first half of the 1620s, they were answered – and swiftly outmanœuvred – by the court pulpit by 1625.

Our understanding of just what was at stake begins by recalling the complex, and increasingly urgent, political necessities felt by the king, the Lords, and the Commons, that characterised the calling of parliaments in this period; issues thoroughly, specifically, and controversially covered in the many competing political histories of the period. Charles's succession parliament was slated to begin on 17 May 1625 and was ill-starred from the first. The arrival of Henrietta Maria in England and the resurgence of plague in London conspired to delay the opening session three times, moving it finally to 18 June. William Laud, recently appointed bishop of St David's in Wales, and fresh from two significant preaching assignments in the waning years of James I's reign, was commanded to preach the occasion.

But the sermon, originally prepared for the opening of parliament, and thus before the king and the usual crowd of lords, diplomats, and other court worthies at Westminster Abbey, had to be temporarily cancelled and then moved, due to the epidemic now ravaging the city and thinning out the ranks of parliament altogether. Charles's future archbishop eventually delivered it at the Chapel Royal at Whitehall the next day, Trinity Sunday.[18] It did not, however, remain the property of the king and his court intimates for long; it went into print within the year.

Laud had prepared his sermon on Psalm 75.2–3, a passage for which he provided alternate readings in parentheses: '*When I shall receive the Congregation,* (or, when I shall take a convenient time) *I will judge according unto right. The earth is dissolved,* (or, melted) *and all the inhabitants thereof; I bear up the pillars of it.*'[19] Once expanded in this way, his text could be parsed to support several intertwining themes with more suppleness. The idea of pillars, of course, lent itself nicely to associated concepts of support, especially in the voting of supply.[20] But more remarkable are Laud's expansive treatments of the concepts of time and dissolution, which first allowed the preacher to offer a poignant observation about the second son who had not been expected to succeed to the throne: 'in very many times, weaker governors, both for wisdom and courage, do prosper . . . to give it to destiny [i.e., attribute success to the vagaries of fate] is to bind God up in chains unworthy for men'.[21] Throughout, Laud made this cautious welcome over into

---

[18] William Laud, *The Works of the Most Reverend Father in God, William Laud, D.D. Sometime Lord Archbishop of Canterbury*, ed. W. Scott and J. Bliss (7 vols, Oxford, 1847–60), i, 92 n. Laud's diary and Heylin's biography of Laud (also cited in Laud, *Works*, i, 62), offer different reasons for the delay, Heylin suggesting that the 18 June date was already long filled by another royal chaplain, Laud stating that the opening sermon and its attendant ceremonial was cancelled due to the pestilence 'lest the great conflux of people should be of ill consequence'.

[19] William Laud, *A Sermon Preached before His Majestie, on Sunday the xix. of June, at White-hall. Appointed to be preached at the opening of the Parliament. By the Bishop of S. Davids* ([1625]), sig. Br.

[20] Laud, *Works*, i, 111, 115.

[21] Laud, *Works*, i, 109.

exaltation: stressing over and again that James I had not died in his own but in God's time – and so this particular moment in divinely-appointed time had introduced a young king fitted to be the prop to Church and state his father had been – a Hezekiah to succeed Great Britain's Solomon, and under whose stewardship the pillars, built by James to support the Church, would not dissolve.[22]

But the tropes of time and dissolution also supported another, less hospitable and less welcoming, theme: an unsubtle reminder to parliament that it met at this young and untested king's command, and could just as easily be sent packing by the same means. Laud expanded on the text's *melting* (for which he had helpfully supplied the alternate *dissolution*) by way of some homely, if alarming, imagery: 'put but a little salt upon a snail and he will drop out of his house immediately'.[23]

And later, more pointedly directive, if less vivid: 'Would you then have a settled and flourishing state? Would you have no *melting*, no *dissolution* . . . ? Why, but if you would indeed, the King must trust, and endear his people; the people must honor, obey, and support their king.'[24] There is room here to suggest that Laud's emphasis on *dissolution* throughout merely may have reflected an acknowledgment of the delays and alarms raised in London during plague time. Such words, however, still sound a surprisingly provocative note from the first, signalling a pre-emptive royal discomfort with parliament's long-cherished prerogatives: to offer advice and present concerns before voting supply. The public provocation came, however, after the preacher exited his privy court pulpit: Laud's sermon went into print by royal command within the month.

Indeed, Charles's first parliament, poor salted snail of Laud's exegetical creation, itself became homeless soon enough, displaced by plague to Oxford, and dismissed soon thereafter in a welter of disputes about Arminianism, the war with Spain, and the influence of the duke of Buckingham. But not before the Commons attempted a resort to divine intervention: three days after Laud's sermon at Whitehall, 22 June 1625, the lower House approved a petition to call a conference with the Lords, in order to 'join in a petition to his Majesty for a general fast'.[25] Given that this was plague time, the Lords swiftly acquiesced both to the conference and the petition. Charles acceded to the joint request of the Commons and the Lords on 8 July.[26]

The Commons, Wilson reports, 'chose its preachers with care' – indeed it needed to – but still the sermons it commissioned, with one exception, were not published. Only John Preston's *Sermon preached at a general fast before the Commons-House of Parliament: the second of July, 1625*, went into in print. But – and this is an essential fact – not until 1633, when, with separate title page and pagination, it was added to a volume of 14 sermons collected and published by the puritan worthies, Richard Sibbes and John

[22] Laud, *Works*, i, 110.

[23] Laud, *Works*, i, 96.

[24] Laud, *Works*, i, 99.

[25] By a margin of 195 to 172: *CJ*, i, 800–1: 22 June 1625.

[26] It is possible that the plague ravaging London and thinning out parliamentary ranks, rather than any concern over the political import of such a request, was the primary reason the issue of a general fast seemed to cause such disquiet and delay: *CJ*, i, 809–10: 2 Aug. 1625, reveals a heated discussion over poor distribution and suspicion that some printers were raising the prices on required purchase to an unreasonable rate; these matters were referred to the archbishop of Canterbury.

Davenport, under the title *The Saints Qualification*.[27] It more properly belongs, then, to what we might call the recycled parliamentary sermon movement of the 1630s, part of a still larger movement to provide books to a godly readership. The 1630s was a decade without parliaments but abundant with parliamentary sermons, as Ussher's of 1621 and Preston's of 1625 began a remarkable round of republication and recirculation in 1631, 1633, 1634, and 1637.[28]

In this way, William Laud became the defining voice of early Caroline parliaments in the absence of other published voices (which, in itself, reflects a censorship campaign spearheaded by none other than Laud himself).[29] Ordered to preach at the openings of all three, he was able to deliver the next two as originally planned, to king and court at Westminster Abbey in 1625 and 1628. All these sermons beat an extraordinarily fast path to publication, with every one printed within months, or even weeks. With no other parliament-identified sermons coming out in print between 1625 and 1628, the king's preacher, with his monopoly on parliamentary sermons, would appear, in fact, to have retaken the initiative for Charles I – and extraordinarily swiftly off the mark.

Generally speaking, Laud preached to score points, and the only point his parliamentary sermons ever made was brutally direct: *a parliament expresses the will of the king*. Laud's parliamentary sermons represent a significant variation on the style pioneered by *avant garde* conformist preachers like Lancelot Andrewes, whose eloquence at court was often deployed in the paradoxical task of preaching artfully against the art of preaching. By the end of the reign of James I, anti-Calvinist preachers had effectively refashioned that art, once so seemingly bound to the ideals of evangelical Calvinist religion, into the startlingly counter-intuitive medium of its own critique.[30]

Similarly, Laud's parliamentary sermons disparage parliaments. On Monday, 6 February 1625/6, Laud, again, preached to king and court assembled at Westminster at the opening of Charles's second parliament. This time, his text was drawn from Psalm 122. Bypassing this chapter's well-known opening line, 'I was glad when they said unto me / let us go into the house of the Lord', Laud commenced with its considerably less resonant verses three to five, once again retranslating for effect: 'Jerusalem *is builded as a* city *that is at* unity with itself (or compacted together). *For thither the* Tribes *go up, even the* Tribes of the Lord, to the testimony of Israel, to give thanks unto the Name of the Lord. For there are the Seats (or the Thrones) of Judgment; even the Thrones of the house of David.'[31] Again, the key to Laud's intentions is in the parentheses: 'compacted together' and 'the Thrones'. These additions signal the beginning of a sequence of linked metaphors, with the alternate translations in place to facilitate connections. Replacing 'throne' to refer to those 'seated' in session is obviously pointed, but Laud's

---

[27] Wilson, *Pulpit in Parliament*, 28–9. Preston's work was reprinted three times in 1637 alone.

[28] Clegg, *Press Censorship*, 145–9.

[29] Clegg, *Press Censorship*, 146.

[30] For Andrewes as the premier architect of this avant-garde approach, see McCullough, *Sermons at Court*, 147–55; for the phenomenon in general, see Lori Anne Ferrell, *Government by Polemic: James I, the King's Preachers and the Rhetorics of Conformity* (Stanford, CA, 1998), 167–76; the quote is from Lori Anne Ferrell and Peter McCullough, 'Revising the Study of the English Sermon', in *English Sermon Revised*, ed. Ferrell and McCullough, 11.

[31] William Laud, *A Sermon Preached on Munday, the sixt of February, at WESTMINSTER: At the opening of the PARLIAMENT. By the Bishop of S: Davids.* (1625), sig. Br.

choice to replace the expression 'compacted together' with 'at unity in itself' reveals subtler interpretive intentions, allowing him to introduce and ally the strange-bedfellow concepts 'mutual agreement' and 'structural integrity'. Jerusalem, Laud told his auditory, was doubly exemplary: "Tis like a City that is *compacted together*. That's for the buildings; no desolation in the midst of it, saith *S. Basil*. 'Tis like a City *at unity in it self*. That's for the Inhabitants . . . When men dwell as near in affection as their houses stand in place.'[32] Proximities made a city, wherein close-set buildings stood representative of the collegial people who dwelled within: 'not scattering, as if they were afraid of one another'. This density of population, housing, and purpose depended on what the preacher called 'artificial joining': a judicious mix of skill and talent surpassing nature. The work, in other words, was not instinctive; it required intention, application – and a kind of fabrication of agreement.

'Let the Citizens break their unity once', warned Laud, and 'they'll spend so much in quarrels that they cannot build the City.'[33] This talk of architecture and artifice prompted a more provocative observation, as Laud cited Tacitus's *Life of Agricola* on the weakness of kingdoms divided by faction: 'they were broken into factions . . . And they smarted for it. But I pray, what is the difference for men not to meet in council, and to fall in pieces when they meet?'[34] The point was not subtle: better no parliament at all than one that could not agree to support the king. After three months of debate over supply, charges against the duke of Buckingham, and Richard Montagu's *New Gagg*, however, the 1626 house of commons did seem to agree on one course of action. On 29 April, it achieved another bicameral success, petitioning the Lords to ask the king to call another general fast, this time with no London-based threat of plague with which to justify its request. None the less, it received assent from both the Lords and the king within a few days.[35]

In the end, fasting did not preserve this parliament either; Charles dissolved it on 15 June. Five days later, he commissioned Laud to preach the fast sermon 'before [him] and the nobility at Whitehall' and, for good measure, elevated Laud to the more eminent bishopric of Bath and Wells the same day. This is the only sermon 'officially' marking the general fast of 1626, and Laud's own account of its publication is nearly breathless in its rush of recall, appearing in his diary as compactly as the account of creation in Genesis 1: 'Tuesday . . . King Charles named me Bishop of Bath and Wells . . . I preached before the king . . . it was Wednesday . . . The King commanded me to print and publish the sermon . . . it was Saturday. . . . Sunday I presented that sermon.'[36]

The intentions behind Laud's choice of text – 'Arise, O God, plead (or maintain) Thine own cause: remember how the foolish man reproacheth (or blasphemeth) Thee daily' (Psalm 74.22) – are so telling, perhaps, that no subsequent commentator has seen fit to explore them further than the bare citation. Once again, we see the parenthetical

[32] Laud, *Munday, sixt of February*, sig. B3v.

[33] Laud, *Munday, sixt of February*, sig. B3v.

[34] Laud, *Works*, i, 69.

[35] *CJ*, i, 84–6: 19 Apr. 1626. The House did debate a bill on contagion, but this is nearly lost amidst the usual welter of concerns related to Arminianism.

[36] Wilson, *Pulpit in Parliament*, 30; see Laud's diary entries for 5, 8, 16 July 1625: *Works*, iii, 192–3. Laud's *Sermon Preached before his Majesty on Wednesday the fift of July at White-Hall At the solemne fast then held* was preached on the 5th of July 1626 and printed on the 8th of that same month by express order of the king. The new bishop of Bath and Wells was able to present Charles with a copy a week later.

expansions on the text which allowed Laud to construct a pointed critique, passages of remarkable contempt towards those who would call for public displays of fasting and penitence. Laud addresses the king: 'And, *Sir*, as you were first up, and summoned the Church to awake, and have sounded the alarum in the ears of your people; not that they should *fast and pray* and *serve God alone*, but go with you into the house of the Lord; so go on to serve your preserver.'[37] With parliament dissolved, Laud effectively rewrote the history of this particular fast; now it was Charles who was 'first up'. The true enemy in this fast sermon is neither plague nor idolatry; here God's visitations come in the form of disobedient subjects. In this context, the line chiding 'the people' would seem to indict a parliament that acts alone – which, indeed, it could not: the men of the house of commons had been dissolved back into the great mass of Charles's subjects. Following Laud's logic, whatever preservation the king had required had surely been ensured by the king's refusal to preserve parliament.

On 17 March 1628, at the opening of what was to be Charles's last parliament until 1640, Laud (still bishop of Bath and Wells but awaiting translation to London, which he had been promised) once again preached at Westminster. His text, 'Endeavoring to keep the unity of the Spirit in the bond of peace' (Ephesians 4.3), was ordered immediately into print by the king, who repeated the scriptural citation to conclude his own speech at the opening of parliament that same day. Laud's own opening lines were anything but peaceable:

> I begin with that which is the matter of the Apostle's exhortation, it is unity; a very charitable tie, but better known than loved. A thing so good that it is never broken but by the best men. Nay, so good it is, that the very worst men pretend best when they break it. It is so in the Church: never heretic yet rent her bowels, but he pretended that he raked them for truth. It is so in the State; seldom any unquiet spirit divides her union, but he pretends some great abuses which his integrity would remedy . . . Unity, then, both in Church and commonwealth, is so good, that none but the worst willingly break it: and even they are so far ashamed of the breach, that they must seem holier than the rest, that they may be thought to have a just cause to break it.[38]

Three days later – again with no particular outbreaks of plague to inspire them – members of the Commons debated a 'motion made to petition his Majesty about a general fast throughout the kingdom . . . and that . . . the Lords to be moved, to join in the petition'. The Lords agreed, requesting an audience with the king for representatives from both Houses to present the petition. On 24 March, Charles agreed to their request (Peter Heylin later observed, acidly, that this acquiescence was almost certainly of necessity, for the king's need for supply was great)[39] setting the date for his and his two Houses' observance, as well as a slightly later date for the rest of the country, so as to allow for the printing and distribution of fast books throughout the kingdom.

---

[37] Laud, *Works*, i, 139.

[38] Laud, *Works*, i, 157–8.

[39] Wilson observes that Heylin spoke in hindsight, but it is still worth noting that he obviously regarded the calling of fasts as a manipulative strategy employed by the Commons: *Pulpit in Parliament*, 33 n.

The Commons moved immediately to extend invitations to preachers, first proposing a 'Mr Dyke of Epping in Essex and Mr [Robert] Harrys of Hanwell in Oxfordshire' to fill the pulpit at St Margaret's, Westminster, that the house of commons had established as theirs since the test communion of 1614. Sir Robert Phelips proposed, instead, that the rota be filled by 'one Englishman and one Scottishman'. The House agreed with Phelips and discussed inviting Walter Balcanquall to preach.[40] Phelips's request ultimately went unrealized (the preacher was, instead, the up-and-coming Cornelius Burges). For its part, the Lords commissioned Joseph Hall, bishop of Exeter, to preach to them at the collegiate church of St Peter at Westminster.

The texts and their publication history eloquently spell the dangers of the times. On 5 April, Jeremiah Dyke preached on Hebrews 11.7: 'By Faith, Noah being warned of God, of things not seen as yet, moved with fear, prepared an Ark, to the saving of his House.' The same day, nearby at St Peter's, Joseph Hall preached a more anodyne sermon, yet the scripture on which he spoke, 'What could have been done more in my vineyard that I have not done in it? Wherefore when I looked that it should bring forth grapes, brought it forth wild grapes, and therefore go to, I will tell you, what I will do to my Vineyard; I will take away the Hedge thereof' (Isaiah 5.4–5), speaks volumes. Both sermons included additional authorial commentary: Dyke stated in a prologue his hope that the 'monument' he had committed to print would contribute to a 'happy, healing' parliament; Hall noted in a postscript that his fellow bishops in the Lords had called his 'poor sermon' into the 'public light' along, and that he had swiftly delivered it so as to avoid seeing transcriptions of it circulated in manuscript. 'I found it not unfit the world should see', Hall observed, 'what preparative was given for so stirring a potion; neither can there be so much need, in these languishing times, of any discourse, as that which serves to quicken our mortification.' The additions grant some insight, at least from the view of the preachers, as to how and why *A Sermon preached at the Public Fast to the Commons House of Parliament April 5th 1628* and *One of the Sermons Preached at Westminster on the day of the public fast (5. April 1628) to the Lords of the High Court of Parliament and by their appointment published* were printed with such impressive celerity.[41]

The other work alluded to on Hall's 1628 title page was, in fact, a copy of a sermon preached to the king at Westminster the week before, 30 March, in preparation for this last fast of the early Caroline sermon season. A Lenten meditation on Galatians 2.20: 'I am crucified with Christ; nevertheless I live', Hall opened with the following: 'He that was once tossed in the confluence of two seas, Acts 27.41, was once no less straited betwixt life and death . . . as there he knew not whether he should choose, here he knew not whether he had.'[42] Historians know better than to find prophecies in the archive, but that is exactly what early modern preachers were trained up to discover in their scriptural archive. In 1628, Laud's parliamentary sermon monopoly was broken. By spring 1629, two more sermons, one preached to the Commons at St Margaret's by John Harris and one to the house of lords at St Peter's by John Williams, preached at the second general fast (held the same month as Charles's third and final parliament

[40] *CJ*, i, 872–5: 20, 21, 24 Mar. 1628; see also Wilson, *Pulpit in Parliament*, 33–4.

[41] Joseph Hall, *One of the Sermons Preached at Westminster on the day of the public fast (5. April 1628) to the Lords of the High Court of Parliament and by their appointment published* (1628), E7v–8r.

[42] Hall, *One of the Sermons Preached at Westminster*, sig. F2r–v.

ended with the abortive second session in February of 1628/9) issued from the presses in rapid succession. All announced the parliamentary occasion and the venue on their title pages; all came out in print virtually immediately. These early Caroline parliamentary sermons thus take on a quick and heady historical momentum and, much as Wilson once argued, conform to the model set by the sermons of the 1640s.[43]

But that is to find precedent before the fact, something the revisionists were right to warn against. The sermon wars of 1628 can, perhaps, be best understood, in the light of the powerfully provocative tone set by William Laud as an initially unchallenged spokesman in print for Charles's 1620s parliaments. This, of course, would require us to read them. Laud's published sermons have generally received very cursory attention from scholars, who tend to dismiss them as political exercises of the most obvious and tedious sort. Even William Scott, the hardly-disinterested editor of the 19th-century Anglo-Catholic Library reprints of Laud's works, calls his sermons derivative, his thinking devoid of significant doctrinal import, and the archbishop 'a statesman more than . . . a theologian'.[44]

Tedious, perhaps; obvious, absolutely; bracingly theological, hardly. But if we relate these to the calling for general fasts by the Commons in July 1625, August 1626, March 1628, and January 1629, we find an interesting pattern, a kind of call and response. Even with its seemingly inarguable rationales – first for plague, and then, in a sense, for the spread of infectious heresy, an offence that had always been described in medical terms as both virulent and contagious – the Commons' call for general fasts on the subject of religion sent a political message that was both provocative and overt.

Any early modern English monarch who called a parliament was already braced to receive a surfeit of unsolicited opinion along with any grant of much-needed supply. But, as the furious reaction of Elizabeth I in 1580 reminds us, a house of commons that requested a regular or general fast was audaciously declaring a state of national extremity, one beyond the reach of human government to address.[45] Yet Charles I did acquiesce to such importuning. What, besides the underwhelming precedent of the private parliamentary communions called in 1621 and 1624, had changed? The recognition of print as a publicising medium, of pulpits as bully, and of the court pulpit as one to be used in parliament time quite deliberately, all make for very plausible answers. Perhaps, then, it *is* fair to say that it was Charles – or at least his spokesman, Laud – who were the ones who started the fight. The Long Parliament simply finished it.

[43] Wilson's account can be found in *Pulpit in Parliament*, 28–34.

[44] Laud, *Works*, i, p. vii. David Cressy's forthcoming work on Charles I and the people of England will assess Laud's work with more specificity.

[45] Trevor-Roper, 'Fast Sermons', 295.

The Street Theatre of State: The Ceremonial Opening of Parliament, 1603–60

JASON PEACEY

This article revisits a fairly familiar topic – early modern ceremonial relating to the state opening of parliament – in order to analyse both new evidence and neglected themes. Thus, while it examines the projection of political authority, and the grandeur of state, it also addresses the audiences for, and popular reactions to, such events, and supplements treatment of James I and Charles I with observations regarding Oliver Cromwell and Richard Cromwell during the protectorate. This involves challenging claims that have repeatedly been made about the 'monarchical' style of Cromwellian regimes, but it also involves emphasizing that different rulers and regimes thought carefully about how best to ensure that their approach to ceremonial accurately reflected their governmental style, and about how to take account of audiences and the political mood on the streets of London. Indeed, the article emphasizes the degree to which Charles I sought to balance the desire to project regal authority with concerns about decorum and disorder, while Cromwellian protectors were more preoccupied with the need to balance grandeur with a civic plain-style.

Keywords: royal ceremonial; state opening of parliament; crowds; disorder; popular politics; London

1

On 30 January 1621, the street between Whitehall and Westminster Abbey rang out with cries of 'God bless you', as James I processed from court to church as part of the ceremony marking the state opening of parliament. Thanks to two eyewitness accounts, by John Chamberlain and Sir Simonds D'Ewes, we know that such cries came from the king, rather than from the crowd that had gathered to witness the spectacle. Chamberlain noted that James was 'very cheerful all the way', while D'Ewes observed that the monarch's behaviour was 'somewhat remarkable'. According to his account, James 'spoke often and lovingly to the people standing thick and three-fold on all sides to behold him', adding that this was 'contrary to his former hasty and passionate custom, which often, in his sudden temper, would bid a pox or plague on such as flocked to see him'. D'Ewes also noted that, in addition to the crowds on the street, the windows of houses overlooking the route were filled with 'many great ladies', who enjoyed a rather better view, although amongst these James spoke only to the duke of Buckingham's mother and wife. In addition, it was also considered significant that he bowed to, and spoke with, the Spanish ambassador, Gondomar. To the extent that James did take notice of those in the posh seats, moreover, he displayed less than regal sophistication, crying 'a pox take ye' at a group which had gathered in one window and who all wore yellow bands – a fashion, and perhaps a coded message of which he did not approve – causing them to withdraw in embarrassment.[1]

This incident raises the issues with which this article is concerned. It aims to analyse the public ceremonial associated with the state opening of parliament in the 17th century. Such events are, of course, not unknown to historians, and scholars such as David Dean, Malcolm Smuts and Elizabeth Read Foster have recognized the importance of political spectacle, and of events which were carefully staged and rich in symbolism. Nevertheless, two key areas have tended to be overlooked by scholars. First, little attention has been paid to the state opening in the context of the 1640s and 1650s, a period for which research has naturally focused upon the politicisation of parliamentary elections, upon political tension within the Palace of Westminster, and upon the constitutional battles and experiments of the civil war and interregnum. The aim, therefore, is to analyse what happened to state openings under Charles I as war approached, and under Oliver and Richard Cromwell during the 1650s, not least because of sustained interest in, and claims about, the regal nature of the Cromwellian 'court'. The argument will be that historians have been too quick to equate the Cromwellian style with quasi-monarchical pomp, and too slow to recognize important differences between the state openings of the 1650s and those of the early 17th century. But the aim is also to address a second neglected aspect of public ceremonial: the audience for state openings. In any number of other settings – parliament, the stage, and public executions – scholars now recognize the importance of studying audience responses to staged events, and the possibility that historians have been misled by static pictorial representations of institutions and events; that we have focused upon what was being presented to the exclusion of how this was perceived. The aim, therefore, is to examine state openings by doing more than merely appreciating that they involved a projection of regal and protectoral power, and by looking beyond the formalities orchestrated by the heralds, and beyond surviving pictorial representations of state grandeur. The argument will be that the reality of state openings could differ significantly from the representation, and that these events may have been less-than-entirely ordered, polite, and decorous. Onlookers, in other words, may not have accepted passively the message which was being projected to them and, as such, these symbolic and carefully-staged events could be fraught with danger.[2] This danger, moreover, could involve more than merely the subversion of official messages and meanings by spectators, and growing public interest in parliament raised the very real prospect of disorder.

The third, and perhaps most important, aim of this article is to connect 17th-century ceremonialism with issues relating to audiences and public perceptions of authority. By exploiting eyewitness testimony and contemporary print culture, in other words, it will be possible to explore how late medieval ceremonialism intersected with the politics of

[1] *The Letters of John Chamberlain*, ed. N.E. McClure (2 vols, Philadelphia, PA, 1939), ii, 338; John Nichols, *The Progresses and Public Processions of Queen Elizabeth; among which are interspersed other solemnities, public expenditures, and remarkable events during the reign of that . . . Princess: . . . with historical notes. (To which are subjoined some of the early Progresses of King James, etc.)* (4 vols, 1828), iv, 649–50; Elizabeth Read Foster, *The House of Lords 1603–1649: Structure, Procedure, and the Nature of its Business* (Chapel Hill, NC, 1983), 4.

[2] R.M. Smuts, *Court Culture and the Origins of a Royalist Tradition in Early Stuart England* (Philadelphia, PA, 1987), 67; R.M. Smuts, 'Public Ceremony and Royal Charisma: The English Royal Entry in London, 1485–1642', in *The First Modern Society*, ed. A.L. Beier, D. Cannadine and J.M. Rosenheim (Cambridge, 1989), 65–93.

the crowd, and to observe how the street theatre of state changed during the mid 17th century, not least in response to audiences, their perceptions, and their behaviour. The article will thus use the changing face of parliamentary 'theatre' as a means of contributing to ongoing attempts to rethink the nature of public politics and popular culture in the turbulent decades of the 17th century.

2

The state opening of parliament, as it developed from the mid 16th century onwards, involved a colourful and dramatic procession from Whitehall to Westminster Abbey. This was intended to convey the idea of continuity with the medieval past, the idea of parliament as a way of bringing together diverse elements of the body politic, and the idea that royal authority was exercised through the institutions of parliament. The procession was invariably followed by the delivery of a sermon, before the monarch was escorted to the house of lords, where peers and bishops took their seats prior to MPs being summoned in order to hear the royal address. Such royal processions were grand and carefully orchestrated. The streets having been cleared and cleaned, messengers and trumpeters led judges, privy councillors, bishops, and peers, as well as leading courtiers and, eventually, the monarch, the latter of whom was generally carried on horseback or in a coach. The monarch was also accompanied by the cap of maintenance and flanked by gentlemen pensioners and a personal bodyguard, and the whole procession was overseen by the heralds, who ensured that order and precedence were observed. All of those involved – and this being a medieval event, MPs were excluded, unless they happened to be members of the privy council or royal officials – were richly attired in formal robes. The pattern of such processions was not entirely set in stone – Queen Elizabeth I travelled by water in 1572, and the 1593 opening was cancelled because of plague, while James I chose to walk rather than ride on at least one occasion – and it was a model which was susceptible to tinkering. Nevertheless, its essence changed little from the mid 16th to the mid 17th century. That we know about these events in such detail reflects the existence of written and pictorial processionals, drawn up by the heralds as part of their preparations, and sometimes termed 'the parliament pomp'.[3]

---

[3] E.R. Foster, 'Staging a Parliament in Early Stuart England', in *The English Commonwealth, 1547–1640*, ed. P. Clark, A.G.R. Smith and N. Tyacke (Leicester, 1979), 129; H. Cobb, 'The Staging of Ceremonies of State in the House of Lords', in *The Houses of Parliament: History, Art, Architecture*, ed. C. Riding and J. Riding (2000), 32–3, 35–6; M.F. Bond, 'A Stuart Parliamentary Processional Roll', in *House of Lords Record Office Report for 1980* (1981); H.S. Cobb, 'Descriptions of the State Opening of Parliament, 1485–1601: A Survey', *Parliamentary History*, xviii (1999), 303–15; T. Milles, *The Catalogue of Honour* (1610), 64–8; David M. Dean, 'Image and Ritual in the Tudor Parliaments', in *Tudor Political Culture*, ed. Dale Hoak (Cambridge, 1995), 253–65; David L. Smith, *The Stuart Parliaments, 1603–1689* (1998), 78–80, 143; A. Wagner and J.C. Sainty, 'The Origin of the Introduction of Peers in the House of Lords', *Archaeologia*, ci (1967), 142–50 and plates xvii–xx; K. Sharpe, *Selling the Tudor Monarchy* (New Haven, CT, 2009), 161, 296–7, 429. A German visitor to London in 1584, Lupold von Wedel, noted that 'all the streets and lanes in Westminster were well cleared and strewn with sand when the queen made her entrance into the house, for it is a custom that on the first and last day of the session the king or queen shall be present in the assembly': Cobb, 'Descriptions', 312. For the absence of MPs, unlike in Scotland, see Dean, 'Image and Ritual', 261–2. For the cancellation in 1593, see Cobb, 'Descriptions', 314. For other pictorial representations, which indicate that James once chose to walk on foot, see Edinburgh University Library, Laing Collection, MS La. III.283, ff. 43v–4, 149v, 150v, 151v, 152v, 153v. I am grateful to Andrew Gordon for drawing this item to my attention.

The aim, however, is not merely to analyse the nature of this procession, but also to explore issues relating to the audience, something which can also be done on a number of occasions during the late 16th and early 17th centuries. The heralds' accounts can be supplemented, in other words, with evidence from other archives and other contemporary observers – not least resident ambassadors of European powers – who provide insights, often tantalisingly brief, into the non-official story of state openings.[4] Such accounts reveal that there was more to the state openings than the formal and decorous procession organised by the heralds. For example, these were events to which spectators themselves often added key elements, and by the early 17th century it is possible to demonstrate that processions came to be surrounded by unofficial paraphernalia, such as the tapestries with which some local householders decorated the route. These seem to have represented a gesture of loyalty and support – the equivalent of bringing out the bunting at a modern royal occasion – and in 1601, it was noted that houses were decorated with 'rich stuff, such as the inhabitants had to furnish the streets as her highness passed'.[5] Beyond this, however, there is also evidence that state openings did not always go as smoothly as the pictorial representations might suggest, and that they did not always offer a formal, orderly and hierarchical display of royal power. Since we are dealing with England, of course, this was partly a matter of the weather, and the opening in 1614 took place on a foul day, which apparently 'marred much of the show'.[6] More importantly, it was also possible for the sense of decorum to be undermined by mishaps and political tension. An account of the opening of the 1614 parliament – the 'Addled' Parliament – thus noted not merely details of the procession and of the king's riding on horseback through Whitehall, but also the curious accident involving the bishop who fell from his horse. More intriguing still is the fact that this mishap apparently prompted a puritan noble, who was himself involved in the procession, to comment that 'at least they had got a bishop down'. When he himself fell from his mount and broke his arm, however, a catholic observer reflected that 'so would fall all the Protestants and Puritans of the kingdom'.[7]

By far the biggest threat to order and decency, however, and to the successful projection of majesty, was the presence of large audiences. Indeed, it is possible to observe how the issue of crowds became more pressing as time passed, and how measures were taken to cope with the number of people that could be expected to appear. Up until the mid 16th century, Tudor monarchs had proceeded in a fairly private fashion, in order to 'escape from the throng of the people'.[8] Thereafter, however, Tudor state openings became much more powerful public spectacles. The 1539 state opening introduced the idea of processing from Whitehall to the Abbey, no

---

[4] For accounts of 1614, e.g., see *CSP Ven., 1613–15*, p. 115; *Letters of John Chamberlain*, ed. McClure, i, 522; Nichols, *Progresses*, iv, 1091–2; BL, Harleian MS 1107, f. 44; Harleian MS 5176, item 20. Little detail has, so far, emerged regarding the procession of 1604: Nichols, *Progresses*, iv, 1062. For the problem of moving from a reconstruction of such events to their reception, see: Dean, 'Image and Ritual', 244–5.

[5] Foster, 'Staging', 129; Cobb, 'Descriptions', 314–15; Dean, 'Image and Ritual', 244.

[6] Nichols, *Progresses*, iii, 2.

[7] *CSP Dom., Addenda, 1580–1625*, pp. 539–40; TNA, SP15/40, ff. 98–104v.

[8] Cobb, 'Descriptions', 305–6. The traditional pattern involved travelling from Westminster to Bridewell Palace by water for robing, and then to Blackfriars for mass, before returning to the king's house by 'a covered way'.

doubt with a sense of public spectacle – in 1554, Mary rode in an open litter 'so as to expose her to the public view'[9] – but this obviously brought with it problems about decency and order. This was perfectly clear from a 1540 memorandum about the need to 'keep out the common people', by erecting rails along the length of the route 'to keep them back'.[10] This, then, became standard practice for subsequent events, and official accounts reveal in precise detail the expense involved in 'railing the streets and passage from Whitehall to the parliament house against His Majesty's coming thither' (1614), and for providing 'posts and rails both sides from the middle of King Street to the great gate leading to Westminster churchyard' (1621).[11] Such accounts itemise the amount of wood required, the number of post-holes which needed to be dug, and the measures which needed to be taken to ensure that nobody walked off with this valuable material.[12] The preparations in early 1624, therefore, involved payments to Ralph Brice, Paul Ward and other carpenters for framing and setting up hundreds of rods, posts and rails 'from Whitehall gate on both sides [of] the street entering into the minister church at Westminster' ahead of the king's 'going to the parliament house' (£9 16s. 3d.), as well as further payments for paving work, including the repairs that were required after the ceremony was over (£6 9s. 10d). Given the bad weather, moreover, money also needed to be spent breaking and clearing ice from the streets and spreading gravel and, when the king then decided to delay the opening, the whole exercise needed to be repeated, at further expense (£5 3s. 4d.). A final payment was made to the beadle of Westminster 'for making proclamation for preserving and bringing out all the rails which were broken down and carried away after his Majesties going to the parliament (2s.).[13]

The public spectacle involving the monarchical procession to the state opening of parliament brought with it, in other words, the danger of disorder. The crowd in 1559 appears to have been well ordered, and people apparently kneeled as the queen passed, shouting: 'God save and maintain thee'.[14] An observer in 1601, however, noted that a stronger guard was added to the back of the procession, behind the ladies of the court, 'to guard them from the press of the people'. It was also observed, perhaps with surprise, that the event was 'this year so well-ordered that nobody received any hurt'. This probably reflected memories of the event in 1597, which had been marred by accidents in which several spectators were crushed 'through the mighty recourse of the people . . . pressing betwixt Whitehall and the college church to see her majesty and nobility riding in robes'.[15] This comment suggests that the order and decency of the state opening, as pictured in processional rolls, may have been somewhat illusory, or at least something which could be achieved only with great difficulty, and this seems to have become an even greater problem as more and more people came to observe the procession.[16] In 1621,

[9] Cobb, 'Descriptions', 309.

[10] Cobb, 'Descriptions', 306–7.

[11] TNA, E351/3248; E351/3254; see also AO1/2424/56.

[12] Foster, 'Staging', 130, 240.

[13] TNA, E351/3257; for similar expenses in 1628, see E351/3261.

[14] Dean, 'Image and Ritual', 243.

[15] Foster, 'Staging', 130, 240; Dean, 'Image and Ritual', 244; Cobb, 'Descriptions', 314–15; Sharpe, *Selling the Tudor Monarchy*, 429.

[16] Dean, '*Image and Ritual*', 256–7, 260. One commentator in 1554 claimed that 20,000 people came to see Philip and Mary, although this may be a wild exaggeration: Cobb, 'Descriptions', 309.

therefore, Chamberlain claimed to have witnessed 'the greatest concourse and throng of people that hath been seen', while D'Ewes noted that the crowd was three deep along the king's route, and that he had been able to secure a 'convenient place' only by arriving very early in the morning.[17] Such a crush led to some people being injured – Chamberlain claimed that 'there was some hurt done by the breaking of two scaffolds', and D'Ewes claimed that he secured his vantage point 'not without some danger escaped' – although the sources provide little hint of overt dissent or active troublemaking.[18] Indeed, these sizeable crowds, with their attendant dangers, seem to have become a feature of early-17th-century state openings, not least in response to the fact that processions became increasingly grand. In 1624, therefore, Chamberlain observed 'greater show and pomp than I have seen to my remembrance'.[19] On this occasion, a larger-than-usual crowd had evidently been anticipated, and the costs involved in preparing for the state opening involved 'taking down the old conduit head in King Street and bringing the same up new again further back towards the common shore to enlarge the street'.[20]

Such popularity continued until the end of the 1620s, perhaps as a result of growing public awareness about parliament, mounting political tension, and heightened antici-pation about what a new session might bring, and it is certainly clear that state openings during this period attracted people from far beyond London. One such visitor was the fellow of Queen's College, Oxford, Thomas Crosfield, who 'went to London to see the pomp of princes and peers going to Parliament' in March 1628, and who recorded the order of the procession.[21] Crosfield's desire to witness the state opening highlights the growing popularity of this particular royal ceremony, but the broader significance of his visit is probably that the heightened grandeur of royal spectacle, based upon an enhanced awareness of the need to project monarchical power, increased the likelihood that orderliness would be undermined rather than reinforced. It is precisely this tension between decorum and disorder that came to preoccupy the mind of Charles I and his courtiers as his reign progressed.

3

The two state openings of 1640, for the 'Short' and 'Long' Parliaments, bring this tension into stark relief, and they highlight the ways in which the monarch reflected upon, and was affected by, both the promise and the problem of state openings, and the growing fear of public disorder.

First, the event in April 1640, marking the opening of the Short Parliament, seems to fit perfectly well into what had become a fairly traditional pattern since the mid 16th century, and one with which historians are fairly familiar. Clarendon later recalled that

---

[17] *Letters of John Chamberlain*, ed. McClure, ii, 338; Nichols, *Progresses*, iv, 649–50; Foster, *House of Lords*, 4.

[18] Foster, 'Staging', 240; *Letters of John Chamberlain*, ed. McClure, ii, 338; Foster, *House of Lords*, 4; Nichols, *Progresses*, iv, 649–50.

[19] *Letters of John Chamberlain*, ed. McClure, ii, 546; Nichols, *Progresses*, iv, 965. Chamberlain seems to have been particularly curious to observe Prince Charles.

[20] TNA, E351/3257.

[21] *The Diary of Thomas Crosfield*, ed. F.S. Boas (Oxford, 1935), 20.

it had been conducted 'with the usual ceremony and formality', and this seems to be borne out by the official archives.[22] Financial accounts thus reveal expenses for 'fitting and preparing of both houses of parliament with degrees and seats against the lords and commons sitting there', and new posting and railing 'on both sides from Whitehall gates to the west end of the Abbey against his Majesty's going to Parliament'.[23] As on previous occasions, moreover, Westminster's JPs were ordered to 'cause watches to be set to preserve the rails to be pitched against the king's going to the Parliament, and to cause the streets to be well paved by the Abbey'.[24] Surviving evidence also reveals that the event was immensely popular, no doubt reflecting the extravagant hopes and expectations people had of parliament after 11 years of 'personal rule'.

This clamour to observe the royal procession is particularly clear from the evidence relating not to the populace, but rather to an elite audience. This was partly a matter of an ambassadorial presence, and the king's master of ceremonies, Sir John Finet, recorded that the Spanish ambassador, the marquess de Velada, 'privately . . . chose (after a hint I had given of the comodiousness of it) the house of the Duchess of Chevreuse for his sight of that solemnity'. Finet added that he also arranged accommodation for 'the better sort of the Marquess's train', in a house 'at the lower end of King Street', where they paid a sum of £14 'for a greater and less window capable of 20 persons . . . where they beheld in front the entire proceedings'. The ambassadors from Venice and the United Provinces, meanwhile, 'hired stands elsewhere, the latter paying for a chamber and the half of a pergola, £10, and the other for a chamber in another house there £5'.[25] Similar preparation and planning is also evident amongst the English aristocracy, and from the correspondence between John Castle and his employer, the earl of Bridgewater. On 9 April, Castle advised Bridgewater that he could find only two rooms for rent in King Street; one 'being a good fair window (that will take 5 or 6 at it) will not be let under £5, and the other that can take but 3 or 4 at most, at £3.10s.'. Castle advised a quick decision, adding that 'if your lordship will have either of them for my lady, your daughter, and your son and Mrs Davys, I wish somebody be sent hither this morning to agree for them'.[26] Bridgewater eventually took a room 'at Hooper's the Barber Surgeon's', which was 'right over Gardiner's Lane end', and as the event approached, Castle advised that 'if my lady Alice and her company do not hasten on Monday morning to be at the room . . . by six o'clock, or presently after, there will be too much difficulty to pass into the House, for the streets will be full before 5 o'clock, and the space within the rails quickly after, choaked up with the press of the multitude'.[27] By examining the papers relating to the elite audience for the state opening, in other words, it becomes perfectly clear that the event attracted, or was thought likely to attract, a mass audience comprised of the 'lower orders'.

[22] Earl of Clarendon, *The History of the Rebellion and Civil Wars in England*, ed. W.D. MacRay (6 vols, Oxford, 1888), i, 173; *CSP Dom., 1640*, p. 59; TNA, SP16/451, f. 31; BL, Harleian MS 4931, f. 46. See K. Sharpe, *Image Wars: Promoting Kings and Commonwealths in England, 1603–1660* (New Haven, CT, 2010), 237.

[23] TNA, AO1/2429/71.

[24] TNA, LC5/134, p. 386.

[25] *The Ceremonies of Charles I: The Notebooks of John Finet, 1628–1641*, ed. A. Loomie (New York, 1987), 279.

[26] Henry E. Huntington Library, San Marino, CA, [hereafter cited as HEH], EL 7830.

[27] HEH, EL 7831. Castle promised to 'give order for a fire and faggots against their coming'.

To a limited degree, moreover, it is possible to observe not just the popularity of the event, but also the reaction of some of those who attended. This is even more important from 1640 onwards, in order to supplement what might loosely be called the 'propaganda' surrounding the event, in terms of its representation – both in pictures and text – in printed literature. Readers were presented, therefore, with an 'exact description' of the April 1640 procession in ballad and image, written by the year's most popular author, Martin Parker, and the order of proceedings subsequently appeared in a printed manual of parliamentary procedure in 1641, both of which naturally stressed order and grandeur.[28] Such literature was not entirely misleading, of course, and it accorded with the impression which the proceedings made on at least some of the spectators. The diarist, John Evelyn, for example, who travelled up from Wotton 'to see the solemnity of His Majesty's riding through the city in state to the Short Parliament', claimed that it was 'a very glorious and magnificent sight, the king circled with his royal diadem, and the affections of his people'.[29] Others were somewhat less impressed, however, and when Sir Thomas Peyton wrote home from Westminster about 'the riding to Parliament' he noted subtle, but important, differences from the conventional pattern, and recorded 'more than what was usual form and state'. Key here was the fact that 'the bishops only did ride, many of them on bob-tailed horses, fitter for Mrs Crayford in my opinion at Bridgehill than for an ecclesiastical baron's gravity and reverence there'.[30]

Oxinden's comment provides the first hint that Charles I and his officials were prepared to tinker with the state opening, something which became much clearer later in the year, at the opening of the Long Parliament. As any number of contemporary commentators noted, but as historians have been slow to recognize, what made this event noteworthy was that the king decided not to process to Westminster Abbey. Instead, he chose to travel from Whitehall to Westminster by water, landing at Westminster stairs before passing through the Star Chamber and Westminster Hall and on to the Abbey. This certainly involved a ceremonial procession, with trumpeters, legal grandees, heralds and peers, who walked ahead of the prince and the king, who wore their parliament robes, and who were accompanied by the cap of estate and sword, and by the earl marshal, the lord great chamberlain and the guards.[31] But this procession involved much less of a public spectacle, and it did not follow the traditional pattern, as Sheila Lambert claimed.[32] According to Clarendon: 'the king himself did not ride with his accustomed equipage or in his usual majesty to Westminster, but went privately in his barge . . . as if it had been to a return of a prorogued or adjourned Parliament'. Another commentator, William Hawkins, informed the earl of Leicester that Charles 'went in a more private way than ordinary'.[33]

[28] M. P[arker], *An Exact Description of the Manner How His Maiestie and his Nobles Went to the Parliament* (1640); [William Hakewill], *The Manner of Holding Parliaments* (1641), sigs G3–4; Sharpe, *Image Wars*, 237.

[29] *The Diary of John Evelyn*, ed. E.S. De Beer (6 vols, Oxford, 1955), ii, 23.

[30] *The Oxinden Letters, 1607–1642*, ed. D. Gardiner (1933), 162.

[31] Foster, *House of Lords*, 5; HMC, *Buccleuch MSS*, iii, 387; *CSP Dom., 1640–1*, p. 242; TNA, SP16/471, ff. 21–2.

[32] S. Lambert, 'The Opening of the Long Parliament', *Historical Journal*, xxvii (1984), 265.

[33] Clarendon, *History*, i, 220; HMC, *De L'Isle and Dudley MSS*, vi, 339; BL, Add. MS 11045, f. 131v; [Hakewill], *Manner of Holding Parliaments*, sig. G4.

There are two ways of explaining the king's decision. First, it seems to fit with the picture that has emerged – not least from the work of Malcolm Smuts and Judith Richards – of a king disinclined to appear in public, and who had withdrawn into an increasingly private court. Smuts has noted the declining importance of royal entries under Charles, not because of a lack of public interest, but rather because the king withdrew from the public gaze, 'so that by the eve of the civil war Charles I almost never appeared in the streets of his capital'.[34] This reflected the king's desire for order and decorum, and his distaste for crowds, something which Charles had inherited from his father – and for which James had dramatically overcompensated in the bizarre performance in 1621 – and which involved acute recognition of the importance of audience response.[35] It might even be possible to argue that this desire to withdraw from public performance was evident as early as the 1625 parliament, when it was reported that the king would go 'privately thither', although this may have been a response to the bad weather and the plague.[36] However, it seems certain that, as time passed, Charles developed an increasingly strong sense of the need for order, hierarchy and decorum; that he refused to become a 'prisoner of ceremony', and that royal entries into London, and public appearances in general, became less common. According to Smuts, therefore, Charles made only one formal entry into London before 1641, and even cancelled his coronation procession in favour of travelling to Westminster Hall privately by water. The conclusion, for Smuts, was that 'great public rituals and formal rules of behaviour gradually declined', even if they left behind a 'delicate ritualism' which pervaded the Caroline court.[37]

Smuts has also demonstrated, however, the value of supplementing, or contextualising, Charles's attitudes towards decorum, and towards royal ceremonies, in terms of his concern regarding the public response to his appearances. According to Smuts, therefore, even crowds which were supportive and loyal were rarely passive and deferential, and the public 'always aggressively asserted its presence, treating the monarch less as an awesome symbol of authority than as a popular hero'. Such noisy and boisterous behaviour was anathema to Charles I, but it was even more troublesome, of course, to the extent that the public response could also be subversive, and this provides the second explanation for the decisions taken at the opening of the Long Parliament.[38] Smuts noted that the royal entry into London in 1641 – made to mark the king's return from Scotland – witnessed notably tighter security, and the fear of disorder seems also to have been uppermost in the king's mind in October 1640.[39] Indeed, official archives indicate that the authorities had certainly *planned* a traditional procession to parliament. In his

---

[34] Smuts, 'Public Ceremony', 68, 84.

[35] L.L. Knoppers, *Constructing Cromwell: Ceremony, Portrait and Print, 1645–1661* (Cambridge, 2000), 76. For James's difficulty in acting like a king who valued the devotion of his people, see Smuts, *Court Culture*, 27. Much earlier, it had been observed that James 'does not caress the people', and that the people 'like their king to show pleasure at their devotion'. James was perceived to have 'no taste for them but rather contempt and dislike': Smuts, *Court Culture*, 27. This naturally fed into unfavourable comparisons with his predecessor, and to the cult of Elizabeth.

[36] *Stuart Dynastic Policy and Religious Politics, 1621–1625*, ed. M.C. Questier (Camden, 5th ser., xxxiv, Cambridge, 2009), 375.

[37] Smuts, *Court Culture*, 199–201, 212; Knoppers, *Cromwell*, 69, 73, 108.

[38] Smuts, 'Public Ceremony', 74–5.

[39] Smuts, 'Public Ceremony', 92.

capacity as lord chamberlain, therefore, the earl of Pembroke had given orders for 'the railing of the streets on both sides from Whitehall to the West door of Westminster Abbey for His Majesty to ride in state thither' (10 October). He also demonstrated concern about the 'confluence and resort of people and coaches', and about the need to clear New Palace Yard of 'undecent and prejudicial structures'.[40] Such preparations indicate that the decision to cancel the procession, and not to proceed 'through the streets', was taken only in late October, perhaps only days before parliament was due to open.[41]

As such, it seems clear that the king feared the reception he would receive, and the possible threat to his safety, and this response was probably not unreasonable given the trouble which London had witnessed since the dissolution of the Short Parliament, and the recent riots at St Paul's Cathedral. Indeed, on the Sunday before the planned state opening, the authorities had apprehended a Scotsman in Whitehall who was apparently attached to the household of the Scottish nobleman, the marquess of Huntley, and who was found to be carrying a newly-loaded and charged pistol. Under interrogation, this character was 'found tripping', and produced an inconsistent story, as a result of which he was incarcerated in the Marshalsea prison.[42] But if the decision to cancel the state opening was justified by the perceived threat to the king's safety, it was also widely criticized because of the political message that it sent out. The Venetian ambassador, Giustinian, wrote that 'the king has intimated that he will not open it with a formal procession, or other solemnity, but privately', and he added that 'the wisest do not approve of this decision, for it shows more clearly than ever to his people that he consented to the summons merely from compulsion by the enemy, and not of his own free will, to please the people'. This is given credence by the fact that, in the truncated procession, the task of carrying the cap of estate was given to the earl of Essex, a known and very eminent critic of the Caroline regime, who had been involved in the petition of the 12 peers which had demanded a new parliament, and who would, in time, become lord general of the parliamentarian army. However, if this represented an attempt to mollify the crown's opponents, it does not seem to have worked, and Giustinian concluded that 'instead of conciliating their good will . . . he alienates them over a matter of outward show which is of no real importance, which at the same time increases the admiration of the steps taken by the rebels'.[43]

The evidence from 1640, therefore, points to a king conflicted over the state opening of parliament, and torn between exploiting the opportunity to project majesty, hierarchy and divine right monarchy on the one hand, and his desire for decorum, and to avoid disorder, on the other. In April 1640, after 11 years without parliament, he opted for a traditional public display, perhaps calculating that the benefits of a formal procession outweighed the risks and the undesirable degree of access which it gave the public to his

[40] TNA, LC5/134, pp. 420, 422; John Adamson, *The Noble Revolt: The Overthrow of Charles I* (2007), 91; Foster, 'Staging', 130.

[41] HMC, *De L'Isle and Dudley MSS*, vi, 337; Adamson, *Noble Revolt*, 92.

[42] BL, Add. MS 11045, f. 131v; HMC, *Buccleuch MSS*, iii, 387. For the riots, see *CSP Ven., 1640–2*, pp. 92–3. For the Scotsman, see: BL, Add. MS 11045, f. 131. The latter story was reported by Rossingham, who also noted happenings at St Paul's, and the concern caused by the discovery of a cache of 36 new muskets at a house in London where catholics were lodging: BL, Add. MS 11045, ff. 131–v.

[43] *Manner of Holding Parliaments*, sig. G4v; *CSP Ven., 1640–2*, pp. 92–3; Adamson, *Noble Revolt*, 92.

royal person. A little over six months later, however, he made a different calculation, even though he and his advisors must have appreciated that a private ceremony – worse, a cancelled ceremony – sent just as powerful a political message as any display of grandeur and pomp.

4

If the state opening of parliament by Charles I has received insufficient attention, the events orchestrated by Oliver and Richard Cromwell have been almost entirely over-looked, even in Kevin Sharpe's recent study of mid-17th-century political culture. This is despite the fairly extensive scholarly interest in Cromwellian ceremonial – particularly Oliver's first and second inaugurations as protector, and his state funeral in 1658 – which has been driven by a debate over how far the protectorate witnessed a return to monarchical style, and a revival of regal trappings.[44] However, it is certainly possible to study the state opening of parliament during the 1650s, and, indeed, surviving sources permit interesting observations to be made about the Cromwellian attitude to pomp and public occasions, and make it possible to compare parliamentary ceremonial in the 1650s with that from Caroline regimes. These sources, relating to both official decisions and contemporary perceptions, no longer revolve around audited accounts and the papers of the heralds, but rather involve printed sources such as pamphlets and newspapers, some of which represented official propaganda, and some of which involved hostile com-mentary. Problematic though these sources may be, they, nevertheless, prove to be extremely revealing about the 'Cromwellian style'.[45]

The received wisdom regarding the interregnum involves the idea that the period witnessed a retreat from republicanism to quasi-monarchical power, and this seems to be justified by evidence relating to public ceremonies, at least superficially. Prior to the establishment of the protectorate in December 1653, much less emphasis seems to have been placed on public displays of grandeur and authority, and the ceremonial of the state opening seems to have been abolished entirely. Evidence from the summer of 1653, for example, indicates that Barebone's Parliament – the 'parliament of saints' – opened in a perfunctory fashion, without pomp or public display. MPs did not even hold their first session at Westminster, but rather assembled in the council chamber at Whitehall, which was, as one newspaper reported tersely, 'the place appointed'.[46] In a similar fashion, Cromwell's inauguration as protector in December 1653 also seems to have been a notably unspectacular occasion.[47]

[44] R. Sherwood, *The Court of Oliver Cromwell* (1977); R. Sherwood, *Oliver Cromwell: King in all but Name* (Stroud, 1997).

[45] Knoppers, *Cromwell*; P.M. Hunneyball, 'Cromwellian Style: The Architectural Trappings of the Protec-torate', in *The Cromwellian Protectorate*, ed. P. Little (Woodbridge, 2007), 53–81.

[46] A. Woolrych, *Commonwealth to Protectorate* (Oxford, 1982), 145; *Severall Proceedings of State Affaires*, no. 197 (30 June–7 July 1653), 3117. This event was not even preceded by a sermon. The newspaper was the uncited source for the earl of Leicester's diary, where this passage was copied almost verbatim: HMC, *De L'Isle and Dudley MSS*, vi, 617–8.

[47] Woolrych argued that the first inauguration 'went off with the rather drab propriety that tends to charac-terise ceremonies unwarmed by traditional sentiment and panache': Woolrych, *Commonwealth to Protectorate*, 360.

This apparent aversion to public ceremony seems to have disappeared, however, once Cromwellian power was established. At the opening of the first Protectoral Parliament in September 1654, Cromwell opted for something noticeably grander, and on 4 September there took place a fairly formal procession from Whitehall to Westminster. This involved, first, 'about 300 gentlemen, with his lifeguard, and divers officers, all bare-headed' and 'richly habited'. They were followed by Cromwell himself, in 'a very rich new coach with six horses', in 'very stately equipage', and surrounded by 'pages and lackeys in their several liveries, most admirable to behold'. Cromwell shared his coach with his son, Henry Cromwell, Major General John Lambert, and Henry Lawrence, lord president of the council of state, who 'rode bare in the coach with him'. Alongside the coach, and on foot, were Lord Strickland, captain of Cromwell's guard of foot, and Mr Howard, captain of the life guard of horse, also bareheaded. Cromwell's coach was then followed by 'two very stately horses with rich furniture', one belonging to the protector himself, and the other being ridden by Mr Claypole, master of the horse. According to one report, the cloth which covered these horses cost at least £500. Next there came a coach containing the lords commissioners of the great seal, and then another which held the commissioners of the exchequer, Colonel William Sydenham and Colonel Edwards. These were followed by Cromwell's foot guard and the wardens of the Tower, 'all in his highness's livery', and as many as 20 other coaches. Upon arriving in Westminster, Cromwell alighted from his coach and entered the Abbey, preceded by the officers of the army and four ceremonial maces, with Lord Whitelocke carrying the purse and Lord Lambert carrying the sword of state. Following a sermon by Thomas Goodwin, Cromwell and his attendants then proceeded to Westminster on foot, again with Lambert carrying the sword of state before him.[48] These details come from contemporary pamphlets and newspapers, and although they were not produced by Cromwellian hacks – notably Marchamont Nedham – they were, nevertheless, approved by the regime, and licensed for publication. They can also be supplemented by evidence from other contemporary observers. According to the Venetian ambassador, Paulucci, Cromwell's coach was 'very gorgeous', and he described Cromwell as having a 'pompous retinue'.[49] The Genoese resident, Francesco Bernardi, commented that the procession from the Abbey to parliament, involving all of the important officials of the regime and many leading army officers, involved '*grandissima dignita*'.[50]

It would be very easy to conclude from such evidence that Cromwell had adopted the trappings of monarchy, on what was evidently a grand and spectacular occasion. S.R. Gardiner argued that Cromwell opened parliament with 'all but royal state', and Sherwood wrote of Cromwell's 'majestic short progress', in an analysis which stressed the drift towards monarchical style – 'the rising tide of royal pomp and pageantry' – after an inauguration which was 'rather short on regal splendour', even if it was 'not without

---

[48] *A Perfect Diurnall*, xxi (4–11 Sept. 1654), 137–8; *The Speech of his Hghnesse the Lord Protector to the Parliament* (1654), 3; *Severall Proceedings*, no. 258 (31 Aug.–7 Sept. 1654), sig. 22M; *The Perfect Diurnall*, ccxlviii (4–11 Sept. 1654), 3797–8; *CJ*, vii, 365. For other accounts, see B. Whitelocke, *Memorials of the English Affairs* (4 vols, Oxford, 1853), iv, 133; *The Diary of Bulstrode Whitelocke, 1605–1675*, ed. R. Spalding (Oxford, 1990), 394.

[49] *CSP Ven., 1653–4*, p. 259.

[50] *Oliviero Cromwell Dalla Battaglia Di Worcester Alla Sua Morte: Corrispondenza del Rappresentanti Genovesi a Londra* (Genoa, 1882), 180.

its royal ritualism and symbolism'. More recently, Kevin Sharpe suggested that the 1654 state opening 'emulated royal practice'.[51] Indeed, many contemporaries were clearly perturbed at such pomp and ceremony, and the Venetian ambassador noted that, when Cromwell summoned MPs to hear his opening speech, 'they obeyed at once, though some of the leading members marvelled at this new fashion', and proved reluctant to attend him.[52] Moreover, this pattern seems to have been repeated in September 1656. At the opening of the second Protectoral Parliament, Cromwell, again, processed to the Abbey, attended by his council and the officers of state and army, the gentlemen of his household, and his guards, and listened to a sermon by John Owen, before making his opening speech before MPs in the Painted Chamber. On this occasion, Cromwell, again, rode in a coach, 'in great pomp escorted by all his guards, horse and foot, by all the gentlemen and others of his court, and by his council also'. Once again, he was accompanied by a series of coaches which contained the secretary of state, John Thurloe, the keeper of the great seal, the judges and the councillors.[53] The Genoese observer, Bernardi, who observed '*l'infinito concorse del popolo*', noted the grand attire of those involved, and the fact that many of those involved wore the protector's livery.[54]

However, the Cromwellian state openings need to be approached with great care. Historians now recognize that the republican regime was acutely conscious of issues relating to imagery and the projection of authority, and that the differences between monarchical, republican and protectoral style ought not to be overplayed.[55] In addition, it is also important to study the Cromwellian style extremely closely, lest the similarities with earlier royal ceremonies attract undue attention at the expense of some very important differences. First, of course, the abolition of episcopacy and the house of lords inevitably altered the imagery, mood and political content of the ceremony, which necessarily became much more secular, and much less medieval. Second, it was much less obvious that MPs were excluded from the ceremony, as they had been in early decades. Strictly speaking, the procession in 1654 took place on the second day of parliament, the first day having fallen somewhat controversially on a Sunday, doubtless because this was 3 September, Cromwell's auspicious day. However, evidence suggests that MPs were present for the sermons on both days (in St Margaret's on 3 September and in the Abbey on 4 September), and that they also took part in the procession between Whitehall, the Abbey and the Palace of Westminster.[56] This fairly dramatic

---

[51] S.R. Gardiner, *History of the Commonwealth and Protectorate* (4 vols, 1903), iii, 178; Sherwood, *Oliver Cromwell*, 16; Sharpe, *Image Wars*, 517. For Sherwood's brief analysis of the opening of parliament in 1654, see Sherwood, *Oliver Cromwell*, 39–40; Sherwood, *Court of Oliver Cromwell*, 60–1, 78.

[52] *CSP Ven., 1653–4*, p. 259; Gardiner, *Commonwealth and Protectorate*, iii, 178; *Diary of Thomas Burton*, ed. J.T. Rutt (4 vols, 1828), i, pp. xvii–xviii.

[53] J. Caulfield, *Cromwelliana* (1810), 158; C.H. Firth, *The Last Years of the Protectorate, 1656–1658* (2 vols, 1909), i, 2–3; *Mercurius Politicus*, cccxxvii (11–18 Sept. 1656), 7254; *CSP Ven., 1655–6*, p. 266. Owen's text, from Isaiah, was 'what shall one then answer the messengers of the nation, that the Lord hath founded Zion, and the poor of his people shall trust in it'. It was printed as J. Owen, *God's Work in Founding Zion* (Oxford, 1656). See also *Calendar of the Clarendon State Papers*, ed. O. Ogle, W.H. Bliss, W.D. MacRay and F.J. Routledge (5 vols, Oxford, 1872–1970), iii, 179.

[54] *Oliviero Cromwell Dalla Battaglia Di Worcester Alla Sua Morte*, 377.

[55] S. Kelsey, *Inventing a Republic* (Manchester, 1997).

[56] *CJ*, vii, 365; *Diary of Thomas Burton*, ed. Rutt, i, pp. xvii–xviii; *The Writings and Speeches of Oliver Cromwell*, ed. W.C. Abbott (4 vols, Cambridge, MA, 1937–47), ii, 431–2; *Oliviero Cromwell Dalla Battaglia Di Worcester Alla Sua Morte*, 180.

innovation – which brought England into line with traditional Scottish practice – also seems to have been a feature of the state opening in 1656.[57] Third, in both 1654 and 1656, the procession had a much more obvious military flavour. As with the protector's installation in December 1653, officers of a standing army not only lined the streets but also took part in the procession itself, replacing, or rather supplementing, Cromwell's personal lifeguard and those with ceremonial military roles.[58] Fourth, Cromwell himself seems to have eschewed both military and regal garb for civilian costume, in a further indication of the plain style which struck at least some visitors to London, like the Scot, James Fraser.[59] Finally, the procession included a decidedly 'common touch', in the form of the participation of a number of tradesmen, including Cromwell's personal draper, just as his funeral would include fairly humble 'officials' such as the protectoral printers.[60]

What we see with Oliver Cromwell's state openings, therefore, is a rather different tension from that which was evident in 1640. Charles I was torn between the desire to project authority and order and the need to preserve order and decorum, but for Cromwell the challenge seems to have been to reinvent public ceremonial, and to strike a balance between, on the one hand, grandeur, pomp and the symbolism of sovereignty, and on the other a non-monarchical and non-religious plain style, and a more simple civil ceremonialism. This balancing act was then complicated, by the fact that Cromwell, like his predecessors, needed to confront issues of security. Indeed, the threat of disorder may have been heightened by the very absence of any hint of sacred government, and by the emphasis on a different kind of government, and one based in some way upon popular consent. Ahead of the 1656 parliament, the Venetian ambassador, Giavarini, certainly reported fears of disturbances at the opening of a new session, adding that this would cause 'embarrassment and trouble'.[61] He also noted the strengthening of the guards in Whitehall and Westminster, and the order 'that others be posted at the approaches of the city, to prevent anyone not having a passport of the state from entering or leaving'. Giavarini also noted that Cromwell had 'increased the number of the troops guarding the Tower of London, and has summoned a council of war of all the officers of the army and the major generals, to meet in his presence'.[62] Such precautions were wise, given that the Genoese resident, Bernardi, observed '*l'infinito concorse del popolo*', and that the 'throng' of people outside the Abbey included would-be assassins such as John Cecil, William Boyes and Miles Sindercombe, although, on this occasion, the size of the crowd may have saved the protector by deterring his assailants.[63]

It is this picture of a modified grandeur, and of ceremonial that was affected by issues of security, which offers the most appropriate way of characterising Cromwell's protectorate, rather than a rising tide of monarchical pomp. Again and again, it is possible to observe public derision, hostility and even violence, and it is necessary to recognize

[57] *Oliviero Cromwell Dalla Battaglia Di Worcester Alla Sua Morte*, 377.

[58] *Writings and Speeches*, ed. Abbott, iv, 258–9; Sherwood, *Oliver Cromwell*, 11; Knoppers, *Cromwell*, 70.

[59] *Writings and Speeches*, ed. Abbott, ii, 432; J. Raymond, 'An Eyewitness to King Cromwell', *History Today*, xlvii, No. 7 (July 1997), 35–41; Knoppers, *Cromwell*, 129.

[60] Sherwood, *Court of Oliver Cromwell*, 114–15.

[61] *CSP Ven., 1655–6*, p. 252.

[62] *CSP Ven., 1655–6*, p. 261.

[63] *Oliviero Cromwell Dalla Battaglia Di Worcester Alla Sua Morte*, 377; *The Whole Business of Sindercome* (1657), 7.

that the regime factored public opposition, and the possibility of disorder and even assassination attempts, into its calculations and plans, at the very same time that it 'appropriated and revised' monarchical forms. Indeed, it seems plausible to argue that concerns about safety were intimately connected with the need to project power in innovative and modified ways. First, although the official government press reported a jubilant response to the inauguration in December 1653 – one newspaper reporting 'great acclamations and shoutings all along the streets' – other evidence highlights perceptions that Cromwell had lost the affection of the people, and that the celebrations were notable for public laughter and derision.[64] Second, and perhaps as a result, Knoppers has detected reduced splendour in Cromwell's entry into London in February 1654. It is true that Cromwell was decked in rich attire, and that the procession involved 'lavishly caparisoned horses', the delivering of the city sword, and Cromwell's adoption of the practice of awarding knighthoods. It is also true that he was attended by 'the companies in livery . . . as was used to the king'. Nevertheless, the procession had a very different atmosphere from earlier entries, both in terms of the official display and the audience response.[65] The regime clearly anticipated large crowds, and one observer noted that, in preparation for the event, 'the streets are railed in from Temple Bar'.[66] The people did, indeed, turn out in droves, but the mood was solemn, perhaps even sullen. One commentator claimed that the episode was 'a triumph made up of dirt and multitude, but the silentest I believe that London ever saw of that kind; not an acclamation, nor one "God save" from Whitehall to the Grocers' [Hall], nay nor so much as a Mordecai to put off his hat'. Such was the downbeat mood of the crowd that this particular witness thought it would be 'no marvel if Haman [Cromwell] could not sleep that night'.[67] Others also noted the absence of applause and cheering, but also claimed to have observed the hurling of curses, and even of dirty cloths and pieces of leather, and of 'tiles and filthy clouts'. The Venetian resident, Paulucci, even claimed that a large stone was thrown at, and hit, Cromwell's coach.[68]

Historians may even have been too hasty in focusing upon the regal aspects of the second inauguration on 26 June 1657. Sherwood described this ceremony as 'to all intents and purposes a king-making ceremony, transforming Cromwell from a *de facto* into a *de jure* king while retaining the title lord protector', and as such it has received a great deal more attention than the state openings of parliament.[69] The second investiture certainly displayed very obvious 'pomp and magnificence' and, following the ceremony in Westminster Hall, Cromwell went to a service in St Margaret's 'in as great state as ever a king of England was', before being conveyed to Whitehall, 'with all that noble train and retinue there from church to his court, the trained band of London in the streets in arms, bells ringing, bonfires burning, and all demonstrations of joy that

---

[64] Knoppers, *Cromwell*, 70–1.

[65] Knoppers, *Cromwell*, 77; BL, Add. MS 70007, f. 40v. See, Sherwood, *Oliver Cromwell*, 17–19. For evidence about companies spending money when monarchs entered the city, see Guildhall Library, London, MS 3054/2 (1641–2), unfoliated.

[66] BL, Add. MS 70007, f. 40v.

[67] Knoppers, *Cromwell*, 79.

[68] Knoppers, *Cromwell*, 79.

[69] Sherwood, *Oliver Cromwell*, 95. For the investiture, see Sherwood, *Oliver Cromwell*, 95–103.

could be contrived'.[70] However, rather than representing 'a clear and complete assimilation of kingship', the episode 'appropriated and revised' monarchical forms, not least by 'transforming a sacred rite into a civil ceremony'. The event sought to make a grand public statement of sovereign power, but entirely lacked traces of sacramental majesty.[71] Indeed, this subtle, but important, modification of tradition was recognized at the time, and one contemporary commentator saw the ceremony very clearly as a compromise between republican and monarchical styles.[72] Here, too, there are grounds for thinking that the nature of Cromwellian ceremonial was affected by the popular mood, and by fears regarding the public response. Once again, it is necessary to treat with caution the claims made by government newspapers like *Mercurius Politicus*, whose editor had favoured a return to kingship earlier in the year, and who may thus have had an interest not merely in stressing the popular acclaim which greeted Cromwell, but also in describing the event using regal language.[73] The Venetian ambassador, while noting that people turned out in 'countless numbers', stressed that the mood was sombre at best, and tense at worst, and noted that onlookers 'would not open their mouths to utter what did not come from their hearts, and which they could not express with complete sincerity'.[74] More importantly, it is hard to imagine that the preparations for the inauguration were unaffected by the 'Sindercombe plot'. This was the term given to the various plans by republican activists to assassinate Cromwell during 1656–7, either by shooting him on his way to the state opening of the second Protectoral Parliament – from the house of Colonel James Mydhope near Westminster Abbey – or by firing Whitehall in January 1657.[75]

Finally, this compromise between sovereign grandeur and civic ceremonialism, and this tension between public display and public order, can also be detected in relation to the parliamentary occasions which came in the wake of Cromwell's rejection of the crown and second inauguration, and in the aftermath of the failed assassination attempts. It seems to have been evident, for example, at Cromwell's opening of the second session of the 1656 parliament, on 20 January 1658. Here again, Sherwood highlighted the grandeur of the occasion, and it is evident that the protector arrived 'under a superb canopy', and that he travelled to the palace by coach 'in great pomp', with 'some magnificent led horses, adorned with superb saddles and cloths, majestic for the gold and jewels they contained, as well as the usual guards on horse and foot'. It is also clear that, although this was a freezing and snowy day, the event drew 'a great crowd of people', not least in order to witness the arrival of the peers who constituted Cromwell's other House. What seems intriguing about this occasion, however, is that this procession began at Westminster stairs rather than at Whitehall, and that the bulk of the journey was made by water, although this seems to have been entirely normal following a prorogation, and it seems to be in this respect that Cromwell 'followed . . . royal

---

[70] Raymond, 'Eyewitness', 38.

[71] Knoppers, *Cromwell*, 107, 123, 124.

[72] Knoppers, *Cromwell*, 126; Bodl., MS Clarendon 55, f. 127.

[73] Knoppers, *Cromwell*, 124.

[74] Raymond, 'Eyewitness', 38.

[75] Sindercombe was arrested in Jan. 1657 and found guilty of treason, although he evaded execution by committing suicide in the Tower: *ODNB*; *Whole Business of Sindercome*, esp. 6–7.

precedent to the letter'.[76] As such, a better example of the conundrum facing the protectorate involves the opening of Richard Cromwell's parliament in January 1659. Here, it is noticeable that Clarendon's account claimed that the protector came 'in the same state that Oliver his father had used to do', and the account in one of the two official government newspapers indicates very clearly that this meant muted and subdued grandeur. Richard, therefore, made his way from Whitehall, accompanied by his privy council, as well as by the 'high officers of state and of his household', as well as army officers and gentlemen of the household, but, like Charles in November 1640, he 'passed by water' to Westminster, albeit 'in a stately new-built galley'. The episode was not without its pomp and, having landed at the parliament stairs, Cromwell processed through the palace to the house of lords and on to the Abbey, preceded by Lord Claypole, master of the horse, who carried the sword before him, with Desborow carrying the sword of state and with the gentlemen of the protectoral household leading the way, 'divers companies of foot being ranked on each side, then followed divers officers of the army, the comptroller of the household, the captain of his highness' yeomen of the guard, the lord chamberlain, the lords of the treasury, the lords of the other House, the lord keepers of the great seal, the serjeants at arms with their maces before his highness, and the whole ceremony was ordered by the heralds or officers at arms attending in their formalities'.[77] However, the event was short on public spectacle and, like his father before him, Richard strove to ensure that the event had a military and civic air, rather than one with regal and religious overtones. He also broke with tradition, by delivering his opening speech to his parliament from a seated position.[78] If such decisions reflected the insecurity of a new and unproven leader, they may have been well founded. Cromwell still found himself harangued by a quaker in Westminster Abbey, who apparently spoke 'a deal of nonsense', which Cromwell was forced to listen to patiently.[79]

5

Comparing the state openings of the 1640s and 1650s thus throws up important discontinuities, which are important for our understanding of both Charles and the Cromwells. Ambivalence and uncertainty regarding public ceremonial seems to have been common across the period, but in different ways and for different reasons. Thus, while security concerns can be argued to have affected the ceremonial practice of all three heads of state, their attitudes at a more fundamental level were rather different, although all three of them seem to have demonstrated a degree of ambivalence and uncertainty regarding public ceremonial. Charles I, more obviously even than his father, demonstrated a concern for order and decorum, and a distaste for public appearances, for

[76] Sherwood, *Oliver Cromwell*, 123; *CSP Ven., 1657–9*, pp. 157–8.

[77] Clarendon, *History*, vi, 99; *Publick Intelligencer*, clxi (24–31 Jan. 1659), 190–1; *CSP Ven., 1657–9*, pp. 287–8; F. Guizot, *History of Richard Cromwell and the Restoration of Charles II*, trans. A.R. Scoble (2 vols, 1856), i, 294.

[78] Guizot, *Richard Cromwell*, i, 294.

[79] *Diary of Thomas Burton*, ed. Rutt, iii, 2.

popularity, and for 'public engagement', and it was this which meant that, however much he valued hierarchy and grandeur, he was more than willing to avoid formal ceremonies whenever possible. As a result, Charles vacillated somewhat in his ceremonial practice, not least by demonstrating a tendency to make last-minute cancellations. For all of the pomp that marked the regime of Oliver and Richard Cromwell, meanwhile, both protectors seem to have been determined to balance different factors, and to reach a compromise between sovereign grandeur and a notably plain civilian ceremonial. Both protectoral regimes seem to have recognized the need for public display, and for grand spectacle, and this inevitably meant a degree of formality, expense and splendour. But this is something which attracted comment because it was thought to be unexpected or undesirable, and because it could be exploited for propaganda purposes by opponents in order to create an image of a hypocritical and Machiavellian Cromwell. It also needs to be balanced by recognition that both Oliver and Richard reworked monarchical style, and 'borrowed only to transform'.[80] The Cromwellian style was resolutely secular and civil, albeit in a way which blended both civilian and military elements, and which also reflected the plain style, and even the common touch, of the Cromwellian court.

However, while the history of state openings in this period is complex, as well as neglected, some important conclusions emerge from this attempt to explore audience reactions as well as official ambitions, and to examine the ways in which they were connected. First, there was widespread recognition, throughout the period, that public performance mattered, not just in the sense that grandeur was desirable, but also in the sense that approaches to ceremonial reflected, and ought to replicate, governmental style. Second, audiences mattered. Examining evidence of the public response, from both elite and popular audiences, indicates that such events were not always as well ordered and decorous as they initially appear from the papers of heralds and from the newspapers produced by government hacks. Third, the presence of large crowds, and their actual or potential behaviour, including the possibility of trouble, played upon the minds of rulers and their advisors, and affected their decisions. What emerges is that, more obviously than their predecessors, but very much like succeeding heads of state, Charles and the two Cromwellian protectors grappled with conflicting pressures in terms of tone and style, and with the fact that their every move was susceptible to contemporary scrutiny and comment.[81] The result was that each respective head of state developed a ceremonial style which, for better or worse, matched their attitude to the institution of parliament.

[80] Knoppers, *Cromwell*, 69, 77.

[81] The full state opening was restored with the Stuart regime in 1660, although Charles II's advisors clearly worried about safety, and reflected back upon the experience and practice of the 1640s: Cobb, 'Staging', 37; *CSP Dom., 1679–80*, p. 71.

Index